REINVENTING DEVELOPMENT REGULATIONS

Relating Development to the Natural Environment

Managing Climate Change Locally

Encouraging Walking by Mixing Land Uses and Housing Types

Preserving Historic Landmarks

Creating More Affordable Housing and Promoting Environmental Justice

Establishing Design Principles and Standards for Public Spaces and Buildings

Implementing Regulations While Safeguarding Private Property Interests

REINVENTING DEVELOPMENT REGULATIONS

Jonathan Barnett and Brian W. Blaesser

Cambridge, Massachusetts

First printing.

Library of Congress Cataloging-in-Publication Data
Names: Barnett, Jonathan, author. | Blaesser, Brian William, author.
Title: Reinventing development regulations / Jonathan Barnett and Brian Blaesser.
Description: Cambridge, Massachusetts : Lincoln Institute of Land Policy, [2017] | Includes bibliographical references and index.
Identifiers: LCCN 2017025707| ISBN 9781558443723 (pbk. : alk. paper) | ISBN 9781558443747 (pdf)
Subjects: LCSH: City planning—United States. | Zoning—United States. | City planning and redevelopment law—United States. | Land use—Law and legislation—United States. | Real estate development—United States.
Classification: LCC HT169.7 .B37 2017 | DDC 346.04/50263—dc23 LC record available at https://lccn.loc.gov/2017025707

Designed by Scott Rattray, Rattray Design

Composed in Adobe Caslon Pro by Westchester Publishing Services in Danbury, Connecticut.
Printed and bound by Puritan Press, Inc., in Hollis, New Hampshire.
The paper is Rolland Enviro100, and acid-free, 100 percent PCW recycled sheet.

MANUFACTURED IN THE UNITED STATES OF AMERICA

For Nory
J. B.

For Grażyna, Brandon, and Alan
B. W. B.

Contents

REINVENTING DEVELOPMENT REGULATIONS

Introduction

Development regulations determine the urban form—the physical shape and structure—of our cities, suburbs, and towns, and have a huge impact on the natural environment. Regulations influence how, when, and where real estate development occurs and affect the legal rights of property owners. Today's pressing development and environmental problems have been created within the current regulatory system, but these regulations also have the potential to help solve these problems if structural deficiencies and biases can be corrected.

Zoning maps still follow a format devised in the 1920s that shows only property boundaries and not topography and other features of land that are part of a living ecosystem. This bias makes it more difficult to plan and implement sustainable development and adapt to the effects of a changing climate. Traditionally, zoning has paid little attention to existing buildings, only to the development potential of each property, making it more difficult to preserve historic buildings and districts. In addition, much of what people find undesirable about suburban growth patterns has been shaped by zoning and subdivision requirements. Narrow strips of commercial zoning along highways have helped create the ubiquitous suburban retail corridor lined with buildings surrounded by parking lots. Conventional zoning and subdivision have mandated the large tracts of suburban houses, hundreds and sometimes thousands of houses all built at once, all a similar size on same-size lots. Walkable communities with a mix of house types can only be created by complicated exceptions and represent a tiny percentage of what is built. Zoning has been a factor in making much new housing unaffordable for those with low and moderate incomes and has become an instrument of social exclusion in many communities. Finally, zoning, with its traditional emphasis on separating the individual structure from its neighbors, has made it more difficult for groups of buildings to shape a desirable Public Realm. The streets and places people experience in the great cities of the world are hard to create today, in part because of unnecessary biases in development regulations.

The problems with current development regulations are familiar. Some people assert that the only answer is to throw out the entire zoning and subdivision system and start over. We do not agree. It is not necessary to replace the existing regulations with a completely new regulatory framework to solve these problems. Attempting to do this would be a time-consuming and politically divisive undertaking for any community. Keeping the existing regulatory framework, while making the necessary changes and additions, limits the creation of nonconforming uses, minimizes infringements on property rights, and avoids significant diminution of property values.

Zoning and subdivision regulations, written originally in the early twentieth century, have already been amended since the 1960s to permit more tall buildings, create more defined land-use zones, provide greater flexibility in decision making, add floor area ratios as a principal bulk control, add special procedures for large properties, and provide more detailed standards for subdivision design. But almost all zoning and subdivision regulations, even with these modifications, are now seriously out of date and no longer relate sufficiently to the current real estate market, to the development needs created by population growth in multicity regions around the country, to an economy changing rapidly in response to advances in telecommunication and transportation networks, and to changes in climate that, over time, will alter the natural environment in which development takes place.

Because some of today's critical problems were created, in part, by the deficiencies and, in some cases, misguided policies of the current system of development regulations, many of these regulations must be modified to implement policies required today. New regulatory provisions are also needed. Improving six critical areas of zoning and subdivision regulation will address most of the problems they have created without disturbing the way other parts of this regulatory system affect property values and the public policies of cities, towns, and suburbs. We address each of the six critical areas for change, and the ways to achieve them, in separate chapters.

Relating development to the natural environment. Geographic information systems (GIS) now make it possible for local governments to adopt zoning district maps that record a wide range of environmental factors, not just property lines. Chapter 1 explains how such a technical and substantive enhancement is a necessary step to enable local governments to translate environmental policies into specific zoning provisions based on the carrying capacity of the land. This chapter also outlines ways to prevent or mitigate the environmental damage caused by current zoning and subdivision requirements, which have had the unintended consequence of causing serious erosion and regional flooding.

Managing climate change locally. Chapter 2 describes measures to slow down—and eventually limit—climate change. The warming trend is a global issue and requires global measures, but there are ways that local governments can use development regulations to reduce greenhouse gas emissions, in addition to the environmental conservation measures discussed in chapter 1. For example, the traditional role of zoning in safeguarding light and air for individual properties can be expanded to preserve access for solar panels and wind turbines. Creating more compact development, as described in chapter 3, also reduces greenhouse gas emissions. A major challenge for local governments is adapting to increasing flood and wildfire dangers that are the inevitable results of climate changes. Chapter 2 describes adaptation through required protective measures and managed withdrawal from areas that become uninhabitable. Adaptation to drought conditions and improving food security can also be achieved through local development regulations.

Encouraging walking by mixing land uses and housing types. Compact, mixed-use business districts and walkable neighborhoods are high on most local government lists of desirable planning and development objectives, but development regulations often have been an obstacle to achieving them. Chapter 3 explains how the strips of small commercial buildings and big parking lots zoned along suburban arterial streets are vast land banks, which can be rezoned into strings of compact, mixed-use centers at approximately one-mile intervals, supported by bus rapid transit if densities are not high enough to repay investing in light rail. The areas between the centers can be zoned for attached houses and apartments related to the adjacent neighborhoods. The chapter also proposes an innovative measure: separating residential density from minimum lot-size requirements. This regulatory approach can permit builders to construct communities with a mix of house types in more walkable patterns without the lengthy and uncertain public review process that is so often involved in planned unit development (PUD) and traditional neighborhood development (TND) projects.

Preserving historic landmarks and districts. Historic preservation and the development permitted under zoning often have been in conflict. Zoning maps based on GIS can add existing buildings, making it easier to understand historic structures in their developmental context. Chapter 4 describes ways to manage what is permitted by zoning when it conflicts with preservation of historic buildings by using zoning overlay districts that can include height limits, build-to and setback lines, and other requirements for the placement of larger, new buildings or additions. The chapter also suggests how to ease land-use restrictions to permit the adaptive reuse of historic buildings for multiple purposes. The use of transfer of development rights for appropriate receiving sites is also discussed.

Creating more affordable housing and promoting environmental justice. Concentrated poverty has been identified by David Rusk and others as a manifestation of social inequality as well as a significant cause of it. Restrictive zoning in many cities and suburbs has prevented the construction of affordable housing and has kept poverty concentrated in older urban and suburban neighborhoods, very often in places least favored by the real estate market. A big obstacle to using existing housing subsidy programs and other incentives for developers to provide affordable housing has been a scarcity of appropriate sites. Chapter 5 discusses how opening up suburban commercial corridors for mixed-use centers with moderate-density housing between the centers, as described in chapter 3, can provide locations for some subsidized units. This chapter also explains how accessory dwelling units can add smaller, more affordable apartments to existing single-family residential areas while benefiting individual property owners. It identifies examples of how such units can be built while maintaining the design and character of the existing neighborhood.

Establishing design principles and standards for public spaces and buildings. What is good design? Experts can argue about this question as an abstract proposition but, as chapter 6 demonstrates, objective design principles can be identified and applied to designing and building communities that can be implemented without causing unreasonable difficulties for developers and investors. In the subdivision ordinance, communities can set the standards for landscaping, green infrastructure, and complete streets in new developments. Placement regulations for buildings can improve public spaces and streets. Regulations can require ground-floor transparency on retail streets and restrict the location of garage and service entrances. Design standards can be required for public open space on private property. And there can be screening requirements for mechanical equipment and loading services. This chapter discusses how such design requirements, in both zoning and subdivision, can safeguard the public interest.

Implementing regulations while safeguarding private property interests. The concluding chapter explains the legal principles that should be followed in preparing and implementing the regulatory modifications and new approaches presented in the previous chapters.

Each chapter identifies problems with current regulations and proposes implementation measures as solutions. Attention is given to aspects of existing regulations that can be modified. Where appropriate, examples are drawn from regulations already adopted in local jurisdictions.

Decisions about regulating development are often made without an understanding of their impact on property rights and their economic consequences for property owners. Realities in the marketplace are not always considered. Therefore, our analysis of the six critical areas includes references to relevant property rights issues, legal principles, and market considerations, as well as the urgent reasons why change is needed. We believe that our proposals are both feasible and necessary.

1

Relating Development to the Natural Environment

Sustainable development means balancing the built and the natural environments to achieve economic growth and a better quality of life while protecting natural resources and ecosystems. Creating and maintaining this balance is an urgent matter today as we experience demands for urbanization of more land to meet the needs of growing populations and smaller household sizes. At the same time, a changing climate reveals that many current development practices have had a destabilizing effect on the environment. A balance is also needed between government regulatory measures intended to protect the natural environment and further the general welfare of communities, and the rights of individual property owners. Our legal system is based on constitutional principles that give citizens and property owners substantive and procedural protections from overreach by government regulatory initiatives.

Zoning and subdivision regulations, first enacted in the 1920s, have been the principal tools of land use and development control and are the regulatory framework for the real estate market. Many zoning and subdivision regulations have encouraged development practices that are harmful to the environment, but these same types of regulations, if properly reformulated, can be a major means to achieve sustainable development design. The real estate market will respond to new regulations based on objectives and policies adopted to promote sustainable development, provided such regulations reflect an understanding of both market constraints and the environmental constraints that shape development options. As always, such regulations must also be founded on sound legal principles, which we outline in chapter 7. As discussed in the introduction, it is a fundamental premise of this book that existing regulations can be modified to correct problems without having to create new regulatory systems. In this and in the following five chapters, whenever we propose changes to development regulations, it is in the context of achieving sustainable development.

The Need to Modify Existing Development Regulations to Protect the Natural Environment

Traditionally zoning has treated land as a commodity assigned to different uses based on projections of future demand, without relating the different uses to the characteristics of the landscape. Often there is a serious mismatch between the type or intensity of development that is permitted and the carrying capacity of the land as a living ecosystem. Within this regulatory framework, developers have a strong incentive to maximize their return on investment to offset the risks that flow from market conditions, financing requirements, and the uncertainty of government approvals. This incentive to maximize return on investment within the traditional regulatory framework of standards that often allowed, and even mandated, development actions that are harmful to the environment, has resulted in development designs and construction practices that destabilize the natural landscape by stripping vegetation, regrading land, and paving large areas. These practices have led to rapid surface runoff, increasing the risk of landslides and severe flooding while lowering water tables as less water penetrates the ground to recharge groundwater and aquifers. Wells run dry, while ground floors and basements flood. The occurrence of hundred-year floods at far more frequent intervals, rapid erosion along stream beds, and the need to expand the boundaries of flood zones as the Federal Emergency Management Agency (FEMA) brings its maps up to date, are all evidence of these problems.

The great landscape architect Frederick Law Olmsted demonstrated in the design of New York City's Central Park and in the Back Bay Fens in Boston that it is possible to create an attractive environment that looks and behaves as if it were natural but is, in fact, almost entirely the outcome of a carefully designed construction and plant selection process. These parks have proved as stable as the original natural environment, while compensating for the degradation that had taken place before the parks were designed. The lessons learned from these parks have helped today's landscape designers understand how to create newly constructed places that are environmentally sustainable. It is also possible to make development fit into the existing natural environment, without significant change to land contours and with minimal destruction of natural vegetation, by carefully selecting building sites and by using building designs that work with the existing land form rather than changing it. Modifications of regulations are badly needed to foster development practices that use one of these methods, or a combination of the two.

Repairing some of the damage to the environment that has taken place in urbanized areas is also feasible. Designs that help restore a natural equilibrium and repair the landscape can be encouraged through regulations that become applicable when a new proposal is made in a place where there is already existing development.

Finally, there are ways to adjust development regulations so they take more account of the variations in the capacity of different segments of the same property to accept urbanization. On a current zoning map, a steep hillside, a wetland, a meadow, and a forest all look the same, but the ability of each to accept development is very different.

How Development Under Traditional Regulatory Frameworks Can Impact the Environment

Impact of Regulations in Residential Subdivisions

Under existing regulations, when residential developments are constructed as large subdivisions on previously agricultural or forest land, the subdivision standards most often produce unintended consequences. For example, these ordinances set standards for street construction within the subdivision. While the text often includes a statement that streets should conform to the existing topography as much as possible, it also contains numerical standards for a maximum street grade—8 percent is a typical figure.[1] That is, the slope of a street may be no more than the specified percentage, and there must be a managed transition from flatter streets to steeper streets. Typically, street grades over 15 percent require special engineering review. A 15 percent grade is a steep street. For comparison, the sloping floor of a continuous ramp parking garage is generally around a 5 percent grade, and building codes generally set a limit of about 6.5 percent for sloping floors in garages.

There are obvious public safety reasons for setting street-grade standards. But keeping street grades to a maximum of 8 percent is not easy on many parcels of property that are large enough to require their own street system. The developer's objective in laying out subdivision streets is to create a design that gives access to the most lots using the smallest amount of street construction. There may not be that many places on the site where existing grades would allow the developer to keep such a street system within the limits specified in the ordinance. And these maximum grades are not the whole issue. A well-known engineering handbook recommends that "at an intersection, grades of more than four percent should be avoided if possible."[2] Most subdivision ordinances also have requirements about how to grade from a relatively level area to a steeper slope and about the visibility of intersections from a distance. All of these street design considerations support a practice of regrading street rights-of-way across a site. In addition, the house lots themselves need to be close to the grade of the street: there can be flooding if the lot is lower than the street and difficult access if the lot is too far above street level. This problem often leads to regrading of the lots as well as the streets, so that the entire site is reengineered.

Planned Unit Development: One Way to Reduce Impacts

One zoning technique—the planned unit development (PUD)—is intended to provide flexibility in site design, placement of buildings, and use of open areas. Designing the streets and buildings under PUD provisions allows a developer to shift the buildings to those parts of the site where construction is easiest and to minimize disturbance of natural terrain and vegetation. This flexibility can enable the developer to simplify the layout of the streets and lots, since the streets may not need to go through areas where the topography presents difficulties. The PUD technique has proved useful in mitigating many of the problems inherent in traditional zoning and subdivision.

The principal limitation of the PUD is that it requires a separate proceeding for approval, and the approval process, including public input, can be lengthy. A second limitation, where the particular jurisdiction restricts the applicant for a PUD permit to a single owner, the property lines may not have much resemblance to the geographic boundaries of various natural resource areas and features. Solving this problem might require retaining walls and other built features that create disjunctions between the planned development and the surrounding area. In some jurisdictions, if property owners are willing to work together, it is possible for multiple owners to be the PUD applicant provided that such control can be established through the use of enforceable covenants on the respective properties, other commitments to the local government by the multiple-party applicant, or both.[3] This approach does not require ownership transfers and allows for the comprehensive planning and development of multiple parcels that can take into account natural resource areas and features. Many communities limit the use of the PUD technique to large parcels. The PUD can be a viable means for creating a design for a large subdivision that minimizes disturbance of natural terrain and vegetation.

Conservation Subdivisions

Conservation subdivision design (CSD) is an approach pioneered by Randall Arendt.[4] According to Arendt, the CSD is different from the PUD in that it employs higher open space ratios with the purpose of creating a community-wide network of open space.[5] Despite the increased open space ratio, the density allowed is the same as that under a conventional subdivision, although small-density bonuses are sometimes given to the developer in exchange for dedicating some or all of the conservation land for public access or use and providing for permanent maintenance of the open space. A CSD is designed around the most significant natural and cultural resources on a site. Its open space network is the first element to be "green-lined" in the design process. Open space is defined to include all "primary conservation areas" (wetlands, floodplains, and steep slopes), plus 30 to 80 percent of the remaining unconstrained land, depending on zoning densities and infrastructure availability.[6] Two principal considerations can result in CSD not being widely utilized. First, where there is insufficient market demand for the smaller lots typical of this type of subdivision and the potentially lower densities that may result from the higher open space requirements, developers may choose not to initiate requests for CSD approval. Second, because CSD works best where it can be applied to create an open space network that includes all or part of a natural system, such as a hillside or a wetland area, it may have the most applicability beyond developed areas, fostering a "leapfrog" or sprawl pattern of development.

In sum, while the PUD and the conservation subdivision design are viable regulatory approaches to ensure that sites are developed to minimize disturbance of natural terrain and vegetation, their use depends on various factors that are not always present in areas subject to conventional zoning and subdivision regulations. There need to be ways to achieve those objectives without having to rely on the PUD or the CSD.

Alternatives to Planned Unit Development and Conservation Subdivisions

In this chapter we suggest some modifications to the overall zoning and subdivision controls that can be applied to make real estate proposals compatible with the natural landscape, including making it easier to lay out streets without extensive regrading of the site. Regrading to meet street design requirements can involve chopping, uprooting, and carting away all the trees and vegetation, putting streams in culverts, and moving topsoil and subsoil around until all the land has slopes not much more than the maximum street grade. The resulting parcel makes it easy to lay out efficient streets that reach the largest number of lots with the least amount of street construction. Some of the topsoil may be sold to help pay for the grading costs. Such prepared sites are a common result under traditional subdivision ordinances.

One of the problems with this kind of site engineering is what happens to other properties in the area, particularly those at lower elevations that are downstream from the storm water that will run off from the newly leveled and denuded land. Leveling one piece of property can leave ragged edges around the perimeter—either steep escarpments or retaining walls. If the next piece of property is subsequently reengineered as well, managing the storm water becomes progressively more difficult. Ultimately, if an entire region is reengineered piecemeal, the whole system fails. This is what has happened in many urbanized areas that flood frequently after rainstorms. Regraded construction sites are also a major indirect source of pollution as the flooding from these sites carries oil, gasoline, salt, and phosphorous nutrients that contribute to algae blooms in waterways.

At the federal level, section 402 of the Clean Water Act (CWA)[7] established the National Pollutant Discharge Elimination System

(NPDES) program for controlling water pollution by regulating point sources that discharge pollutants into waters of the United States.[8] Because of the large amount of potential pollutants associated with nonpoint sources—those that come from diffuse locations and enter into the groundwater or surface water through indirect processes such as the application of fertilizers or pesticides, construction activities, irrigation practices, septic system failures, or other means—Congress in 1987 also created the Nonpoint Source Management Program under section 319 of the CWA.[9] The NPDES program is implemented through the states under a discharge permit known as the State Pollutant Discharge Elimination System (SPDES). A NPDES/SPDES permit is required for construction sites that disturb one or more acres of land and discharge storm water to any surface water of the United States or to a municipal separate storm-sewer system (referred to as an MS4) that discharges to any surface water of the United States.[10]

At the local level, storm water runoff is addressed for new development in jurisdictions that have adopted storm water control ordinances. These ordinances include a standard that, generally defined, requires that on new construction sites, the annual average volume of storm water runoff that flows from a development site during and following development not exceed the predevelopment average volume of runoff, when the natural equilibrium of soil and vegetation, which had evolved over a long period of time, slowed the flow of water on site so it was absorbed into the ground.

Meeting the volume runoff standards can be difficult, however, particularly if there had been streams on the land and the obligation has to be met within the boundaries of an individual property. Developers typically address the problem by including detention ponds within the subdivision to hold rainwater until the storm subsides. Dealing with storm water management at a more regional level can take some of the burden of compliance with runoff standards from individual developments. We come back to such regional measures later in this chapter.

We also recommend that grading requirements within broad specified limits simply require that the street system conform to existing topography as much as possible, leaving the safety determinations to the subdivision review process. Setting the street requirements in this way should reduce the amount of drastic regrading that developers will need to do, as will more flexibility about lot sizes in residential zones, which we discuss later in this chapter.

Impact of Regulations on Large Commercial Development

Figure 1-1, an aerial photograph of the Mill Creek Mall and surrounding development, located outside of Erie, Pennsylvania, near the junction of Interstates 90 and 79, shows a typical situation in urbanized areas that have been developed since World War II. This complex first opened in 1975. There is a suburban mall, now 1.3 million square feet, surrounded by separate retail buildings, including big-box stores and several strip shopping centers, along with separate smaller structures for such uses as

Figure 1–1 An aerial view of a typical regional shopping center, this one near Erie, Pennsylvania, shows how the required parking ratios in the zoning regulations result in large areas of paved surfaces. Each of the other retail buildings around the center must also satisfy official parking requirements on their own sites, so their land is mostly pavement also. In a heavy rainstorm water will run off rapidly from these impervious surfaces into such places as the stream visible on the edge of the development, possibly causing erosion and flooding. Reflected sunlight will also create areas of concentrated heat in the summer. The first question is whether so much parking is necessary, as the parking ratios found in most ordinances have surprisingly little objective justification. As this photograph shows, parking lots like these are rarely full. We advocate removing fixed parking ratios in high-intensity commercial zones, to allow the amount of cars provided to be a business decision. It is also possible to reduce parking if businesses will share spaces, and the adverse effects of parking can be mitigated by landscape designs using such elements as pervious surfaces and areas of trees and other plantings.

fast-food franchises. This kind of development requires substantial regrading of land and adds large areas of rooftops, paved access roads, and paved parking lots in place of what had been a natural or agricultural landscape—in this case, areas along Walnut Creek, which surrounds the development on three sides. Having so much impervious surface makes water run rapidly off the site, as there is little opportunity for the storm water to be absorbed into the ground.

Existing regulations are the reason why impervious parking lots cover so much of the developed landscape. Parking requirements in zoning codes require that a retail building provide a minimum number of parking spaces per 1,000 square feet of gross leasable area. This ratio is typically 4.5 or 5.0 cars per 1,000 square feet, although some authorities recommend 5.5 to 6.6 cars per 1,000 square feet. A ratio of 6.0 cars per 1,000 square feet is recommended for big-box stores and 15.0 for fast-food restaurants, both of which can be seen in the photograph to have been built close to the mall. Interestingly, fine dining requires 21 cars per 1,000 square feet, presumably because patrons linger over their meal and reduce turnover in the parking lot. Including fast food or fine dining in a mall raises the overall parking requirement.[11]

Each car space and its related road space takes up 350 to 400 square feet, meaning that close to twice the area of a typical one-story retail building is required for parking and circulation, even at a relatively low parking ratio of 5.0. The Mill Creek Mall would require, at a 5-car ratio, about 100 acres of cars, and the surrounding developments have even higher parking requirements. Although almost universally accepted, these parking ratios turn out to be far less scientific than they sound, and we consider whether these ratios distort development and are even necessary later in this chapter. But first we review the impact of these typical parking requirements on the natural environment.

Regardless of the number of cars that need to be parked, the parking lots need to be close to flat; a 5 percent grade is often a maximum for a parking lot.[12] Retail buildings are normally built on level land as well, so the mall and its parking need to be on a site that is close to flat. Big, flat sites are rarely found in nature, so, as allowed by the subdivision, grading, or site plan regulations, the vegetation is removed and the land regraded, and the edges of the site are lined with retaining walls. The strip shopping centers and other separate stores also require regrading for their parking. The parking lots and the roofs of the buildings are all surfaces that do not

Figure 1–2 This commercial corridor, Dodge Street in Omaha, Nebraska, looks better than most as there are no utility wires in view. However, the combination of wide, paved traffic lanes and the parking lots for businesses along the street, plus the regrading of the residential subdivisions on either side of this commercial corridor, produces a new unnatural landscape, with much more storm water runoff and a hotter microclimate in the summer.

absorb water, and they also reflect a large amount of sunlight, making such commercial areas much more of an environmental problem than the lawns and trees of a residential neighborhood, which can absorb water and some of the heat from the sun, or a natural or agricultural landscape. Because the microclimate in and around large parking lots is especially hot in summer, air conditioners in the retail buildings have to work harder, more power is used, and even more heat is released into the atmosphere as a result.

Figure 1-2 shows a typical suburban commercial corridor lined with retail buildings and at-grade parking on both sides and surrounded by residential subdivisions on regraded land. This is a design that has been shaped by development regulations that do not take the natural landscape into account.

Modifying the Structure and Substance of Existing Development Regulations

What can be done to stop the repetition of such familiar situations, and what can be done to repair what is already there? Organizational and substantive changes can be made to existing regulations that can result in major improvements in the way development takes place.

Incorporating Environmental Information into Development Regulations

Most development regulations were enacted when environmental issues were less well understood and when the technical means for managing information about the environment were much more limited. The typical zoning map shows land as a blank page on which only streets and large bodies of water are delineated. The boundaries of the various zoning districts are overlaid on this simple, schematic diagram. Most of the areas covered by official zoning maps have now also been mapped in a local government's geographic information system (GIS). A typical GIS map is composed of layers such as land contours, soil conditions, hydrology—including watershed boundaries—and large areas of natural vegetation, as well as property lines and building locations. A GIS can also incorporate the floodplain maps issued by the Federal Emergency Management Agency (FEMA), the location of earthquake faults, and maps of forest-fire danger in places where these issues are significant. Zoning maps can be modified to incorporate GIS maps. Having ready access to this information can make a significant difference in the way regulations are written and administered.

Zoning and subdivision ordinances may include regulations pertaining to land contours, hydrology, or other aspects of the natural landscape. But implementation of these environment-related regulations typically depends on a survey of existing conditions being submitted for review by the owner or developer of the particular parcel. Consequently, regulatory decisions about construction on slopes or at the edges of bodies of water are made only for individual properties, whose property lines rarely encompass a larger geographic area that may be relevant to the decision. As a result, important environmental issues may not be addressed at all. In addition, because the soils, topography, water resources, and other natural characteristics were not considered at the time of the original adoption of the zoning and subdivision regulations, environmental factors relevant to appropriate land uses and densities are unlikely to have been considered in making those land-use determinations.

Review of development impacts that affect larger geographic areas may be addressed through state environmental policy acts modeled on the National Environmental Policy Act (NEPA). But many states do not have these kinds of environmental regulations.[13] Generally, these "little NEPAs" or "mini NEPAs" require the preparation of an impact statement on all actions that significantly affect the quality of the environment. This "significantly affect" requirement for determining when an impact statement must be prepared is addressed somewhat differently in each state. Some states, such as Massachusetts and Minnesota, use review thresholds that serve as the basis for determining when impacts are considered significant enough to require preparation of an impact statement.[14]

Even in those states that have mini NEPAs, environmental reviews tend to be triggered only by relatively large projects because review is only required for projects above defined thresholds. Environmental review seldom takes place for separate, smaller projects that, cumulatively, can have significant environmental impacts for a larger geographical area. Most zoning and subdivision ordinances do not include information on which substantive provisions about these environmental issues can be based. Introducing reasonable environmental considerations into the review of smaller projects under local zoning and subdivision ordinances is a badly needed improvement, and incorporating GIS information in the zoning map can make doing this much easier.

Whether local governments are able to consider most or all of these environmental issues in the development project review process depends on state law. In states where local government regulatory authority on land use is prescribed by state statute or in the state constitution (known as Dillon's Rule states),[15] the ability of local governments to consider such issues depends on whether there is a state statute that authorizes local environmental review. In states where local governments have home rule powers,[16] this authority may be found within the power of local communities to govern their affairs.

Whether the planning and regulatory framework of the local jurisdiction is governed by state statute or is a function of home rule powers, it is most useful for property owners and local government officials if the relevant environmental information needed for a development decision can be viewed in advance of any development proposal. GIS data concerning environmental features such as wetlands, hillsides at varying slopes, soils, earthquake zones, flood zones, fire hazard zones, and other relevant environmental information can be shown both on plans and on zoning maps.

Create environmental zones as part of comprehensive plan. In state jurisdictions that require local comprehensive plans and the adoption of implementation measures consistent with those plans, it is possible to conduct extensive environmental analysis at the planning stage.[17] The local planning body could divide the local jurisdiction into land-use planning zones in which the environmental constraints in those zones would be documented with GIS layers of information. Within these zones, development proposals of various types and intensity of use consistent with the planning policies for those zones would be identified. For each of these development proposals, mitigation measures would be formulated. In this way, developers would know early in the development process what measures are necessary for project approval. The extent to which an individual developer would be required to undertake mitigation measures would depend on the extent to which the mitigation is attributable to development. As long as developers have included the appropriate mitigation measures in their development proposals, further environmental project review would not be necessary. This approach avoids the additional time and cost created by duplicating environmental reviews and development reviews.[18]

Incorporate GIS information into zoning district maps as an administrative technique. Where development regulations are not required to be consistent with a comprehensive plan, it is possible to incorporate the GIS information into the zoning district maps by overlaying the zoning districts on a GIS-based map of the actual terrain to show the relationship between the geometric boundaries of the land-use zones and the natural resources and environmental features within each zoning district. Taking the data concerning environmental features such as wetlands, hillsides at varying slopes, soils, earthquake zones, fire hazard zones, and other important information for the local jurisdiction and creating GIS map layers that relate to the individual zoning districts of a jurisdiction is a necessary technical step, but it is not a regulatory step.

While environmental information incorporated on a GIS-based zoning map may indicate land constraints that could affect the location and intensity of use on parcels, identifying those constraints does not empower local government to impose restrictions or mitigation requirements without first carefully considering policies and implementation measures for each environmental resource or feature. Legally, a developer cannot be required to mitigate more than the proportionate impact of its development on natural resources and environmental features. Consequently, the GIS-based analysis and resulting dialogue between the planning authorities and the developer may result in the need for the local government to share in the sustainability measures necessary to ensure that the natural systems, as public resources, are not irreversibly compromised.[19]

In those communities that have existing environmental regulations, the GIS-based zoning map can be keyed to those regulations and enable the local government staff and the developer to focus on the combination of zoning and environmental regulations applicable to a specific parcel. Communities that lack local policies and implementation measures for environmental resources and features will need to undertake the necessary technical analysis, policy formulation, and drafting and adopting of implementation measures related to the GIS-based zoning information. This undertaking could lead the local government to consider comprehensive land-use policy and related zoning changes to reflect environmental considerations. Where environmental resources and features encompass more than one parcel of land, for example, a watershed area, any policies and implementation measures based on the broader geographical area must be designed so as not to impose a disproportionate burden on individual property owners who seek to develop their property in accordance with zoning.[20]

Development decision making through environmental zones or a GIS-based zoning map. The GIS-based zoning map, or development zones based on environmental considerations, will not eliminate the need for individual site surveys when considering specific projects, but relating development to a comprehensive plan based on GIS data, or showing land-use zones with information layers that describe land contours and streams as well as streets and property lines, will make it possible to understand the effect that a decision on one property will have on neighboring properties and also on properties farther away where there may be an environmental connection—being downstream, for example. If a new subdivision, a planned development, or a new big-box store and associated parking are being considered for approval, local officials, other property owners, and the public can understand much more clearly, when they see the proposed development displayed on a GIS-augmented zoning map, what the potential environmental consequences of the development are for the surrounding area. This new understanding will help improve the development review process so that it is possible to anticipate and address potential environmental impacts for local developments whose size is below the thresholds for an environmental impact statement at state or federal levels, consistent with established legal principles for imposing impact mitigation measures.[21]

The GIS data can also be used by the developer to analyze and, if appropriate, question the types or scope of environmental mitigation measures imposed under the local development regulation. For example, a local environmental impact regulation or ordinance should include a process by which the developer can perform its own project environmental-impact analysis using GIS data, or any other environmental analysis, and present that analysis to the local administrative body (for example, a planning commission or conservation commission) to explain why the environmental mitigation imposed is either not accurate or not proportionate to the impact of the proposed project. The review process should include a hearing before the administrative body, with findings of fact and conclusions. If the administrative body concurs with the developer's analysis, the project would be granted an appropriate variance from the environmental mitigation measures. If the administrative body disagrees with the developer's analysis and the request for a variance, the developer would have the right to appeal that decision to court. Depending on state law, the appeal may be based on the record that was developed before the administrative body or may be de novo, meaning the evidence that can be introduced in the court proceeding is not limited to the record.

Establishing Predevelopment Standards and Guidelines

Ensuring that development relates to the environment means that the natural resources and environmental features that are on site should still be on site at the point that a development proposal is presented for review. One practice that undermines that predevelopment status quo on the site is the practice of clear-cutting, the removal of all trees from a tract or parcel of land. While few would openly advocate clear-cutting and grading of an entire site before submitting a development proposal, it is a practice that causes tension between the right of property owners to use their properties as they see fit, subject to not causing any nuisance to their neighbors,[22] and the public concern for protecting significant natural resources and features that, if lost or degraded, can result in negative environmental impacts to the community.

Require grading permit. One way to stop predevelopment grading of a site is to require a grading permit before any earth-moving operations commence and to require that the grading is done pursuant to an approved development plan, with the objective of preserving, to the extent possible, the site's natural hydrology and retaining existing natural contours and significant natural resources.

Implement tree preservation measures. Traditionally, tree preservation ordinances have limited their scope to the protection of trees located in public rights-of-way, streets, avenues, and public parks. Such ordinances also provide for the regulation of privately owned trees when they are dead, diseased, or a threat to public safety. The legal authority for this type of tree preservation ordinance is derived from the common law of nuisance[23] and the police power—the legislative power that resides in each state and is delegated to municipalities—to establish laws and ordinances to preserve the public order and to promote the public health, safety, and other aspects of the general welfare.[24]

Because the concern in this chapter is with the exacerbation of storm water runoff and erosion that can result from predevelopment clear-cutting and severe regrading of private land, the question is, how can a tree preservation ordinance be drafted that prevents such practices but also meets constitutional standards? The answer is to stay within the traditional police-power purposes of public health and safety, and craft provisions that address the potential negative impacts on a community's public health and safety that result from storm water runoff and erosion. The public health and safety purposes encompass environmental concerns. Specific environmental reasons for tree preservation are: (1) protection against soil erosion through stabilization of the soil and the creation of wind breaks; and (2) reduction in storm water runoff and water pollution. Other environmental objectives could include (1) air quality enhancement; (2) energy conservation through the cooling effects of a tree canopy; (3) water conservation through reduced evaporation and runoff; (4) noise buffering; (5) woodland and wetland wildlife habitat and ecology maintenance; and (6) resistance against colonization of an area by non-native plant species.[25]

A tree ordinance can be part of a community's environmental policies without implicating the takings clause under the federal and state constitutions.[26] One means of doing this would be to apply the tree ordinance only to undeveloped parcels large enough to be considered for PUD or subdivision approval. Tree cutting on such properties should, like the grading ordinance, be required to be done in accordance with an approved plan.

We are skeptical about a new generation of tree preservation ordinances that have as their premise that *privately* owned trees are a "public resource" that may be subjected to local government control for the benefit of the community.[27] This new type of tree ordinance typically requires that for each tree removed from the landowner's property, another tree like it be replanted elsewhere on the site.[28] If that is not feasible, the ordinance may also require payment of a fee in lieu to a community tree preservation fund. Other ordinances condition the issuance of every building or land development permit on an applicant's submission of a tree survey and a tree protection plan for approval by the local government arborist.[29] Some ordinances may also provide that removing, cutting, or severely overpruning a tree protected under this new type of ordinance constitutes a public nuisance, punishable by criminal penalties.[30]

This "public resource" regulatory approach to preserving trees on private property can impact private property owners in two ways. First, where the regulation monitors and imposes penalties, or a fee in lieu, on private property for those owners whose properties are already developed with residences or commercial uses and who propose to remove trees on their properties, this type of local government regulation, in effect, creates a constructive easement in trees over their private properties. Second, where development is proposed on undeveloped private property, and the regulation requires the maintenance, replacement, or other planting of trees on that property before the development will be approved, the regulation imposes a condition on development. Both the constructive easement in the first instance and the development condition in the second instance are forms of exaction that are vulnerable to being challenged as takings under U.S. Supreme Court's *Nollan/Dolan* Dual Nexus Test[31] and the Court's most recent decision on exactions in *Koontz*.[32] The *Nollan/Dolan* Dual Nexus Test requires that there be an "essential nexus" between the exaction and a legitimate governmental purpose and that the exaction be "roughly proportional" to the impact of the proposed action by the property owner or the developer. This means that whatever the local community believes are its public purposes in adopting this broader type of tree preservation ordinance, it must undertake the technical analysis to be able to show how its tree preservation provisions as applied to private property satisfy the two prongs of the *Nollan/Dolan* Dual Nexus Test.[33] We provide a more complete explanation of these legal principles in our discussion about implementing development regulations in chapter 7.

A tree preservation ordinance directed at stabilizing the soil and reducing storm water runoff and water pollution, to be effective and legally defensible, must be based on a comprehensive study of the negative impacts of storm water runoff and soil erosion on neighboring properties and wetlands, as well as the added municipal storm water management costs, and a demonstration of how tree preservation can stabilize the landscape to prevent or reduce these negative impacts.

Allow variations in lot size while maintaining the same number of units per acre. An important reason why it is difficult to lay out efficient streets in subdivisions without regrading the natural contours is that the area covered in the proposed subdivision is generally part of a single residential zone. These residential zones are almost always written to require every building lot to be the same size, so that the same kind of access pattern must be evenly spaced across the whole site. Rather than define residential density as, for example, four houses to the acre, including the acreage occupied by streets, most ordinances achieve this objective by requiring each lot to be a minimum of a quarter acre, or 10,000 square feet. It should be possible when approving subdivision plans, without changing the overall density, to permit a more limited version of the flexibility in lot sizes that is possible in PUDs, thus avoiding some of the complexities of applying for a PUD. There should be a minimum overall development density requirement, just as there generally is for the PUD. Flexibility in lot size opens up many more possible ways to lay out the streets.

Requiring same-size lots is the cause of what are often criticized as cookie-cutter subdivisions. Defining density in terms of number of houses or apartments per acre rather than by lot size creates other possibilities for improving subdivision designs. In addition to making it easier to organize the street system, it can create a more varied and interesting community that can accommodate different age groups and family structures. The original intent, back in the 1920s, when many ordinances were first written, might well have been to perpetuate social distinctions: families living in a bungalow with a front porch on a 50-foot-wide lot were perceived as a different social class from people living in a center-hall colonial on a 100-foot-wide lot. But the scale on which subdivision took place in the 1920s is nothing like the scale of hundreds, or even thousands, of houses that can make up a subdivision today, so these residential zoning categories have had the effect of making distinctions more rigid at a time when society is much more fluid. Today, people want houses of different sizes at different stages of their lives and are often drawn to older neighborhoods where a mix of lot sizes and house types had originally been permitted or grew up over time. The option to create new neighborhoods with the same flexibility does not exist under conventional zoning regulations.

The legal question of whether lot size can be varied while maintaining the same overall density per acre in a zoning district is a question that is analogous in many ways to the legal question that was raised in connection with the PUD technique when it was originally introduced. The flexibility allowed in the mix of uses and location of density within a parcel under a PUD raised the question of whether such flexibility violated the so-called "uniformity provision" found in most state zoning enabling statutes. That provision requires that regulations within each zoning district be uniform, while regulations in distinct zoning districts may differ from one another.[34] The idea behind the uniformity requirement is that zoning regulations should equally and impartially impact owners whose land is similarly situated. But the concern of the requirement was not to prevent different regulations from being applied in the same zoning district to owners who chose to develop their property under differing circumstances. For example, one court rejected a uniformity objection to a

PUD ordinance that allowed for clustering of the density on the site, explaining that the PUD ordinance "accomplished uniformity because the option [of clustering] is open to all developers."[35] Similarly, where the maximum development density is established within a zoning district in terms of number of houses per acre, rather than by lot size, the fact that varying lot sizes and corresponding housing types are allowed, as long as the overall district density is not exceeded, would be an option open to all developers. It does not run afoul of the uniformity requirement. While we believe that such a zoning district would satisfy the uniformity requirement under the Standard State Zoning Enabling Act adopted by many states, state zoning enabling legislation could also be amended to provide for this type of zoning district.

In chapter 3, we discuss in more detail the permitting of a mix of lot sizes within the same overall density, as this approach to regulation not only promotes land conservation but also can make communities much more walkable.

Use environmental information to inform and shape subdivision design. As the ability to vary lot sizes makes it much easier to relate development to the natural environment, awareness of this flexibility can be incorporated in the kinds of studies, using GIS information, that can be made of areas that are likely to develop in the future. As discussed previously, the studies can either be part of the comprehensive planning process or part of the formulation of zoning districts. In this way environmental issues are identified in advance for both prospective subdividers and adjacent property owners. Subdivision designs already go through an extensive review process to make sure that proposed streets and related infrastructure, which are going to be turned over to the local government, meet all the construction and operating criteria of the various governmental departments. The environmental information from the local government's GIS, available as overlays on the zoning districts, enables planning department staff to evaluate environmental constraints as part of the review of proposed subdivisions. This information is not to limit the density of the subdivision as allowed under the applicable zoning district but to address questions of how best to lay out a subdivision in relation to the topography and natural resources on the site.

Environmental information displayed by geographic information systems can suggest places where a subdivision's streets should not be laid out because the topography makes it difficult to meet street-grade standards. It is also possible that some of the smaller access streets could be steeper than the 7 or 8 percent target for important streets. For example, they could be approved up to 12 percent, depending on review made possible by GIS information. Places of special environmental sensitivity can also be identified in advance of development. Such places should perhaps be avoided in the overall plan or will need special design treatment. Compliance with these criteria will be easier if the density is set by the number of houses or apartments per acre rather than by lot size.

Additional Subdivision Standards for Protecting Environmental Resources and Features

Additional standards can be added to subdivision ordinances to reduce storm water runoff from streets, driveways, and house roofs. The principle is to make the behavior of the completed subdivision in a rainstorm come as close as possible to the way the land would have managed the water before it was developed.

Prepare environmentally friendly street and driveway standards for subdivisions. Standards for street rights-of-way in subdivisions are often criticized for making the streets too wide. Traffic engineers have favored wide lanes to permit cars to move faster in both directions, and they also have preferred space for street parking on both sides. As neither high traffic speeds nor big quantities of street parking are desirable within most residential neighborhoods, more recent technical studies call for narrower streets. However, having a wide street right-of-way, as distinguished from the paved area, which is called the cartway, can be an advantage, and it would be unwise to reduce the right-of-way just because the area devoted to traffic lanes should be smaller. The right-of-way should be wide enough to permit a utility easement, a sidewalk at least five feet wide, and a tree lawn, also at least five feet wide, on both sides of the street (figure 1-3). To make the street design more compatible with the natural environment, the tree lawn, traditionally a strip of grass reserved for planting street trees, can be designed as what is called a rain garden, a planted area designed to help rainwater be absorbed into the ground instead of flowing along the surface. Trees can and should be included at an appropriate

Figure 1-3 This street in the Kenwood Historic District in St. Petersburg, Florida, has a generous tree lawn between the street and the sidewalk, a design often found in older residential neighborhoods. Providing this kind of landscaping is significant now that controlling storm water runoff has become such an important issue. As designed, this tree lawn will allow rainwater to percolate down into the aquifer as well as create a gracious environment. If the lawn were to be lowered below curb and sidewalk to become a drainage swale, it could also retain and filter water that would flow in from the street and sidewalk. Building a swale instead of a tree lawn is a useful technique for new development.

spacing. The right-of-way can also include a drainage swale on both sides of the pavement, designed so that storm water from the street will flow into the rain garden and thus into the ground. This kind of environmentally friendly street design will reduce the amount of water that runs off during storms and reduce the need for costly hard infrastructure, especially piping systems. Traditional curbs, gutters, and drainage pipes could well be unnecessary in most subdivisions (figure 1-4).

Make pervious driveways a standard for new developments. There is now unitary paving material that allows rainwater to soak through it but has a smooth continuous surface. It is strong enough to be used in small local

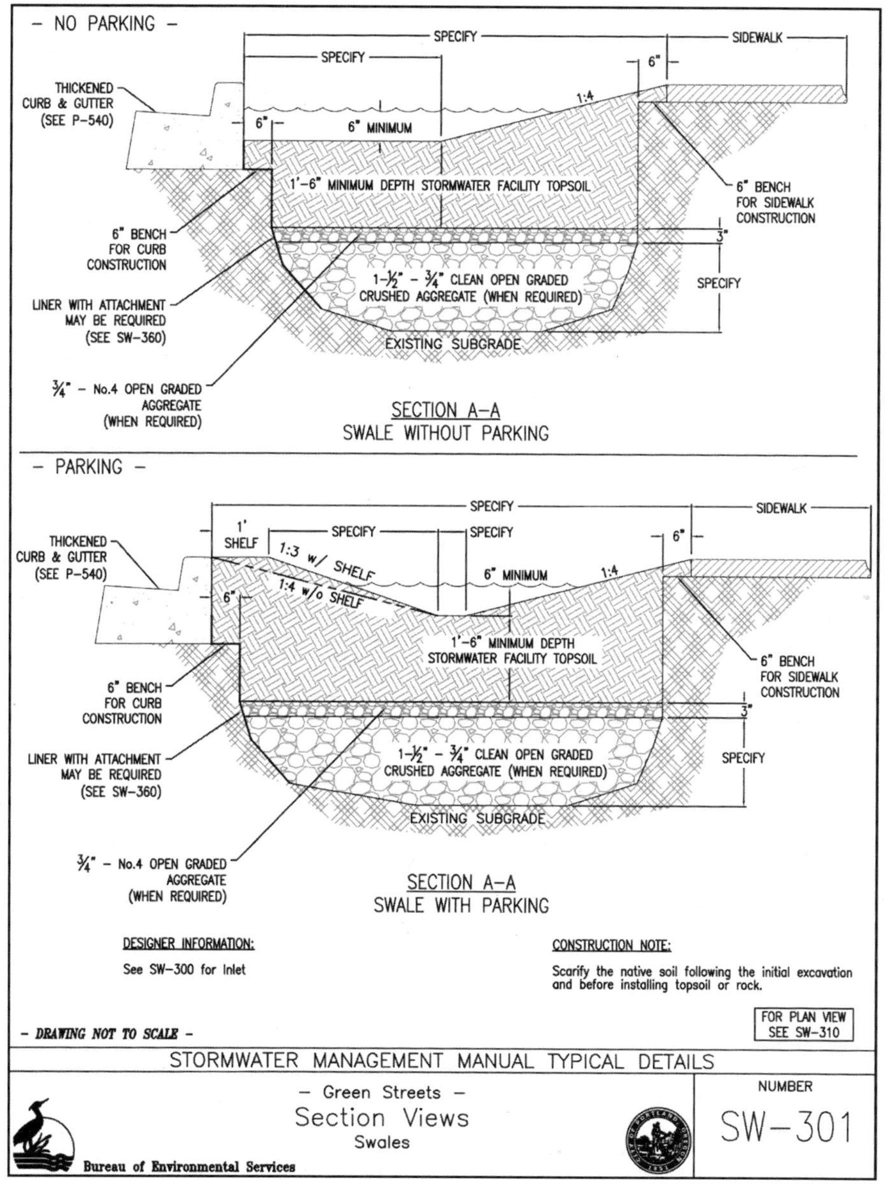

Figure 1-4 These construction details from the Bureau of Environmental Services of the City of Portland, Oregon, show preferred methods for designing drainage swales in the tree lawn position between the street paving and the sidewalk.

streets and thus is appropriate for driveways and parking areas in residential subdivisions. This kind of paving can be adopted as a standard for subdivision approval.

Establish standards and guidelines for water harvesting. Water harvesting refers to techniques used to capture and collect rain from roofs and storm water runoff from paved surfaces on site, which can then be redirected into the landscape or retained for purposes such as longer-term storage or groundwater recharge.

In addition to streets, driveways, sidewalks, and walkways, the roofs on houses are a major impervious surface area in a residential subdivision. Rainwater can be harvested from the roof to rain barrels at the foot of each drainpipe. This is an inexpensive way to prevent rain from flooding yards and flowing into the street. It does require some maintenance. Householders have to either drain the water after the storm has gone past or use the water for the garden, perhaps by attaching the rain barrel spigot to a soaker hose. In the winter, if there are freezing temperatures, the rain barrel should be disconnected from the downspout until spring. A more expensive, but more convenient, solution is to attach all the downspouts on a house to an underground cistern which is equipped with a pump. The water from the cistern can be used for watering the lawn or for washing outdoor deck areas or cars, saving purified drinking water for more appropriate uses. The cost of including such a cistern in new developments could easily be included in the house price.

Implementation of water retention techniques through existing development regulations is likely to be most effective if applied to new development rather than in an effort to retrofit developed areas. In either case, however, there are certain considerations and implementation strategies that should be undertaken.

Of first importance is to conduct the analysis necessary to prepare a water conservation plan. The purposes of such a plan would include managing water as a scarce resource, retaining storm water until a flood danger has passed, supporting economic activity, and maintaining a sustainable water supply for which changes in land-use patterns and behavior are required. This plan also provides the rational basis[36] for both standards and guidelines in the subdivision ordinance, or possibly in a separate water conservation ordinance. The plan should include an evaluation of current water usage, contain goals and criteria for long-term water usage and conservation in relation to projected population growth and development, and identify both voluntary measures, including incentives, and mandatory measures to promote water conservation.

For new developments, incentives could be provided in the form of tax rebates to developers who incorporate water conservation measures, such as rainwater harvesting, pursuant to a water-harvesting plan for roofs and paved areas that is tied to landscape irrigation. For existing residential areas, rebates on water bills could be given to homeowners for the installation of cisterns.

The subdivision ordinance in most jurisdictions would need to be amended to provide for mandatory design regulations for conservation, which would include harvesting water and other requirements for the efficient use of water. Again, the legal basis for mandating water conservation would need to be a water conservation plan that documents the status of water resources and projects future water needs in terms of a planning horizon. If a community were to require developers to pay a fee for every new single-family home or apartment unit built, and dedicate the fees collected for water conservation programs to benefit the community, that fee would have to satisfy the *Nollan/Dolan* Dual Nexus Test.[37]

Another consideration in the initial implementation of water conservation measures would be to limit the mandatory provisions to those developments that require a discretionary permit, such as a special permit or a PUD approval. As the changes suggested here make it less necessary to secure a discretionary permit, the regulations should also provide that the mandatory water conservation measures apply only to subdivisions of a minimum size (for example, five or more units).

Incorporate maps of flooding and other special hazards. Incorporating FEMA flood maps in the GIS-based zoning maps, as discussed earlier, can make it easier to understand the relationship between FEMA maps and the proposed development. Some local governments permit developers to solve floodplain problems by using fill to raise the grade, or perhaps by constructing a parking garage as a base for other development. Such actions can have consequences for property owners downstream, again an issue that may once have passed unnoticed but can now be identified because floodplains and land contours have become part of the zoning map.

Proximity to forest areas that might burn, soils prone to landslides, and the location of earthquake faults are other hazards that can and should be incorporated in GIS-based zoning district maps, making it easier to make these issues, if they are present, part of the review process when a subdivision or a planned development is approved.

Many places at risk for earthquakes already have special building-code regulations, but earthquake fault areas are not always given more specific attention in zoning regulations. Earthquakes are extremely difficult to predict except by broad measures of statistical likelihood. However, it is possible to map earthquake fault zones where the locations of faults are known. For example, under a 1972 California law[38] the state's Department of Conservation provides local governments and state construction agencies with maps showing zones of required investigation for possible earthquake faults, landslides, and liquefaction to help identify where higher building standards may be necessary for safe development. Depending on the historical record of the intensity of earthquakes along these faults, there can be higher construction standards for buildings and possibly height limits and building spacing requirements for these zones. In addition, buildings, especially places of public assembly, should not be constructed over a fault zone. Mapping known fault lines should be part of the GIS-based map for all development regulations.

Require a solar and wind access plan for all subdivision and planned development approvals. Preserving access to light and air is a traditional purpose of zoning, which can be extended to preserve access to sunlight for solar energy panels and to preserve access to air currents to permit the operation of wind-driven generators. Again GIS makes it possible to add sunlight patterns at different times of the year as an overlay to the zoning map, so that, instead of requiring the calculation from the developer, the guidelines will already be in the ordinance and can be followed when the initial plans are being proposed. Wind patterns can also be mapped, although winds are much more variable than sunlight.

Remove parking requirements in commercial districts to make development more compatible with the natural environment. The most significant land-use component in retail development is parking, especially when it is built as an at-grade parking lot. As discussed earlier, meeting the minimum parking requirement for various kinds of retail use can take at least twice the land area of the building—and more if the building has multiple floors or is a big-box store or a restaurant. The comparable requirement for offices is a ratio of 3.0 or 3.5.[39] As office buildings are usually multistory, providing about 1,200 square feet of parking for every 1,000 square feet of leasable office space means that every office building where parking is provided at grade is completely surrounded by parking lots. As the grading and paving of parking lots have a significant environmental impact, are all these spaces necessary?

Donald Shoup, a distinguished research professor at the University of California, Los Angeles, asks the question, "Where do minimum parking requirements come from?" in an article published in the journal, *Transportation Research*. His answer is: "Nobody knows."[40] There is no backup in standard planning texts for the setting of parking ratios, and the subject is not normally covered in a planning curriculum. Shoup quotes another researcher, Richard Willson, who surveyed 144 cities in 1996 to find out how they determined their parking ratios. Willson found that the two most common methods were looking at the ratios used by other cities and referring to *Parking Generation*,[41] a handbook on parking ratios compiled by the Institute of Transportation Engineers (ITT). Looking at other ordinances creates a closed, self-referential system. Shoup quotes a study by the American Planning Association's Planning Advisory Service (PAS) that relying on other ordinances for parking ratios without independent verification may turn out to be a way of repeating someone else's mistakes. ITT does do its own research on parking use. The question then becomes, how good is this research? Shoup is skeptical. Using data summaries from *Parking Generation*, Shoup observes that half of the 101 reported parking-generation rates are based on four or fewer surveys of parking occupancy, and 22 percent are based on a single survey. Shoup notes that the surveyors go out of their way to pick places where there is only a single land use, no access to transit, and no shared parking in order to get clear data, but that selection also restricts the sample to relatively isolated suburban locations. Shoup goes on: "No information is provided on several key issues. Why and where were the surveys conducted? How long did the surveys last? How long did the peak parking occupancy last? Finally, nothing is said about off-peak parking occupancy."[42]

Shoup is on his way in this article to making a much larger point, namely, that the widespread availability of free parking, whose costs are covered by development, distorts the economics of all transportation. This argument is developed more completely in his 2011 book, *The High Cost of Free Parking*.[43]

Are the required parking ratios necessary for retail businesses? Many people would say no. It is rare to see a completely full retail parking lot. Retailers counter by saying that they need the parking for the peak selling season between Thanksgiving and New Year's, which can be as much as 40 percent of their business. Although increasing amounts of shopping take place online, shopping is also taking place in the brick and mortar stores, often by online shoppers who first visit the stores to see the merchandise before purchasing. As long as parking is still needed, lenders for retail development will require it. In the long run, will the retail parking requirements established many years earlier, before online retail became important, always be necessary? Certainly, the environmental damage caused by grading and paving the parking lot in newly developing areas will be permanent. So what should be done?

Eliminate minimum required parking ratios in commercial zones. The simplest way to determine whether current required parking ratios are really needed would be to require that all parking for retail development be located off street, but without a minimum required number of parking spaces. If business owners and lenders need parking to be at a particular ratio, developers can provide it, just as they can now. But if development is unconstrained by parking ratio requirements, and if developers have to make a decision about the number of spaces they are willing to pay for, the total number of needed parking spaces may prove to be lower than today.

In established commercial districts, businesses could satisfy their parking needs by participating in an association that would provide the necessary parking spaces within walking distance of their business. Today, many businesses post signs in their parking lots saying parking is for their customers only, so that people are supposed to drive from one store to another, even when the distances between them are easily walkable. If owners pooled their parking in a single district, all participants could benefit from the added flexibility. Parking districts would be particularly useful in places where the businesses are close together along a main street with sidewalks. The association could maintain an overflow parking field for the small number of peak retailing days, with frequent shuttle buses back and forth during that time. This land could be used for other purposes, like recreation, the rest of the year. On-site parking requirements in these zones could be eliminated, conditionally, if a business can show it is participating in a parking association with the necessary capacity. Potential spillover into the streets of neighboring residential areas could be prevented by issuing parking permits on these streets to residents only, something that is already done in many communities.

Managing Storm Water Runoff in Commercial Districts to Enhance the Environment

Large commercial developments usually require some kind of official review: subdivision, planned development, and, very often, some kind of zoning change or discretionary decision allowing for variation from the regulations. Once environmental factors are officially recognized as part of the zoning districts, environmental standards can be incorporated in these reviews. The biggest environmental issues for these developments are created by the storm water runoff from the parking lots and the rooftops. The usual engineering solution is to dig detention ponds or large ditches at the perimeter of the property. This can delay runoff, but it is not the best way to recharge groundwater; it uses up valuable land and sets up large barriers between streets and buildings, making walking from one place to another more difficult. There are alternatives that can be adopted as review standards.

Terrace the parking. While parking lots need to be flat, flattening the entire acreage needed for parking to a single level is not necessary. Each double row of cars can be relatively level, but the next double row of cars can be at a slightly lower or higher elevation, with a strip of landscaping retaining the grade between them. By terracing parking in this way, the change in grade across a property can be accommodated without drastic reconfiguring of the whole site. The driveways between rows of cars will be steeper than the parking rows, but they can be kept to a grade of 5 percent or less. There should then be no need for massive retaining walls at the perimeter of the property. The actual design of such a site plan has to be suited to the particular local conditions, but standards can be written and compliance reviewed as part of the overall review process.

Use permeable paving for parking. As we noted in discussing residential driveways, improvements in technology have made paving materials available that can be put down as a single, unbroken layer, like conventional asphalt, but permit water to filter through the paving to the ground below. Before, to have equivalent permeability, it was necessary to use gravel or special pavers, both of which have maintenance issues. This new kind of pervious paving can be used for the parking spaces and parking aisles, as well as roadways within a site where low impacts are expected. Areas with heavy truck traffic will still need conventional paving. Adding standards for this kind of parking lot construction will help manage storm water runoff and will permit recharge of groundwater over a larger area than would conventional retention ponds.

Use landscaping to reduce heat island effects. Providing shade trees in parking lots can greatly reduce heat island effects. Trees can be planted at the ends of parking rows or in strips between files of parking—an alternative that would fit well with terraced parking lots, as the trees can be planted in the boundaries between the terraces. A ratio of shade trees to number of parking spaces should be a requirement in the zoning and reviewed according to tree planting standards when individual site plans are proposed.

Require cisterns for roof water in commercial districts. Water from the large, flat roofs of retail development should be retained in cisterns and used for cleaning roadways and parking lots and watering landscaping. Cisterns can be installed under landscaped areas, walkways, and parking lots. The aggregate of retaining storm water in this way will greatly diminish the negative effects of commercial development on surrounding streets and properties.

Retrofitting Previously Developed Areas for Environmental Compatibility

Land already urbanized under outmoded zoning ordinances can gradually be brought back into a better relationship with the natural environment through regulations that apply when changes are made to existing buildings or building sites that reach or exceed defined thresholds. Retrofit implementation can include the following provisions.

Add rain barrels and cisterns in residential developments. Requirements that water from rooftops be retained in rain barrels or cisterns can be added to all the residential zones in a locality. The regulations apply to all new development and all changes to a building of more than a defined level of expenditure. In addition, local legislation could require all residential buildings to meet this requirement by a deadline. The local water utility can do the installation, and householders could pay a one-time charge or meet the cost through an addition to their water bill—much as people pay for a new hot water heater through an increment to their electric bill. As noted previously, if rain barrels or cisterns reduce water usage, they should make the homeowner eligible for rebates on the water bill.

Require residential driveways to be made of permeable material. Requiring permeable paving for driveways can be added to residential zone requirements, so that when a driveway is replaced as part of a larger renovation, it must be paved in a permeable material, such as the new pervious paving that can be put down as a single, unbroken layer.

Retrofit existing commercial parking lots. When parking lots in commercial districts are repaved as part of a major renovation, the old paving should be broken up and taken away, and replaced, where appropriate, with the new type of permeable parking material that can have a unitary surface. Landscaping standards should also be met as far as practicable.

On established commercial properties where runoff has been managed with large retention ponds or drainage swales, if parking lots are rebuilt as terraces, using permeable surface materials and with appropriate landscaping, some of the land devoted to water retention can be repurposed for additional buildings, possibly using underground cisterns as part of the foundations for these buildings. Eliminating minimum parking requirements makes such intensification of development more likely.

The aggregate effect of rooftop water retention and more permeable paving over large areas can transform the management of storm water, reducing the load on sewage treatment plants and making the landscape more environmentally balanced.

Legal considerations in implementing retrofits. A local government's ability to require retrofitting of existing developed sites to bring them more in compliance with standards designed to reduce their impact on the natural environment is possible when an owner initiates a proposal to redevelop or renovate an existing use that requires a rezoning, a special permit approval, a variance, or some other type of discretionary approval. At the same time, the implementation of retrofit standards, whether in the form of environmental standards or urban design standards, must be reasonable and must not significantly impact the economic viability of the use. For example, in a Missouri case,[44] the owners of property used as a gas station and car wash proposed to rebuild their station, which was permissible under the applicable base zoning district. However, the city had adopted a corridor overlay district, with neo-traditional requirements, called the Main Street Corridor Special Review District (MSSRD). The district imposed a build-to line of 10 feet from the street for all buildings in the corridor as well as other building-design and materials requirements. The owners challenged the ordinances establishing the corridor overlay district on the ground that the MSSRD regulations effectively modified their "use." The appeals court agreed with the trial court that "requiring a new service station to have its building within ten feet of the street is clearly a modification . . . [and] that the effect of Ordinance #59380 with the ten-feet setback requirement is so burdensome as to these plaintiffs as to be confiscatory."[45] While a state or federal takings claim is unlikely to prevail so long as a property that is impacted by the retrofit requirements is not rendered unproductive, such requirements may still be challenged as unreasonable under state or federal law. And if the property owner is in a state that has adopted property rights legislation, the local government may also face a claim for compensation based on substantial loss of property value.[46]

By way of contrast to this example, in later chapters of this book we recommend build-to lines for several types of situations where complying with a build-to line is not difficult. In the Main Street Corridor case, the property owner was not proposing an entire new building but simply a plan to rebuild an existing structure. The build-to line would have had operational impacts with significant economic consequences and would have required moving the entire building to a new location, imposing high costs, especially as service stations are subject to EPA cleanup requirements when the redevelopment on the site alters the location of the building.

This case is a good reminder that circumstances can make it difficult to apply new regulations to a specific existing development. But retrofitting roof drains with cisterns, requiring a permeable material for new driveways, and modifying parking lots to improve storm water management all clearly benefit the community and, in most cases, are unlikely to be determined to impose significant economic hardship on the property owner.

Incorporating Environmental Considerations into Development Approval Decisions

Because GIS now makes it possible to map environmental conditions, they can be included in the considerations for defining and mapping land-use zones and intensity of development. Provided the necessary GIS-based environmental and planning analysis is done through the comprehensive planning process to support implementation measures, the carrying capacity of land can become a consideration in zoning and other types of regulatory measures, along with more traditional considerations such as transportation access. Where the plan identifies steep slopes or river edges that are subject to flooding, these areas can be mapped at lower permissible densities than other parts of the landscape that are more appropriate for development. If it is not feasible to undertake a comprehensive rezoning to implement the environmental factual findings and policies adopted in a comprehensive plan, establishing environmental overlay zones could be a shorter-term implementation measure. The overlay could require development to address underlying natural conditions like steep slopes or flood-prone areas, subject to the previously discussed legal principles for imposing mitigation requirements on individual developments.[47]

The analogy to this GIS-based overlay zone approach can be found in development impact fee programs, in which a local government must first decide what level of service for a facility or service (for example, roads or sewer) it wishes to maintain for the community. The local government has the initial obligation to fund improvements necessary to bring the facility or service up to the desired level of service; after that, the developer may be required to pay its proportionate share of improvements to maintain that level of service when its project is developed. The obvious distinction to be made in the case of the environment is that, to preserve natural systems, there are certain levels of protection that cannot be compromised. Because these natural systems benefit the public generally, but typically do not conform to zoning or local government jurisdictional boundaries, intergovernmental agreements to invest public funds to preserve these systems may be necessary.

Planning for and Managing Development on the Basis of Watersheds

The logical next step from establishing a comprehensive plan for environmental protection or GIS-based environmental overlay zones within local jurisdictions is to recognize the importance of watershed-based planning and regulation. Watersheds are the natural systems made up of streams and their tributaries and the sloping land that forms a drainage basin that feeds storm water into a common outlet point, such as a larger stream or lake.[48] Watersheds seldom have the same boundaries as property lines or even the jurisdictional boundaries of a community. It is hard to manage storm water and other environmental issues effectively if planning and regulation are not coordinated across an entire watershed.

Intergovernmental Agreements. For a watershed approach to be effective, the local governments, whose jurisdictions cross one or more watersheds, should enter into intergovernmental agreements to address non-point-source pollution within the watershed and to coordinate land use and development regulations directed at protecting surface waters. These local governments would also need to engage in partnerships with private stakeholders. But as ecologically desirable as watershed-based planning and zoning is, it is precisely because watersheds do not conform to local jurisdictional boundaries that such an approach can be politically difficult to achieve. Lack of funding, lack of trust among neighboring communities, and the concern by communities for their respective home rule powers, are often-cited obstacles to achieving multijurisdictional watershed management.[49]

In the absence of formal intergovernmental agreements to coordinate planning and land-use regulation on a watershed basis, some communities have formed watershed associations, which comprise the relevant jurisdictions and can promote coordinated actions and reduce the burden on individual property owners. This practice should be adopted more widely.

Storm Water Management Districts. The existence of a watershed association to which a community can belong makes it easier to create cooperative associations among property owners who form a storm water management district, so that retention requirements do not fall unequally on different property owners and storm water is managed as part of a watershed, and not just for an individual property.

Notes

1. Of course, local ordinances will each use different figures. But the people writing the ordinances tend to consult similar sources. A publication of the American Association of State Highway and Transportation Officials (AASHTO) sets recommended maximum grades for local streets at 7 percent in largely flat areas and up to 10 percent in rolling terrain, both at a design speed of 30 miles per hour. The recommended maximum allowable grade for wider, collector streets is 9 percent in relatively flat terrain and up to 11 percent when the land is steeper. American Association of State Highway and Transportation Officials, *Geometric Design of Highways and Streets* (Washington, DC, 2004).
2. Myer Kutz, *The Handbook of Transportation Engineering*, 2nd ed. (New York: McGraw Hill, 2011), chap. 10, sec. 8.
3. See, for example, Daniel R. Mandelker, *Planned Unit Developments*, Planning Advisory Service Report No. 545 (Chicago: American Planning Association, March 2007), 65.
4. See Randall Arendt, *Conservation Design for Subdivisions* (Washington, DC: Island Press, 1996).
5. However, it is possible to include conservation subdivision design standards within PUD provisions. Ideally, there should be a local comprehensive plan that identifies where CSD is appropriate and then, through the PUD provisions, addresses what percentage of a project must be protected as open space and which provisions of the zoning and subdivision ordinances (for example, number of lot splits, lot size minimum, setback requirements, types of utilities allowed, road widths, and so on) can be modified through the PUD process.
6. Randall Arendt, "Conservation Subdivision Design: A Brief Overview," n.d., *www.greenerprospects.com/PDFs/CSD_Overview.pdf.*
7. 33 U.S.C. §§ 1251 et seq.
8. The Clean Water Act defines "discharge of a pollutant" to mean "any addition of any pollutant to navigable waters from any point source." 33 U.S.C. § 1362(12). Point sources are discrete conveyances such as pipes or manmade ditches. 40 C.F.R. § 122.2—Definitions.
9. 39 U.S.C. § 1329.
10. See U.S. Environmental Protection Agency, "National Pollution Discharge Elimination System" (Washington, DC, 2017), *www.epa.gov/npdes.* See also

Brian W. Blaesser and Alan C. Weinstein, *Federal Land Use Law & Litigation* (St. Paul, MN: Thomson-Reuters, 2017), §§8:20–8:25.

11. The Institute of Transportation Engineers (ITT) recommends 5.5 cars per 1,000 square feet of gross leasable area for weekday operation and a ratio of 6.0 on Saturdays in its *Transportation Planning Handbook*, 3rd ed. (Washington, DC: Institute of Transportation Engineers, 2009). The planning and urban design standards prepared by the American Planning Association (APA) follow the Urban Land Institute (ULI) suggestion of car ratios of 4.0 for smaller centers and 4.5 for larger centers but otherwise adopt the *Transportation Planning Handbook* numbers, including 6.0 for big-box stores and 15.0 to 21.5 cars for restaurants. See American Planning Association, *Planning and Urban Design Standards* (Hoboken, NJ: Wiley, 2006), 246, table.

12. The actual grading requirements are contained in local codes, but the 5 percent maximum figure can be found in many documents that summarize planning practice—for example, the standards of the General Services Administration for Federal Buildings and the American Institute of Architects' *The Architect's Handbook of Professional Practice* (Hoboken, NJ: Wiley, 2011). "Most passenger cars are not affected by uphill or downhill grades of less than 5%," according to Kutz, *The Handbook of Transportation Engineering*, chap. 9, sec. 10.

13. There are state environmental policy acts in fifteen states and the District of Columbia. See Daniel R. Mandelker, *NEPA Law and Litigation* (St. Paul, MN: Thomson-Reuters, 2016), chap. 12.

14. For example, the Massachusetts act establishes cutoff points over which impacts are considered significant enough to require the preparation of an impact statement. See Mass. Regs. Code tit. 301 § 11.01(2)(b). Minnesota has categories of actions that define whether impact statements are required. See Minn. Stat. Ann. § 116D.04 subd. 2a(a). Examples of these types of thresholds from the Massachusetts act are (1) direct alteration of fifty or more acres of land; (2) creation of ten or more acres of impervious area; (3) conversion of land in active agricultural use to nonagricultural use; (4) alteration of a designated significant wildlife habitat; (5) alteration of one or more acres of salt marsh or bordering vegetating wetlands; or (6) alteration of ten or more acres of any other wetlands. Mass. Regs. Code 301 § 11.03.

15. Dillon's Rule is used to construe statutes that delegate authority to local governments. The rule states that local governments have no inherent powers and are limited to those powers granted by the state constitution or state legislature. See, for example, *Merriam v. Moody's Ex'rs*, 25 Iowa 163, 170 (1868). In states that follow Dillon's Rule, courts construe the rule to require strict adherence by local governments to the scope of land-use regulations and procedures established by the state.

16. A state constitution or state statute may grant local governments home rule authority, which gives local governments broader powers of self-government. The scope of home rule can vary by jurisdiction. Some states broadly define what

are matters of local concern; others broadly define what are matters of statewide concern or define municipal functions narrowly. Still other jurisdictions allow home rule only where there is an affirmative grant from the state. More permissive home rule jurisdictions have what is called legislative home rule, under which local governments may exercise all powers the state legislature is capable of delegating to them even though the legislature has not delegated the power. Local governments typically implement their constitutional home rule powers through the adoption of a charter that specifies their home rule authority.

17. This approach is discussed in American Planning Association's *Growing Smart Legislative Guidebook* (Chicago: American Planning Association, 2002), chap. 12.
18. See discussion of the goal of efficiency in chapter 7 of this book.
19. See discussion of relevant legal principles in chapter 7.
20. The legal principle of proportionality is discussed in chapter 7.
21. See chapter 7.
22. See, for example, Herbert Hovenkamp, *Principles of Property Law* (St. Paul, MN: West Academic Publishing, 2005); Herbert Thorndike Tiffany, *A Treatise on the Modern Law of Real Property* (Chicago: Callaghan, 1940), sec. 29.
23. The term *nuisance* refers to the use of one's property in a manner that seriously interferes with another's use or enjoyment of his or her property (a private nuisance) or is injurious to the community at large (a public nuisance). Unlike the concept of trespass to land, nuisance does not require a physical invasion of others' property. See, generally, Brian W. Blaesser and Alan C. Weinstein, eds., *Land Use and the Constitution* (Chicago: Planners Press, 1989), 9.
24. See discussion of relevant legal principles in chapter 7.
25. Christopher J. Duerksen and Suzanne Richman, *Tree Conservation Ordinances: Land-Use Regulations Go Green* (Chicago and Washington, DC: American Planning Association, 1993), 10–15, 36, 400. Scenic America, "Strategies for Tree Conservation," *www.scenic.org/issues/tree-conservation/strategies-for-tree-conservation*; Elizabeth Brabec, "Trees Make Sense," in Duerksen and Richman, *Tree Conservation Ordinances*, appendix B, 99; Thomas Hayden, *Hot Ways to Cool Down Our Cities*, *City Trees* 36 (6), *www.urban-forestry.com/citytrees*; E. Gregory McPherson et al., "Benefit-Cost Analysis of Modesto's Municipal Urban Forest," *Journal of Arboriculture* 25, no. 235 (1999); Michael F. Galvin, Becky Wilson, and Marian Honeczy, "Maryland's Forest Conservation Act: A Process for Urban Greenspace Protection During the Development Process," *Journal of Arboriculture* 26, no. 275 (2000); Jim Schwab, ed., *Planning the Urban Forest*, PAS Report No. 555 (Chicago: American Planning Association, 2009).
26. See discussion of takings clause in chapter 7.
27. For example, one county tree ordinance in Georgia states as its purpose: "The protection of the public health, safety, general welfare, and aesthetics of the

County and all of its citizens; the promotion of several environmental benefits for the citizens and their communities; the protection of specimen and historical trees; the prevention of the loss of mature trees and the ensuring of appropriate replanting; and, the enhancement of the quality of life in the County." Code of DeKalb County § 14-39(a).

28. See Georgetown County, South Carolina Tree Protection Regulations, art. IX, §§ 1102–1103 (draft of proposed regulations dated June 14, 1999).
29. See Code of DeKalb County, GA §§ 14-39 (e)(1)(b) and (e)(2).
30. See, for example, City of Jacksonville, Florida Landscape and Tree Protection Regulations, pt. 12, chap. 656, sec. 656.1210 (proposed amendments to regulations dated July 7, 1999).
31. *Nollan v. California Coastal Comm'n*, 483 U.S. 825 (1987); *Dolan v. City of Tigard*, 512 U.S. 374 (1994). See discussion of these cases in chapter 7.
32. *Koontz v. St. Johns River Water Management Dist.*, 133 S. Ct. 2586 (2013). See discussion of *Koontz* in chapter 7.
33. See, for example, *Greater Atlanta Homebuilders Association et al. v. DeKalb County et al.*, 588 S.E.2d 694 (Ga. 2003).
34. See *Mayor and Council of Rockville v. Rylyns Enterprises, Inc.*, 372 Md. 514, 814 A.2d 469, 482 (2002). See also discussion in chapter 7.
35. *Chrinko v. South Brunswick Tp. Planning Bd.*, 77 N.J. Super. 594, 187 A.2d 221, 225 (Las Div. 1963).
36. See discussion of concept of rational basis in chapter 7.
37. See discussion of this test relative to tree preservation ordinances noted earlier and of legal principles in chapter 7.
38. Alquist-Priolo Earthquake Fault Zoning Act, California Public Resources Code, div. 2, chap. 7.5.
39. See table in American Planning Association, *Planning and Urban Design Standards* (Hoboken, NJ: Wiley, 2006), 246.
40. Donald Shoup, "The Trouble with Minimum Parking Requirements," *Transportation Research Part A: Policy and Practice* 33A (7/8, 1999): 349–374.
41. Institute of Transportation Engineers, *Parking Generation*, 4th ed. (Washington, DC: Institute of Transportation Engineers, 2010). This is the edition currently available. The criticisms by Richard Willson and Donald Shoup relate to earlier editions.
42. Donald Shoup, "The Trouble with Minimum Parking Requirements," *Transportation Research Part A: Policy and Practice* 33A, no. 7/8 (1999): 551.
43. Donald Shoup, *The High Cost of Free Parking* (Chicago: Planners Press, 2005, revised 2011).
44. *Dallen v. City of Kansas City*, 822 S.W.2d 429 (Mo. App. W.D. 1991).

45. Ibid., 433.

46. See, for example, Bert J. Harris Jr. Private Property Rights Act, sec. 70.001, Florida Statutes; Arizona Private Property Rights Protection Act Ariz. Rev. Stat. Ann. § 12-1131 et seq. See also discussion in chapter 7.

47. See discussion in chapter 7.

48. For a good introduction to watershed management, see Kenneth N. Brooks, Peter F. Folliott, and Joseph A. Manger, *Hydrology and the Management of Watersheds*, 4th ed. (Oxford, UK: Wiley-Blackwell, 2012).

49. See Jim Schwab, "Crossing the Home-Rule Boundaries Should Be Mandatory: Advocating for a Watershed Approach to Zoning and Land Use in Ohio," *Cleveland State Law Review* 58, no. 463 (2010).

2

Managing Climate Change Locally

The American Association for the Advancement of Science published a report in 2014 entitled *What We Know: The Reality, Risks, and Response to Climate Change.*[1] "Climate Change is happening now. And it is going to get worse." is a headline in the introductory part of the report, which concludes that rising global temperatures will increase the frequency and intensity of natural disasters, including droughts, heat waves, forest fires, and flood surges, and that, as the world population keeps growing while droughts and changing temperatures make crop failures more likely, climate change will also increase the risk of serious food shortages.[2]

Many critical actions about climate change are being undertaken at the international,[3] national,[4] and state levels.[5] The role of local regulations in managing climate change is limited because of the global nature and scale of the problem. But there are significant regulatory initiatives that local governments can take to mitigate climate change and to adapt to changes that have already begun—initiatives that concern real estate development and urban growth management. Mitigation strategies are directed at the activities that help cause climate change. Adaptation strategies deal with the existing and predicted future impacts of climate change.

This chapter focuses on the local government regulatory initiatives that can at least help slow down climate change and help local governments manage its current and long-term effects.

How Local Development Regulations Can Help Manage Climate Change

Mitigation strategies at the local level can help limit motor vehicle emissions and consumption of energy for heating and air-conditioning buildings. Regulations can include measures to reduce vehicle miles through land-use planning and by making buildings more energy efficient through building codes, which can also require the use of green building techniques. Policies and regulations for making development relate to the natural environment, as discussed in chapter 1, can help temper climate change by reducing warming created by urbanized areas. Compact development, considered in chapter 3, can reduce auto use by making transit and walking more feasible. Preserving older structures, a focus of chapter 4, reduces the need to draw on natural resources for new building materials. While such modifications to development regulations have other important benefits, they also serve as mitigation strategies that moderate the forces creating climate change.

Sun and wind energy reduce the need for fossil fuels, heading off factors that contribute to global warming. The right local development regulations can make using such renewable forms of energy more effective.

Adaptation strategies, directed at the existing impacts of climate change, are more of a local issue than mitigation because the best methods to deal with these effects will vary substantially depending on geographical location. Adaptation strategies can address local impacts of climate change, such as wildfire, sea level rise, drought, and heat waves, while also reducing vulnerability to future climate change. Revising development regulations, although not the only tool for adapting to climate change, will be essential.

Local Adaptation to Increasing Risk of Natural Disasters

Traditionally, natural disasters have been considered inherently unpredictable, and the potential for future disasters has been managed by insurance policies. When a disaster occurs, there are also special programs from the federal government and individual states, after a state of emergency has been declared, and money is provided in annual budgets to deal with such emergencies. According to the Insurance Information Institute, the total of insured losses from extreme weather events between 1995 and 2014 in the United States, adjusted to 2014 dollars, was just under $400 billion.[6] If, as experts predict, climate change continues to intensify the frequency and severity of these weather-related events, insurance companies will need to reevaluate the risks of providing insurance in places where natural disasters have become more likely. The companies can raise premiums, and, at some point, the premiums may become unaffordable for most people. Eventually insurance companies may refuse to write policies for properties in some areas. The budgets for disaster relief will also be increasingly strained. While natural disasters remain unpredictable, as their probability increases, it is prudent to do whatever is possible to protect the landscape and property and to minimize the damage from such disasters, which, of course, endanger human life as well. People and property in vulnerable locations can be protected before a disaster in three ways:

1. Create a protective system that covers an entire area.
2. Institute protective measures on individual properties.
3. Limit development in locations where an overall protective system is not feasible or cost effective and where protections on individual properties prove insufficient.

In the discussion that follows, we apply these three general propositions to forest-fire and flood risks, and then consider drought, heat waves, and food security.

Adapting to Increased Wildfire Risks

As warmer weather and longer summers advance northward (and southward in the Southern Hemisphere), trees become less adapted to their environment because of changes in seasonal temperature and rainfall patterns. Trees begin to die, particularly if warming weather is accompanied by drought. Insect populations, once held in check by the onset of cold weather, have more time to feed on tree trunks and leaves. Dry and dying trees have recently increased the fire danger in the United States, particularly in the western states. According to Thomas Tidwell, the chief of the U.S. Forest Service, in 2015 congressional testimony, fires have increased since 1995 in severity, intensity, and cost as fire seasons have lasted on average more than 70 days longer. Drought and increased temperatures have contributed to dangerous conditions, compounded by more people moving into fire-prone areas. In 1995, wildfire funds made up 16 percent of the Forest Service's annual appropriated budget; in 2015, for the first time, more than 50 percent of the Forest Service's annual budget was dedicated to fighting wildfires.[7]

More people have moved into fire-prone areas. Tidwell states that the number of housing units within half a mile of a national forest grew from 484,000 in 1940 to 1.8 million in 2000. Housing units within national forest boundaries rose from 335,000 in 1940 to 1.2 million in 2000. Forest Service estimates indicate that a total of almost 400 million acres of all vegetated lands are at moderate-to-high risk from uncharacteristically large wildfires, more than 70,000 communities are at risk, and fewer than 15,000 communities have a wildfire protection plan.[8] Building in fire-prone areas, and creating places where the built environment interacts with fire-prone areas, has led to the use of the term *wildland-urban interface* (WUI). The federal definition of WUI is "the area where structures and other developments meet or intermingle with undeveloped wildland."[9]

Wildfire protection for large areas. Comprehensive measures to protect large areas from wildfire have proved difficult to implement. Public education programs remind people that they can prevent forest fires by being careful with fire in wilderness areas. Thomas Tidwell, in a 2013 testimony before a Senate committee, described programs to restore or create fire-adapted ecosystems by thinning trees or conducting controlled burns. Another technique he mentioned is removal of leaf litter and debris on the forest floor as well as the branches and foliage of small trees that provide "ladder fuels," allowing surface fires to transition to the entire tree, which is otherwise less susceptible to burning—management techniques once used by Native Americans. Forty-two percent of the national forests need such preventive treatment, according to Tidwell. Unfortunately, he went on to say, the increasing costs of fighting fires has caused the Forest Service to transfer funds from fire protection programs to pay for fighting the increasing incidences of forest fires.[10]

Local wildfire protection plans. After the 2000 wildfire season, as a result of increased public pressure on Congress for greater federal attention to problems in the WUI, Congress passed the Healthy Forests Restoration Act of 2003 (HFRA).[11] One of the stated purposes of the HFRA is "to enhance efforts to protect watersheds and address threats to forest and rangeland health, including catastrophic wildfire, across the landscape."[12] The HFRA gives priority to the development of community wildlife protection plans (CWPP). A CWPP "identifies and prioritizes areas for hazardous fuel reduction treatments and recommends the types and methods of treatment on federal and nonfederal land that will protect one or more at-risk communities and essential infrastructure; and recommends measures to reduce structural ignitability throughout the at-risk community."[13] These wildfire protection plans are prepared in accordance with a planning process that involves the Forest Service and the Bureau of Land Management working with a local community to prepare a community base map that establishes the WUI and displays inhabited areas at risk, forested areas that contain critical infrastructure needed by the community, and areas at risk for large-scale fire disturbance—all basic factors to be used by the community in developing a plan. The CWPPs, however, are consensus documents and do not have any legal force, although they include a process for setting community priorities for dealing with risks.[14]

Development regulations can be used to implement a wildfire protection plan. Using data from aerial photos, historic records of wildfires, and contour maps, local governments in forested areas can employ expert analysis to map potential fire-hazard areas and attempt to quantify wildfire risks for specific geographical areas and properties within those areas. A complex array of factors contributes to wildfire risk, including type and distribution of vegetation, proximity of structures to fire-prone vegetation and other combustible structures, weather patterns, topography, hydrology, average lot size, and road construction. GIS-based zoning maps would make it easier to delineate fire-hazard zones because factors such as prevailing wind directions can be incorporated in the maps, using such sources as the wind data available from the Natural Resources Conservation Service of the U.S. Department of Agriculture.

To ensure both the comprehensiveness and the legal defensibility of any regulatory implementation measures, a CWPP for a community that is located within a potential fire-hazard area should be tied to the local comprehensive planning process. Dealing with fire hazards constitutes one component of planning for natural hazards. For local community areas within the WUI, the comprehensive plan's natural-hazards element should be based on studies that support policies for approving building materials, creating and maintaining defensible space, and clearing dead and dying trees and other vegetation.

Based on these studies, wildfire overlay zones can be adopted that delineate one or more GIS-based zoning districts for areas with high wildfire risk. Within a wildfire overlay zone, development can be required to comply with wildfire mitigation standards that are factually based and proportional to the impact a development will have within the defined zone.[15] These requirements may include creating defensible space around buildings by reducing vegetation and other elements that might fuel a fire, providing emergency vehicle access and water supply, constructing houses on sites that will be less vulnerable to wildfire, and using fire-resistant materials in construction. It may be necessary to create tree-free areas or firebreaks to prevent the spread of forest fires to developed properties. If these firebreaks are established on private property, the land may need to be purchased through local or state funds.

Defining wildfire hazard risk areas. States are developing methodologies to classify wildfire hazard risk areas because the task of identifying wildfire hazard zones is complex. Because of the implications for property owners in the WUI, it is important that these methodologies be reliable in identifying wildfire risk. For example, in 2013, the governor of Colorado created a task force to "identify and reach agreement on ways to encourage activities, practices and policies that would reduce the risk of loss in the WUI and provide greater customer choice and knowledge of insurance options."[16] The task force prepared a report[17] that recommended the mapping of the WUI areas within Colorado and identifying the wildfire risk for properties in these areas.[18] The Task Force Report focused primarily on the Colorado State Forest Service's Colorado Wildfire Risk Assessment Portal (CO-WRAP) to determine a property's risk, but acknowledged that CO-WRAP was not sufficiently developed to operate as a statewide disclosure tool at the individual parcel level.[19]

Despite the undeveloped state of this tool, the task force recommended requiring that a property's CO-WRAP wildfire risk score be disclosed to potential homebuyers, financial institutions, and insurance companies at the time the property is sold. This requirement would be implemented through an amendment to the standard form real estate contract. Under the real estate contract, if the score indicated a high-risk property, that would trigger a wildfire risk audit.[20] However, this approach—scoring individual properties to identify wildfire risk and making this information available through a time-of-sale wildfire risk audit on residential sales—has not been effective in achieving the desired public safety benefit.

Real estate transactions occur relatively infrequently, with only a small percentage of the total existing housing inventory being sold in any given year. Therefore, the public safety benefit of a time-of-sale requirement is questionable, as it would affect only a small percentage of properties each year. Moreover, the benefits of an audit, which would force some mitigation, are temporary, as this requirement would not force a buyer to consider the wildfire risk after the purchase has been made. Responsible buyers and lenders will obtain the wildfire risk information and factor it into their purchase or financing decisions in any case.

The Task Force Report also recommended the imposition of fees on properties proposed for development in the WUI. As in other examples discussed in this book, such fees are a form of exaction that must satisfy the *Nollan/Dolan* Dual Nexus Test that requires that there be an "essential nexus" between a legitimate governmental purpose and the imposition of a fee, and that there be "rough proportionality" between the fee and the impact of the particular land use or development. It would not appear difficult to establish an essential nexus between the state's interest in controlling wildfires and the imposition of a fee on WUI property owners under a wildfire risk program. However, the actual amount of the fee imposed as a condition of approval for a home built in the WUI must be roughly proportional to the home's impact, as established by a methodology that may take into account a wildfire risk score, but also any other factors that ensure that the resulting fee satisfies the "rough proportionality" requirement under *Nollan/Dolan*.[21]

Dealing with places that are too hazardous to protect from fire. Some locations may prove to be too hazardous to be protected by local measures or comprehensive forest management or cannot be protected with sufficient certainty. In such locations or zones, local government may have to prohibit or strictly limit new development and seek to purchase at-risk properties. Such properties could be acquired through offers of purchase by a local government fund or fire-protection trust, concepts that are comparable to measures established for buying out property owners in flood-prone areas. Ideally, all owners would eventually be bought out and these hazardous zones could become firebreaks or be returned to forest management.

As forest-fire dangers increase, the capital costs for buyouts will be less expensive than the cumulative costs of firefighting, evacuating residents, and property damage, and a buyout policy will be preferable to leaving residents in harm's way and sending teams of firefighters into danger.

Adapting to Increased Flood Risks

As discussed in chapter 1, FEMA flood maps should become part of GIS-based local zoning maps. Incorporating this information will facilitate mapping flood-risk zones in each jurisdiction. In coastal areas, these maps would include both boundaries for areas affected by flood surges and for areas where the velocity of the flood surge will introduce significant horizontal forces that can damage or destroy buildings. For inland locations, flood-risk zones would primarily identify the boundaries of areas subject to flooding.

Traditionally, flood maps have delineated the areas of 100-year and 500-year floodplains. The numbers reflect probabilities: a 100-year flood has a likelihood of occurring once in 100 years. Of course, this means there could be two 100-year floods in a row, but the probabilities are against this happening. The problem with relying on the maps of floodplain boundaries is that the criteria for drawing them depend primarily on the measurement of past floods. Increased urbanization speeds up and amplifies flooding and puts more development in the way of possible flood damage. In the future, climate change is likely to make storm events more frequent and raise sea levels—which feed back into river estuaries and affect shorelines. The Federal Emergency Management Agency manages a continuous process of bringing floodplain and flood-surge velocity maps up to date. It is important for local regulations to have accurate maps showing the potential for flood surges and flash floods.

In 2007 the Intergovernmental Panel on Climate Change predicted a rise in average sea level of as much as .59 meters by the year 2100, which is about two feet, with most of the change taking place in the latter part of the twenty-first century. That prediction seemed comfortably far off. However, the panel did not include the potential effects of glacial melting when the ice is situated over land, as the models for predicting this change were not yet sufficiently developed. The German scientist Stefan Rahmstorf suggested a way to compensate for the lack of defined information about glacial melting by relating sea-level rise to overall temperature changes, leading him to predict a range with a mean of just a little less than a meter more than 1990 water levels by 2100.[22] The panel's 2014 report put the upper end of average sea-level rise at about one meter by 2100.[23] These predictions are still not that alarming. Since then, however, observations of melting glaciers, and of Arctic and Antarctic ice, have shown melting to be taking place much faster than anyone predicted even a few years ago. New measurements have caused noted climate scientist James Hansen, formerly of NASA and now at Columbia University, to state: "My conclusion, based on the total information available, is that continued high emissions would result in multi-meter sea level rise this century and lock in continued ice sheet disintegration such that building cities or rebuilding cities on coast lines would become foolish."[24]

Hansen is careful to say that he does not consider this prediction to be inevitable. There is still time for worldwide intergovernmental action to stop "continued high emissions" but the available time to do this is growing short.

Hansen and other scientists make it clear that, whatever measures are taken to reduce or halt global warming, a substantial sea-level rise by 2050 is inevitable. Communities in vulnerable locations such as Miami Beach and Norfolk, Virginia, are already seeing unprecedented flooding after what used to be ordinary high tides. An increase in world average sea-level of even one meter might appear to be something that could be managed with a small sea wall; but the problem is the augmentation of high tides and storm surges, which can become more forceful and spread the effects of a big storm over a much wider area than is reached today. Rising sea levels can also infiltrate subsurface areas, contaminating the water table and possibly causing the land above it to subside. And 2050, while it may also seem to be a long time from now, is actually a much more immediate deadline, as it took until the 1980s to put together effective protections for London and the Netherlands after a devastating North Sea storm in 1953.

There are three choices for how to deal with flood risks comparable to the choices for fire risks. First, it is possible to create collective protection for densely populated areas that will shield everyone from the worst effects of flooding, saving individual property owners within the protected area from having to make substantial changes. Second, for flooding in unprotected areas, raising the height of habitable floors and making sure that mechanical equipment is above flood levels could be effective. Third, in places where collective protection is considered too costly and effective action on individual properties is not practical, it will be necessary to phase out allowing people to live in such areas, beginning with a ban on new development, followed by buyouts when properties come up for sale, and eventually by buyouts of entire areas. All of these alternatives are disruptive and costly, but may eventually become necessary in some coastal areas and along some rivers.

Protecting all properties within large areas. The U.S. Army Corps of Engineers has built levees along many major U.S. river systems, beginning with the Mississippi and Sacramento River basins in the late 1920s and extending now to flood protection throughout the United States. Properties within the protected area generally are not required to have other defenses from flooding under local development regulations, although there may be FEMA flood requirements for some of these areas because of times when levees were breached or overtopped. The issue now is whether a comparable level of engineered protection can be extended to newly vulnerable areas, such as coastal cities at increasing risk from flood surges.

After disastrous floods in London in 1953, a movable flood barrier was installed in the Thames River downstream from central London. It was completed in 1983. Since the Thames Barrier began operating, it has been raised more than 150 times, sometimes to control flood surges coming up the Thames estuary and sometimes, by keeping the tidal water out, to create a temporary reservoir to help manage floodwaters coming down the Thames after a heavy rain. The use of the barrier has become more frequent in recent years. There are engineering studies in progress of ways to enlarge or replace the barrier in preparation for anticipated future sea-level rise. There is also a long array of coastal flood barriers, the Delta Works, constructed in the Netherlands after extensive damage from the same 1953 storm. The existence of these protections has meant that development behind these barriers has continued to have its traditional relationship to waterfronts and ground levels.[25]

New Orleans is the only major city in the United States to have flood-surge barriers. They failed during Hurricane Katrina in 2005, and the result was devastating damage. The cause of the failure turned out to be both faulty design and improper construction, and the barriers have now been rebuilt to provide the protection from a category 3 hurricane, as was originally intended, although they are still not designed to manage a category 4 or 5 storm.[26]

Superstorm Sandy (not quite a category 1 hurricane) caused storm surges that invaded lower Manhattan in 2012. Waters poured into vehicle and subway tunnels, flooded streets and stores, and swamped an electrical substation, blacking out most of the lower Manhattan area. Basements flooded, and elevator machinery and heating and air-conditioning equipment were incapacitated, rendering office buildings unusable and apartments uninhabitable. The same storm brought very damaging flood surges and flooding to other coastal regions of New York City and the surrounding coastlines in New Jersey, New York, and Connecticut. Recovery has been paid for partly by insurance and disaster relief, and for the most part the recovery objective has been to put everything back the way it was before.[27]

After Superstorm Sandy, New York City mayor Michael Bloomberg ruled out seeking funds for anything like the flood barriers that protect London and the Netherlands, judging that there would be no political support for the capital costs required, and instead prepared a plan to make New York's infrastructure more resilient, including recommendations for what owners could do to make their individual properties safer.[28]

The U.S. Department of Housing and Urban Development, along with the Rockefeller Foundation and other private funders, supported Rebuild by Design, an effort to bring together teams of top designers, engineering experts, and climate scientists to prepare proposals for the New York City metropolitan area that would help protect it from a future disaster. So far, none of the selected proposals has been funded at a level that could create significant protection from the course of a future storm.[29]

As far as we can ascertain, there are no plans for vulnerable East Coast cities like New York, Boston, Baltimore, Norfolk, Charleston, South Carolina, and Miami, or Gulf Coast cities like Tampa or Biloxi, that would give them the kind of engineered protection given to New Orleans, London, or the Netherlands coastline, although the investment could be justified by the ratio of capital costs for protection to the property values of the areas protected.

In sum, individual property owners in vulnerable coastal cities are on their own, with insurance and regulations being their only protection right now.

Protecting individual properties subject to floods and flood surges. The big question in places that are likely to become more vulnerable to flooding because of climate change is how soon and how often will flooding be a problem? “Restore the Shore” was the slogan in New Jersey after Superstorm Sandy hit the New Jersey coast in 2012. Some rebuilding has been required above new estimated flood levels, but the priority has been to get everything back in operating condition as soon as possible. In some places small seasonal cottages are being replaced with big new houses. If there is no comparable storm for another generation, restoration will have turned out to be the right choice. If another similar or worse storm comes along much sooner, which climate science tells us is increasingly likely, then an opportunity has been missed to rethink what it means

Figure 2–1 Illustration from a Federal Emergency Management Agency (FEMA) handbook showing homeowners how to bring their properties into compliance with new floodplain requirements, a necessary step if the property owner wishes to have flood insurance. The illustration is intended to show a desirable outcome, and—at one level—it does. The house is much as it was before, except that it now can only be reached by a long flight of steps. And what happens after the next storm if the floodplain requirements are raised again? At some point an elevated house ceases to be a manageable alternative. And all the services that make the house habitable remain at ground level, where they are still vulnerable to storms.

to develop towns in low-lying coastal areas and on barrier islands. FEMA now requires that habitable floors be raised above predicted flood levels for buildings that have already been more than 50 percent damaged by floods[30] and for new buildings in the flood zone. It is an easy requirement to add to development regulations (figure 2-1).

But it makes a big difference how big a change of elevation is required. If the rise is a story or less above ground level, a relatively comfortable relationship can be maintained with the street and surrounding buildings. Larger buildings can be placed above a level of parking or above other uses that are not considered to be habitable places, which is a permissible use in a flood zone (figure 2-2).

Raised structures for individual houses, even if the elevation is relatively moderate, can create problems for livability. A substantial enclosure under the house can divert floodwaters and make things worse for neighboring property owners. In velocity zones—the areas likely

Figure 2-2 The guest rooms of the Beau Rivage Casino in Biloxi, Mississippi, are raised above a massive base, built after Hurricane Katrina damaged the building in 2005. The base serves as a bulwark against storm surge and is built to accept some flooding. Massive structures along a coastline can deflect storm surges on to other properties, so they should be constructed as part of a coordinated storm protection strategy.

to receive a storm surge—regulations do not permit such enclosures. A carport and a porch under the raised house, which should be permitted, can create an appearance more like an ordinary house, but utilities still have to connect up from the ground level. If the house is used during the winter in a cold climate, these vertical connections will need to be carefully protected from freezing. In a storm, although the raised house may not be flooded, the water, sewer pipes, and other connections can be swept away. The supporting structure under the house can also be damaged by the velocity of a flood surge.

Raising buildings more than a story makes problems worse. While larger buildings can be placed on two levels of parking, doing this can make a massive disconnect between street and building. Individual houses raised on an open supporting structure as much as two stories high are difficult to access, and the undersides of houses and a forest of supports along both sides of a street are difficult maintenance problems. Raising buildings will not always provide protection from the violent lateral forces that come with a flood surge. After Superstorm Sandy hit the New Jersey Shore, many houses already raised up on open supports were left tipping at crazy angles or even swept off their pilings (figure 2-3).

Although raised buildings may be safer from rising waters, a location that requires such massive precautions is not going to be an easy place to maintain the streets and utilities necessary to support development. If utility companies and local government departments need to repeatedly replace downed wires, repair broken pipes, and repave streets, taxpayers and utility managers will question whether it continues to make sense to have permanent development in such an area.

In some cases, raising individual houses may be the only practical alternative, although this is far from ideal. Local governments need to add flood hazard zones to the regulations. Within these zones, habitable floors in new construction must be built above predicted flood levels. Substantial remodeling of older buildings must also meet the new-building standards. In addition to being above flood levels, new buildings should meet standards for lateral stability in case of high winds or flood surge, and utility connections must be protected.

Regulations for flood hazard zones are best implemented through using overlay districts that require a site plan review process for proposed development. There are five basic regulatory policies that may be the basis for regulations in such zones:

Figure 2–3 Raising buildings on structural columns will not protect against the velocity of a storm surge. This photo shows the forty-unit Spinnaker Point condominiums in Pascagoula, Mississippi, after flood tides and a storm surge from Hurricane Katrina in 2005. Raised houses along the New Jersey Shore suffered comparable damage from flood surges during Superstorm Sandy in 2012.

1. Uses that are dangerous to health, safety, and property because of water or erosion hazards or that result in damaging increases in erosion, flood heights, or velocities should be restricted, conditioned, or prohibited.
2. Uses vulnerable to floods, including facilities that serve such uses, should be protected against flood damage at the time of initial construction.
3. Changes to natural floodplains, stream channels, and natural protective barriers should be minimized to preserve the way they accommodate or channel flood waters.
4. Filling, grading, dredging, and other development that may increase flood damage should be limited to the extent possible.

5. Construction of flood barriers that will divert flood waters from natural systems or may increase flood hazards in other areas should be prohibited or made subject to performance standards.[31]

Buyout zones in flood-prone locations. Under current funding for buyouts from FEMA, always administered through a state program, the property owner must apply for a buyout. Not every buyout request is accepted. A city or county must have participated in developing, and have formally adopted, a local hazard mitigation plan which has been approved by FEMA and the state to be an eligible location for a federally funded buyout.[32] The proposed flood buyout project must conform to this plan and solve, or help solve, a problem connected with it. The buyout should also be cost-effective in that it saves money over repetitive funding to restore the property after successive floods or helps eliminate future risk by removing development on the property.

These buyouts are intended to deal with a relatively small group of properties that have been shown to be regularly endangered by storm events. Future conditions could be very different. Climate change threatens to increase the scale of the places that will need to be bought out, raising the possibility that it will no longer be economically viable—or even possible—for local governments and utility companies to deliver services to these places.

Locations that have experienced repeated and damaging flood events, and where there is no possibility of regional engineered protection, may ultimately have to be remapped as buyout zones. Within a buyout zone, regulations should say that new construction is not permitted, and properties, when they are sold, should be offered for purchase by the local government. When city services and public utilities need to be discontinued in buyout zones, the properties affected should be able to remain in the buyout zone if the owners are prepared to go off the grid, generating electricity from solar panels and using wells and septic tanks. Properties in this situation should be exempted from property taxes and would need to be self-insured.

These are drastic remedies, and no one would wish to enact them unless necessary. However, there are many places along East and Gulf Coast coastlines, and some on the West Coast, where, if current projections are accurate, local governments will need to help manage an orderly retreat. A buyout zone would be one way to deal with this situation.

Local Adaptation to Drought Conditions

Climate change is also likely to accentuate periodic drought conditions. Eventually, some localities may have to adjust to lower availabilities of water, especially for agriculture, the major consumer of water resources, but also of safe, drinkable water for household use.

Large-scale adaptations to drought. Water supply in much of the United States is managed regionally, and sometimes water is drawn from long distances. Most groundwater resources are in full use and often under stress. The newspapers frequently carry stories about low reservoir levels and dropping water tables. We will need to rely more on rivers for new sources of water, which will require additional purification plants, and desalination plants may be needed in coastal locations. The technology to purify the water in sewage treatment plants has been developed to the point where the effluent is pure enough to drink. Understandably it is not an option people like to contemplate, but some localities that draw their water from rivers are already treating the water to remove pollutants from sewage outfalls upstream. Local governments can also help regions adapt to drought conditions by adopting regulations to promote water conservation.

Adapting to drought on individual properties. In areas subject to drought, the development regulations can include requirements to save water. The rain barrels and cisterns required to hold water in areas subject to heavy rains and flooding can also be required in dry areas. What rainwater is collected can be used for irrigation or cleaning of cars and decks, so that purified drinking water is not wasted on such tasks. The grass lawn, a tradition in damp and rainy Great Britain and much emulated in other English-speaking countries, may not continue to be viable in drought areas. Xeriscaping, the use of drought-tolerant plants for landscaping, is a term invented by the Denver Water Department[33] and can be the standard. The specific palate of trees and plantings to be permitted can be selected based on local conditions. A more complicated water-saving measure is the reuse of water from sinks, bathtubs, and showers to flush toilets. The cost of the additional piping and fittings for an individual property is more than most people would be willing to pay, but housing developments in a few locations are reusing greywater. An often mentioned example of this is in Hammarby-Sjostad, Stockholm.[34]

Local Adaptation to Heat Waves

Death rates spike during heat waves in urban areas. This problem will become worse as periods of high summer heat become longer and more intense. In urbanized areas the effects of heat waves can be mitigated by building and development requirements that can help offset increasingly hot weather.

Regulations to help safeguard lives during heat waves. Urban heat islands, where the effects of warm weather are intensified, are created in places with high percentages of building coverage, streets, and paved parking lots. The following measures for individual properties can make significant improvements.

Light-colored roofs. In warm climates, roofs of light-colored material reflect rather than absorb heat into buildings—an effective and simple measure. Such roofs can reduce the need for air conditioning, which transfers heat from buildings into the surrounding atmosphere. Conversely, in cold climates, roofs should be dark-colored to absorb the sun's heat in winter and reduce use of fuel for heating. The geographical line dividing the places where it makes the most sense to use light-colored roofs rather than dark ones has been moving northward in the Northern Hemisphere, and that movement can be expected to continue. Local governments should require light-colored roofs, especially on large buildings, in geographic areas where it will be helpful in mitigating summer heat.

Green parking lots. The paving in parking lots absorbs a great deal of heat. Temperatures in the parking lot of a shopping center will be much higher than a nearby residential neighborhood with landscaped streets and yards. The measures discussed in chapter 1 to make parking lots more pervious to rainwater can also reduce their heat-absorbing characteristics. A highly effective way to reduce parking lot heat islands would be to require rows of shade trees to be planted in pervious parking lots, which would help irrigate tree roots.

Urban forests. The tree cover in developed areas is sometimes described as the urban forest. Increasing urban forest coverage can be a major factor in mitigating summer heat. Making the paved portions of streets narrower in newly developed subdivisions reduces the amount of paved area, which absorbs more heat than natural landscape. Narrower paving also provides more room for street trees and makes it easier to separate tree-planting areas from utility easements. Subdivision ordinances can and should require tree planting on streets, and set design standards to make sure the trees have room to grow. As discussed in chapter 1, planned unit development (PUD), or an as-of-right provision that reduces the required lot size, can be used for subdivisions proposed on large parcels, and any tree planting or cutting on such properties should be in accordance with a landscaping plan approved as part of the PUD or subdivision approval.

Adapting to Future Food Shortages

The United States is used to a culture of food abundance supported by an international food supply system. But the combination of climate change and rapidly increasing world population is likely within a few years to create worldwide food scarcity brought on by desertification or flooding of former agricultural land. Countries that have been exporting food may need to change their agriculture to feed their own populations.

To protect future food supplies, agricultural land needs to be preserved as a positive resource, not left to be a potentially interim use before an urban area expands. Silvaculture—tree nurseries or land where trees are grown to be cut down for lumber—should also be protected. Much of the remaining prime agricultural land in the United States is situated near cities because successful cities usually developed in places where there was a substantial "foodshed" to support the population. Drought can also reduce the productivity of land when agriculture is based on irrigation. Food security could become a significant problem in years to come. It is prudent to take land out of agriculture only after careful consideration, and not let urbanization be the default decision.

Agricultural zones. One of the most effective tools for preserving prime agricultural land is an agricultural protection zone (APZ). In an APZ established by a municipality, agriculture is the exclusive or principal allowed use; other uses that could be incompatible with farming, including nonfarm residential developments, are prohibited.[35] However, an APZ could allow for some uses deemed compatible with agricultural use as accessory uses. These zones typically require much larger lot sizes or allow much lower development densities than other zones.[36] In some jurisdictions, APZ ordinances place limitations on the ability to subdivide agricultural parcels, often with an exemption for agricultural worker housing or for family members of the farmer.[37] APZ provisions may also make it more difficult than usual to rezone land from the agricultural protection zone to a classification in which development is allowed.[38]

APZ ordinances may include provisions that address the conflict between farming and nonfarming uses, including enhanced setbacks, site design review of nonfarming development, required buffers, or mechanisms designed to protect farmers against nuisance claims.[39] The designation of agricultural protection zones should be based on considerations of soil quality as well as the location, character, and current use of the land.[40] APZ regulations serve a number of purposes, including protecting areas with prime agricultural soils from development, protecting against conflicts between farming and nonfarm land uses, and maintaining a critical mass of agricultural land in a given jurisdiction. It can also be used to forestall land speculation by nonfarmers.

Some local jurisdictions use an alternative to agricultural zoning: mapping farmland as residential with a large minimum lot requirement. This category may fill a need in some places, but it should not be mapped on operating farms. Farmers borrowing money to manage their cash flow from season to season can find that their borrowing power is enhanced by their farm's status as future residential land. But if they cannot pay back all their loans, foreclosure may precipitate conversion to building sites. Considering farmland as future residential land can also raise property taxes on farms. It is possible to have property taxes abated or to transfer or purchase the development rights from farmland, but, if possible, agricultural land should be protected by APZ regulations.

Urban agriculture. The expansion of urbanized areas has reduced the amount of nearby agricultural land. Food comes from greater distances, which makes it less fresh, and the transportation adds costs as well as negative environmental effects.

Rooftop greenhouses. While it is almost impossible to restore urbanized land to the kind of productive agriculture that existed before land was prepared for development, there are many places within cities and suburbs where restoring food production is still feasible. Meadows on top of buildings, usually referred to as green roofs, can be a beautiful feature if the building has a structure capable of supporting it. Green roofs retain rainwater and mitigate heat effects. But farming on the limited area of a rooftop is difficult. Rooftop greenhouses are a far more efficient way of establishing food production in cities and suburbs, and, if widely distributed, they can make a significant difference in the amount and quality of food available.

Many existing warehouses and parking garages have structures capable of supporting heavy rooftop loads. A greenhouse roof framework can be built above warehouse buildings with the necessary supporting columns an extension of the existing structure. Losing the rooftop parking spaces, if they exist, will permit construction above parking garages that have structures designed to accept heavy loads. The weight of planting boxes should be well within the capabilities of the structure. Irrigation systems can be partly based on rainwater collection. There are some rooftop urban greenhouses already in business, either supplying exceptionally fresh food to restaurants and specialty grocers or to households on subscription. Regulators should make sure rooftop greenhouses are permitted uses in commercial and industrial zones. These greenhouses should be exempted from being part of the floor area ratio (F.A.R.) calculation to encourage wide adoption of urban greenhouse agriculture. As F.A.R. is essentially an occupancy control, and as greenhouses would not have many employees, providing for F.A.R. exemption would be consistent with the purpose of the regulations.

Other buildings with large, flat roofs, like big-box retail stores and factories, could also be adapted to include rooftop agriculture. New buildings can be designed to support greenhouses; older buildings may require additional supporting structure.

Residential food production. During World War II, people were encouraged to dig up their lawns and plant "victory gardens" to add to the food supply and mitigate some of the hardships of food rationing. Today many local ordinances and rules of homeowner associations require ornamental front lawns and side yards, although vegetable gardens in backyards are generally acceptable. As good-quality food becomes scarcer and more expensive, more people will become interested in raising food themselves, and pressure will increase on local governments to permit it.

Restrictions in the existing zoning ordinances can become impediments to urban agriculture. Until June 2010, the city of Los Angeles prohibited residents from growing crops in residential zoning districts and from selling produce on-site. Such regulations also typically prohibited keeping farm animals as they were deemed inherently incompatible with urban life. Raising chickens on residential properties used to be precisely the kind of use that development regulations were invented to prohibit. It was almost proverbial: "If you didn't have zoning, there would be people with chicken coops in their backyards." Interest in "slow food" and concerns about additives in commercially raised chickens have caused residents in some neighborhoods to want raising chickens to be permitted, and they have been agitating to make sure regulations allow them to do it. As food becomes scarcer and more expensive, interest in home-grown food is likely to increase.

Zoning regulations, therefore, need to be amended to allow for growing plants and certain crops. The same zoning regulations that exclude agriculture also contain lot size and setback requirements that could impact agricultural activity. These regulations could be amended to allow people to grow food. Sometimes regulations do not address whether an agricultural use is allowed either as a primary or accessory use within a city zoning district. This results in ambiguity in the implementation of the regulations and sometimes creates confrontations between landowners and their neighbors. The easiest way to remedy these impediments within traditional zoning is to adopt an urban agricultural zoning ordinance that allows for urban greenhouses, urban farms, and some animal keeping as accessory uses with specified setback and scale limitations. Of course, the intensity of agricultural use allowed need not be the same in every agricultural zoning district. In Jersey City, New Jersey, the city council amended its land development ordinance to enable urban agricultural practices. These amendments permit community gardening, rooftop gardens, and raised planters in all zoning districts and exempt these uses from site plan approval. The amendments also allow commercial agricultural operations in commercial, industrial, and mixed-use redevelopment plan area zones.[41]

Temporary agriculture in parking lots. Many parking lots are not used for long periods of time, such as lots at football stadiums rarely used to capacity except for a few games during the fall. Parking lots belonging to educational institutions are often lightly used during summer vacations. During the growing season, planting boxes can be placed in unused or partially used parking lots and maintained and harvested by voluntary organizations. Again, local regulation can make sure that this kind of ad-hoc agriculture is a permitted use.

Local governments are on the front line for adapting to changes in climate, and development regulations will be an important method of adaptation.

Notes

1. *What We Know: The Reality, Risks, and Response to Climate Change* (Washington, DC: American Association for the Advancement of Science, 2014). The chair of the panel of authors was Mario Molina of the University of California, San Diego, and Scripps Institution of Oceanography, with cochairs James McCarthy, Harvard University; and Diana Wall, Colorado State University. Other panel members were Richard Alley, Pennsylvania State University; Kim Cobb, Georgia Institute of Technology; Julia Cole, University of Arizona; Sarah Das, Woods Hole Oceanographic Institution; Noah Diffenbaugh, Stanford University; Kerry Emanuel, Massachusetts Institute of Technology; Howard Frumkin, University of Washington; Katharine Hayhoe, Texas Tech University; Camille Parmesan, University of Texas, Austin, and University of Plymouth, United Kingdom; and Marshall Shepherd, University of Georgia. The report can be downloaded from the association website.
2. See the "Climate Reality" section, ibid., 2–5.
3. In December 2015, in Paris, 195 countries adopted a Climate Agreement, also known as the Paris climate accord, that sets out a global action plan to put the world on a course to limit the increase in global warming to below 2°C above pre-industrial levels and to limit the temperature increase to 1.5°C above pre-industrial levels. The text of the agreement is available online at *https://unfccc.int/files/essential_background/convention/application/pdf/english_paris_agreement.pdf.* On June 1, 2017, President Trump announced that the United States would withdraw from the Paris climate accord. The president said the United States will not implement any aspect of the accord, including the carbon emissions reduction pledges, known as nationally determined contributions, or funding for the Green Climate Fund. Although the president later expressed a willingness to renegotiate the agreement or negotiate a new agreement, there is no clear means under the agreement to restructure the terms of the United States' involvement, nor at this point any indication that the other countries that signed

the agreement would be willing to engage in such negotiations. Under the terms of the Climate Agreement, no party may file a notice of intent to withdraw until three years after the agreement became effective (November 2016). Because the process to withdraw after notice is given takes another year, the earliest the United States could withdraw is November 2020.

4. In 2015, the Obama Administration and the Environmental Protection Agency released a final Clean Power Plan, which is intended to reduce carbon emissions from the power sector by 32 percent (870 million tons) below the 2005 levels by the year 2030. See Clean Power Plan, 80 Fed. Reg. 205 (Oct. 23, 2015); and Environmental Protection Agency, "Overview of the Clean Power Plan," *https://19january2017snapshot.epa.gov/cleanpowerplan/fact-sheet-overview-clean-power-plan_.html.* The plan establishes state-specific goals reflecting CO_2 emission performance rates and guidelines for the development and implementation of state plans to establish reduction measures to meet state performance rates and reduction goals. On February 9, 2016, the U.S. Supreme Court stayed implementation of the Clean Power Plan pending judicial review. The Supreme Court's decision overrode the D.C. Circuit's January 21, 2015, decision not to put the Clean Power Plan regulations on hold. Challengers claim the EPA does not have the authority under section 111 of the Clean Air Act to craft the rule. On March 28, 2017, President Trump signed an "Energy Independence Executive Order" that, among other things, directed the EPA to review the plan and, "if appropriate," suspend, revise, or rescind the plan. If the EPA begins a new rule-making process pursuant to the Executive Order, it could petition the D.C. Circuit to hold off issuing a decision pending completion of the rule-making process. The Executive Order also rescinded the White House Council on Environmental Quality (CEQ) August 2016 guidance that had been issued to show federal agencies how to quantify greenhouse gas emissions when conducting National Environmental Policy Act (NEPA) reviews and provided a common approach for assessing regulatory actions.

5. The Regional Greenhouse Gas Initiative (*www.rggi.org/*) in 2009 became the first U.S. cap-and-trade program designed to reduce CO_2 emissions from power plants, an agreement signed by the states of Connecticut, Delaware, Maine, Maryland, Massachusetts, New Hampshire, New York, Rhode Island, and Vermont. California has its own cap-and-trade program and is a participant in the Western Climate Initiative, along with Arizona, Montana, Oregon, Utah, Washington, and several Canadian provinces. There is also a Midwest Greenhouse Gas Reduction Accord, signed in 2007, agreed to by the states of Illinois, Iowa, Kansas, Michigan, Minnesota, and Wisconsin, plus the province of Manitoba, but it is not currently pursuing an active agenda. For more information about state climate-change initiatives *see* the Center for Climate and Energy Solutions (*www.c2es.org/*), the successor to the Pew Center on Global Climate Change.

6. Insurance Information Institute, New York, New York, *Catastrophes*, *www.iii.org/fact-statistic/catastrophes-us.*

7. To review the 2015 fire season and long-term trends, *Hearings Before the House Committee on Agriculture, Subcommittee on Conservation and Forestry,* 114th Congress, 1st Session (Oct. 8, 2015) (statement of Thomas Tidwell, Chief, USDA Forest Service).
8. *Wildland Fire Management: Hearings Before the Senate Committee on Energy and Natural Resources*, 113th Congress, 1st Session (June 4, 2013) (testimony of Thomas Tidwell, Chief, USDA Forest Service) (hereafter, "Tidwell testimony").
9. See "Wildland Urban Interface Communities Within the Vicinity of Federal Lands That Are at High Risk from Wildfire," notice issued by the Secretary of Agriculture and the Secretary of the Interior pursuant to title IV of the Department of the Interior and Related Agencies Appropriations Act, 2001 (114 Stat. 1009) (66 Fed. Reg. 753, Jan. 4, 2001).
10. Tidwell testimony.
11. 108 Pub. L. No. 148, 117 Stat. 1887 (codified at 16 U.S.C. §§ 6501–6591).
12. Ibid., § 6501.
13. Ibid., § 6511(3).
14. See Communities Committee, Society of American Foresters, National Association of Counties, and National Association of State Foresters, *Preparing a Community Wildfire Protection Plan: A Handbook for Wildland–Urban Interface Communities* (Columbia Falls, MT, Bethesda, MD, Washington, DC, March 2004).
15. See discussion of legal principles in chapter 7.
16. Governor of Colorado, Executive Order B 2013—0002 (2013).
17. Kaplan Kirsch Rockwell, *Report to the Governor of Colorado, the Speaker of the House of Representatives, and the President of the Senate* (Colorado Department of Regulatory Agencies, Denver, September 2013) (hereafter the Task Force Report).
18. The Task Force Report states that "Colorado needs a standardized method to identify the wildland-urban interface and wildfire risk for properties across the state. This identification system is a foundation for the entire system of recommendations set forth in this Report" (ibid., 11).
19. Ibid., 14. In the "Barriers to Progress" section, the report indicates that updating the model will take approximately five years and cost $600,000 per year along with additional costs for data gathering and training (ibid., 15).
20. Ibid., 16–17.
21. See discussion of the *Nollan/Dolan* Dual Nexus Test in chapter 7.
22. Stefan Rahmstorf, "A Semi-Empirical Approach to Projecting Future Sea-Level Rise," *Science* 315, no. 5810 (2007): 368–70.
23. See International Panel on Climate Change, "Is Sea Level Rising?" FAQ 5.1. (2007), *www.ipcc.ch/publications_and_data/ar4/wg1/en/faq-5-1.html.*

24. James Hansen, *It's Time to Stop Waffling So Much and Say That the Evidence Is Pretty Strong . . . Multi-meter Sea Level Rise Is an Issue for Today's Public, not Next Millennium's*, comment made in an open-access discussion journal published by Columbia University, July 27, 2015. See also James Hansen et al., "Ice Melt, Sea Level Rise and Superstorms: Evidence from Paleoclimate Data, Climate Modeling, and Modern Observations That 2°C Global Warming Is Highly Dangerous," *Atmospheric Chemistry and Physics* 16 (2016): 3761–3812, *www.columbia.edu/~jeh1/2015/20150704_IceMelt.pdf.*
25. For a more detailed description of engineering defenses against flood surge, see Jonathan Barnett and Larry Beasley, *Ecodesign for Cities and Suburbs* (Washington, DC: Island Press, 2015), 24–34.
26. See Mark Fischetti, "Is New Orleans Safer Today Than When Katrina Hit 10 Years Ago?," *Scientific American*, August 27, 2015.
27. This conclusion is drawn from review of a survey of rebuilding plans in the Connecticut, New Jersey, and New York areas most affected by Superstorm Sandy, conducted at the School of Design at the University of Pennsylvania in 2013. See *Alternative Futures for the Jersey Shore*, Department of City and Regional Planning, University of Pennsylvania (Philadelphia, 2013).
28. New York City, plaNYC, *A Stronger, More Resilient New York*, *www.nyc.gov/html/sirr/html/report/report.shtml.*
29. According to the Summary of Federal Register Notice Published October 16, 2014 Regarding Rebuild by Design Projects, $930,000,000 has been allocated to six selected projects. The projects as designed will require billions of dollars more to reach the state of completion shown in the renderings for each project.
30. "The minimum NFIP [National Flood Improvements Program] requirements for new construction, substantially improved, and substantially damaged buildings affect the type of foundation that can be used, establishes the required height of the lowest floor to or above the BFE [Base Flood Elevation], establishes the criteria for the installation of building utility systems, requires the use of flood-damage-resistant materials, and limits the use of the area below the lowest floor. In recognition of the greater hazard posed by breaking waves three feet high or higher, FEMA has established minimum NFIP regulatory requirements for Zone V buildings that are more stringent than the minimum requirements for Zone A buildings. Therefore, the location of a building in relation to the Zone A/Zone V boundary on a FIRM can affect the design of the building. In that regard, it is important to note that if a building or other structure has any portion of its foundation in Zone V, it must be built to comply with Zone V requirements." *FEMA Coastal Construction Manual* (Washington, DC: Federal Emergency Management Agency, 2011).
31. Adapted from Kent City Code, chap. 14.09.
32. See, for example, FEMA's *Property Acquisition Handbook for Local Communities.*

33. According to the *Merriam-Webster Dictionary*, which says the Denver Water Department invented the term in 1985.

34. There has been an extensive amount written about Hammarby-Sjostad in books and magazines. See, for example, Barnett and Beasley, *Ecodesign for Cities and Suburbs*, 56–57.

35. See American Farmland Trust, *Saving American Farmland: What Works* (Northampton, MA, 1997), 49.

36. See Lara DuMond Guercio, "Local and Watershed Land Use Controls: A Turning Point for Agriculture and Water Quality," *Planning and Environmental Law* 62, no. 3 (2010). See also Robert E. Coughlin, "Formulating and Evaluating Agricultural Zoning Programs," *APA Journal* 57, no. 183 (2007); Arthur C. Nelson and James B. Duncan, *Growth Management Principles and Practices* (Chicago, Washington, DC: Planners Press, 1995), 52.

37. See American Farmland Trust, *Saving American Farmland*, 61.

38. Ibid., 65–66.

39. Ibid., 62–63.

40. Ibid., 49, 56–57.

41. See generally, Madeline Fletcher, Jennifer Rush Low, and Jennifer Schwartz Berky, "Overcoming Barriers to Cultivating Urban Agriculture," *Real Estate Law Journal* 41 (Fall 2012).

3

Encouraging Walking by Mixing Land Uses and Housing Types

Public health researchers have found that moderate physical exercise, a half hour a day, preferably every day, can improve general health and lower the risk of chronic illnesses and premature death.[1] Moderate exercise, such as walking or riding a bicycle, can be programmed into daily life, making it easier for more people to commit to exercising. Of course, running and other vigorous physical activities have major health benefits, but many people find it difficult to exercise regularly or do not have the physical capacity.[2]

Health professionals began considering where they could recommend that people walk or bicycle. They discovered that there are far fewer suitable locations in many parts of the country than there were two generations ago, or even more recently. Children used to be able to walk or bicycle to neighborhood schools and parks, neighboring families were within strolling distance, and convenience shopping was only a short walk away from where people lived. In city and suburban centers, people could walk from the office to where they had lunch. Hotel guests could go out in the evening to restaurants and entertainment right down the street. While all these walking trips are still possible today, they are available to a much smaller proportion of the population. Dr. Richard Jackson, chair of the Environmental Health Sciences Department at UCLA, notes that "in 1974, 66 percent of all school children walked to school, and, by 2000, that number had dropped to 13 percent."[3] Today's suburban tract housing developments, office parks, strip shopping centers, drive-in restaurants, and motels are all far less walkable places, and much farther apart than in older urban and suburban centers. This, despite the fact that surveys show that the selling prices of homes in walkable neighborhoods are

15 percent higher than similar homes in less walkable neighborhoods and that a majority of Americans—retiring baby boomers and Generation Yers, in particular—would prefer to live in a walkable neighborhood.[4]

Short trips that people used to make on foot are now made by automobile. According to the most recent National Household Travel Survey, 28 percent of all daily travel consists of trips of less than one mile, and 60 percent of those trips are taken by car.[5] The numbers vary from place to place, but 17 percent of all trips of any length and by any mode of transportation (a category that includes walking) are trips of less than a mile made by car. Short vehicle trips are a significant contributor to air pollution and traffic congestion. Auto engines pollute most when cold, as it takes the catalytic converter several miles of operation to reach peak operating efficiency.[6] People driving from one parking lot to another running errands along a commercial strip or driving from home to a convenience store and then back, are a significant source of air pollution. About half of all traffic congestion is caused by too many cars for the capacity of the road, as opposed to such temporary factors as construction, bad weather, or an accident. Traffic congestion caused by too many cars on local roads tends to occur at peak hours for commuting and, in suburbs, on Saturdays, when many people are out doing errands. Short trips can contribute to traffic congestion, especially when people drive their children to school at the same time that others are driving to work and when many cars are driving in and out of parking lots along commercial corridors.

When considering time expended door to door, walking is the most efficient form of transportation for distances up to a quarter of a mile (a five-minute walk) and very competitive with buses and even taxis for up to half a mile. And walking only requires fossil fuels for preparing food consumed by the pedestrian. Bicycles are even more efficient than walking, in terms of physical energy expended to distance covered, and make it easy to cover longer distances. But bicycles require more supporting infrastructure, designated bicycle-ways in urban areas, and bicycle storage and changing rooms for cyclists who commute to work.

Jan Gehl, the Danish architect who has devoted his professional life to improving conditions for pedestrians in cities and towns, asserts that walking is a necessary part of what creates a successful society. His aphorism is "Life takes place on foot." When conditions are favorable for walking, people will engage in what Gehl calls optional activities, that is, they will sit for a moment on a convenient bench, look into a shop, stop and buy a coffee. This makes it more likely that people will run into someone they know or start a conversation with a stranger—the social activities that Gehl says are what living in a community is all about. Walking without a specific destination can also have benefits. Gehl quotes the Danish philosopher Soren Kierkegaard as inspiration: "Above all, do not lose your desire to walk. Every day I walk myself into a state of well-being and walk away from every illness. I have walked myself into my best thoughts, and I know of no thought so burdensome that one cannot walk away from it."[7]

At a more pragmatic level of consideration, places where distances are walkable have to be more compact, which has both environmental and cost advantages. Compact development urbanizes less new land, which puts less stress on the natural environment while saving some costs for developing new infrastructure.

All these diverse considerations make walkable and compact neighborhoods and business centers important planning and policy objectives for local governments. Although there are some notable new walkable neighborhoods and business centers, walkable places are not being built very often. A major reason is the prevalence of overly strict land-use and building-density separations in zoning ordinances. Many ordinances go too far in separating commercial land uses into separate zones, when some of these activities are perfectly compatible and can, in fact, reinforce one another. Ordinances also go too far in separating different kinds of residential development, so that one size of single-family lot is placed in one zone and a slightly different lot size for a single-family house is in a completely different zone. Many jurisdictions do not allow apartments in commercial zones, although this mix seems to work well in older loft districts where former office and industrial buildings have been converted to housing. The proliferation of single uses and separate zones has caused cities and towns to spread out far more than is necessary and has made it much more difficult to walk or cycle between destinations in the newer parts of cities and suburbs. As zoning is a big part of this problem, changes to zoning can do much to correct it.

Restoring walkability in residential neighborhoods and business centers can be viewed as a conservative policy because it aims to restore relationships that were commonplace two generations ago. However, separating some land uses continues to be important. No one wants to live near heavy industry or have a noisy bar open on a quiet residential street. People who live in a neighborhood of single-family homes do not want to see houses torn down and a motel, or a high-rise apartment house, go up in their place. So we favor continuing to separate land uses that are clearly incompatible. And we also favor maintaining development densities at compatible levels within residential districts. In this chapter we propose some simple changes to regulations for commercial development along arterial corridors and in new residential neighborhoods that will allow for more compact development that, in turn, encourages walking and cycling.

Modifying Zoning for Commercial Corridors

The long multilane street, with commercial buildings and parking lots stretching out for miles, is a familiar sight in our cities and suburbs today (see figure 3-1). These ubiquitous commercial strips are an expression of the current real estate market and are designed to provide easy access for shoppers driving cars. However, in a more fundamental way, they reflect a real estate market that has been drastically reshaped by the standard requirements of zoning. Frequently, commercial use has been mapped along these highways for most of their length, creating a surplus of land zoned for commerce, so that many parcels are undeveloped or underdeveloped. At the same time, the commercial strips are narrow, sometimes no more than 100 feet deep, and are mapped to back up to residential districts where it would be difficult to acquire additional property and even more difficult to rezone the additional area for commercial or mixed use. In sum, too much land along highways is zoned commercial to be used efficiently, and narrow commercial zoning districts, whether located along highways or on arterial streets adjacent to residential districts, do not leave enough room for denser, walkable commercial destinations with a variety of different uses.

As discussed in chapter 1, parking requirements satisfied by relatively inexpensive at-grade spaces are a major shaping force in these commercial districts. Zoning regulations typically require that each building satisfy a minimum parking requirement on its own property. The parking lots become the dominant feature of commercially zoned land along these corridors. Cars traveling to these separated destinations conflict with traffic that is going farther along the route, with frequent left turns into parking lots being made against oncoming traffic in the middle of long blocks. The familiar result is a traffic jam. The wide separation of buildings caused by their parking lots makes it difficult to walk from one destination to

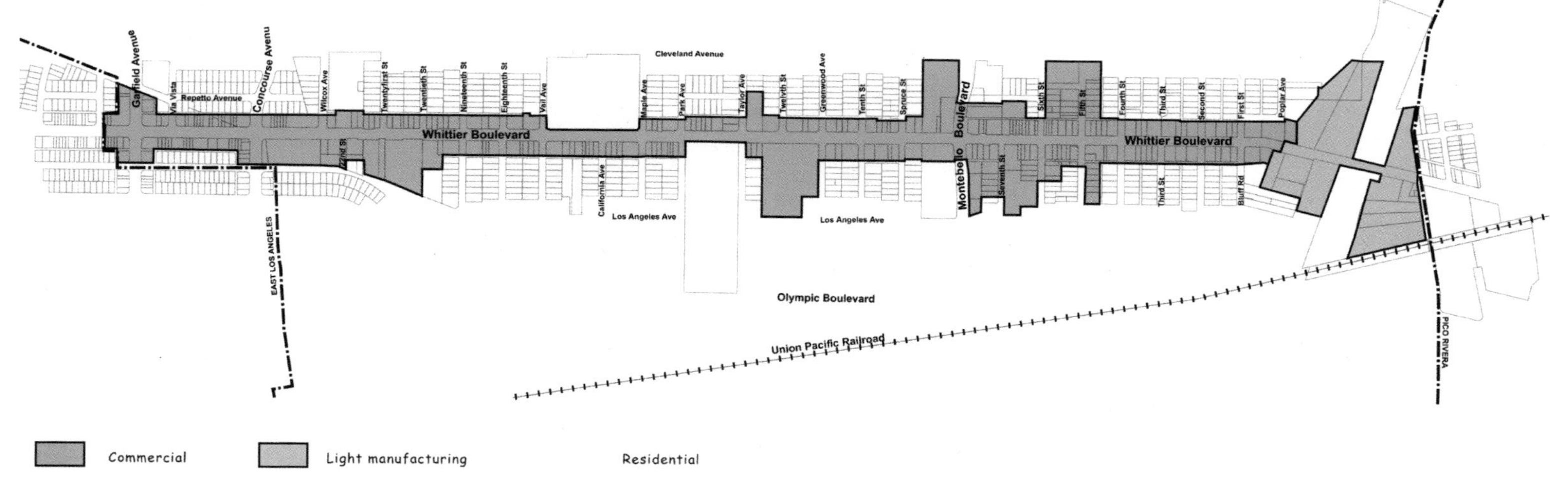

Figure 3–1 The zoning map for a typical commercial corridor, Whittier Boulevard in Montebello, California, shows that, while the whole corridor is lined with commercially zoned land, there is not enough at any given place along the corridor to permit more intensive development such as a town center.

the next, so that people are forced to drive. The short trips add to the traffic; and the frequent stops and starts increase the emission of greenhouse gases such as carbon dioxide.

Anyone setting out today to invent commercial-district zoning for cities and suburbs would not come up with such a dysfunctional pattern, but these commercial areas are already built, represent huge amounts of investment, and are generally accepted, despite the obvious drawbacks in design and functionality. What can be done to improve this situation?

Realizing the Redevelopment Potential of Commercial Corridors

The at-grade parking lots and the prevalence of relatively low-cost one-story buildings make commercial corridors vast land banks. They already have their utilities in place and access to established services, unlike open land at the perimeter of urban areas where developers and local governments must pay for expensive infrastructure and community facilities to support new development. If four critical changes were made, existing commercial corridors could absorb some of the growth that now goes into perimeter areas while creating walkable neighborhoods and business centers.

Create walkable, mixed-use, park-once districts at intervals along commercial corridors. Not all locations along a commercial corridor have equal potential for redevelopment. The capacity is higher at the intersections with significant cross streets, and, as there is frontage around the intersection on more than one principal street, there is likely to be more space available for commercial and mixed-use development. Intersections along a commercial strip with traffic signals should be evaluated to see if they could support higher density development (see figure 3-2). At almost every mile along a commercial corridor it should be possible to identify an intersection where a significant street meets or crosses the commercial street. These places, with their superior accessibility, have the potential to support higher density development. Land around these intersections can be "up-zoned" to permit both a mix of residential and commercial uses and a bigger floor area. The intent should be to create a walkable, commercial and residential center in accordance with design guidelines for public spaces, which should be adopted at the same time as the rezoning (see chapter 6). The zoning can permit offices and hotels as well as stores, town houses, and apartments (see figure 3-3).

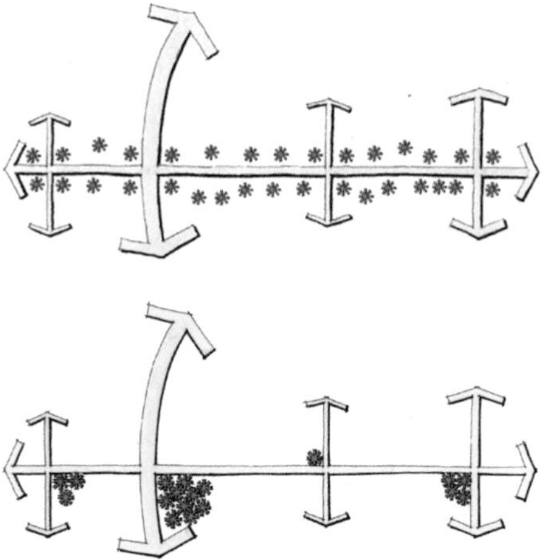

Figure 3–2 These diagrams suggest that, instead of the dispersed development commonly found along commercial corridors, areas of concentrated commercial activity can occur at places where there are important intersections. The greatest amount of development is shown at the intersection with the most important street. Note that the diagram calls for development in only one quadrant of the intersection.

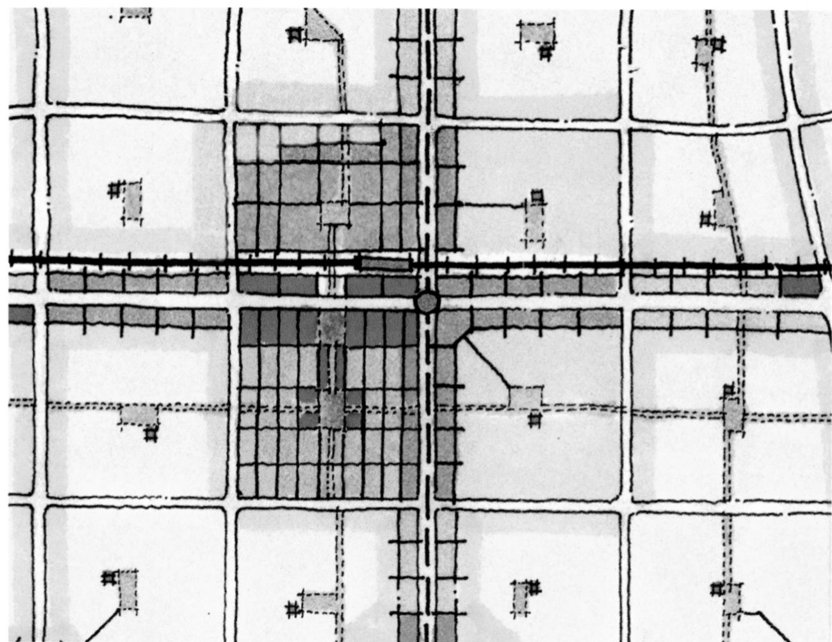

Figure 3–3 Conceptual diagram of a retail center, in red, located in one quadrant of an important intersection along a commercial corridor.

Although there will always be local opposition to any zoning change, there are benefits for adjacent residential districts: easily accessible concentrations of useful services and alternative places for younger and older family members to live without leaving the neighborhood. Increased development potential is also a benefit for the property owners in the commercial corridor. Over time, the creation of relatively intense, mixed-use centers at approximately one-mile intervals should enable the construction of an improved transit system, such as bus rapid transit, which could in turn help reduce some of the demand for parking, making the higher mapped densities more feasible.

Some commercial uses can share parking. A park-once district permits someone to park in a lot, including one belonging to an individual business, and walk to other destinations. Retail uses can agree to share parking within a district, provided there is enough parking to support overall demand. A garage built by a local parking authority can be a component of a park-once district where all the destinations are within walking distance of one another. Peak parking demand also varies throughout the day. A hotel has its peak parking needs at times when an office building's parking spaces are mostly vacant.

To create mixed-use, park-once districts at intersections along commercial corridors, the best approach is to start at the planning level and establish goals and policies for existing corridors. A primary goal should be to reconfigure streets and properties around the intersections along these commercial corridors so that these places can function as true mixed-use centers. Land-use policies that could be established in the land-use element of a comprehensive plan should include the following:

- Allow for new high-density mixed use at intersections mapped on the plan.
- Use shared parking and parking structures where possible, and to the rear or side of buildings.
- Encourage arrangement of buildings to create distinctive spaces and focal points at the intersections and provide for pedestrian access.
- Emphasize the continuity of the district by relating buildings as directly as possible to the street; minimize setbacks.
- Allow a mix of commercial, office, and multifamily uses.

Zoning provisions that are amended to be consistent with these planning policies would be incorporated into an overlay zone for each selected intersection along a commercial corridor. Within these mapped areas there should be design standards for building placement, signs, landscaping, and the location of aboveground local utilities and utility service connections. The ability to retrofit buildings and uses to conform to the new zoning standards for these commercial corridors will depend on whether owners or developers apply for rezonings or permits in these newly mapped commercial corridor intersections.

This change in the configuration and mixture of uses will occur over time. Once the new overlay provisions are adopted, the existing uses in the mapped locations along the corridor would technically become nonconforming. There are two approaches to avoid this problem. One is to have the overlay district provisions supplement rather than replace the requirements of the underlying zoning, which would mean that the existing uses would remain conforming while the retrofitting process occurs. A second approach would be to provide in the provisions of the new zoning overlay district that existing uses are deemed conforming. Giving existing uses in these commercial intersections a conforming status is a way to avoid creating financing problems with lenders concerned about the stigma of a nonconforming status. The reconfiguration of these intersection areas along corridors into walkable mixed-use districts can be expected to occur because density is being increased and there is ample incentive for owners of these intersection properties to undertake redevelopment of their properties. The shift to online shopping makes it even more likely that building owners with failing retail tenants will start looking for new ways to redevelop their properties. Requests for redevelopment approvals will then trigger the requirement that the proposed uses comply with the comprehensive plan policies and the new zoning and design requirements.

Allow apartments and town houses along commercial corridors. A second necessary change is to permit apartments and town houses all along commercial corridors, including locations that are not up-zoned to higher densities. The market demand for multifamily housing and for attached houses is often satisfied by building on greenfield sites at the edges of cities and towns. If the zoning were modified to permit apartments and town houses along commercial corridors, some of this market demand for housing could be accommodated as horizontal mixed use or as apartments above retail in denser locations. The economics of residential development can include structured parking, which means higher density building is possible on land that is now mostly parking lots. It could

Figure 3–4 An image showing how multifamily residences can replace low-density commercial development in commercial corridors at places without important intersections. The size of the residential buildings becomes smaller on the side closest to the adjacent residential neighborhood.

prove to be more desirable to live in residentially developed areas within commercial corridors that run through established neighborhoods than to live in the same kind of housing out on the urban fringe (see figure 3-4).

The parts of the commercial corridor that do not support high-density, mixed-use development should also be rezoned to permit moderate-density residential development, but not increased density for commercial development. Town houses with internal garages, or garden apartments over a one-level parking deck, can be designed to face into adjacent residential neighborhoods, again adding housing options for current or prospective residents. There still can be commercial frontage along the main street, but over time there should be fewer entrances for commercial properties and less interference with traffic movement on the main street.

The implementation approach for guiding moderate residential development along commercial corridors would also require adopting planning policies that support the use of zoning overlay districts along specific stretches of the corridor. Because these auto-oriented corridors typically have large building setbacks, low density, buildings separated and isolated from one another, and surface parking, appropriate planning and design policies would include the following:

- Relate buildings as directly as possible to the street; minimize setbacks.
- Reduce the number of curb cuts along the corridor.
- Align sidewalks near the curb.
- Provide pedestrian connections from the corridor to the adjacent areas.
- Increase landscaping along the corridor (that is, trees along the right-of-way).

These policies can be implemented through zoning overlay districts similar to the commercial corridor intersection overlay districts. The zoning overlay districts would contain a combination of development standards that would apply to any application for a redevelopment permit, and design guidelines to ensure that the proposed development is consistent with the redesign objectives for the corridor.

Eliminate specific required parking ratios. As discussed in chapter 1, the uncertain basis for required numerical parking ratios in development regulations, plus the ability of some uses to share parking, support the conclusion that the simplest and best regulatory solution when redeveloping a commercial corridor site is to require off-street parking, but to leave the decision about the number of spaces needed to the developer or owner of the property. If no new development takes place, the existing parking would remain. Development that responds to the changes in the zoning would begin with plenty of existing parking, and the property owners have years of experience in seeing how these spaces are used. If housing is added, the economics often include parking: garages in individual town houses and structured parking for apartments. The land cost for accommodating the housing on what had formerly been parking lots then becomes the cost of decanting the parking from commercial uses into structured parking. Permanent lenders and prospective tenants will have their own ideas about how much parking they require, but these requirements are more easily modified by experience than through mandated ratios. So, in these mixed-use locations, the parking ratios can be decided by market considerations. The answer to the argument that parking could overflow into the streets of neighboring residential communities is to require parking-zone windshield-identification stickers on those streets, a simple administrative answer to neighborhood parking concerns that is used in many communities.

Reduce the number of commercial zones and consolidate the commercial uses. Many local zoning ordinances have ten or more different commercial zones, although, when you look up what is permitted in the table of uses, the same use can often be found in several different zones. Traditional distinctions among many commercial uses have little functional utility today and unnecessarily spread out commercial activities that could benefit from proximity to one another. So in remapping commercial corridors, it makes sense to reduce the number of commercial zones and make them more inclusive. It also is not necessary to create a closely calibrated range of permitted densities. Low, medium, and high commercial densities ought to be sufficient for most development situations, with the highest densities reserved for important central locations. Low-rise apartments, town houses, and live-work units should be permitted uses in all commercial zones. Apartment buildings of four stories or more should also be permitted in the denser, mixed-use, park-once districts.

Creating New Walkable Neighborhoods

The older parts of cities and suburbs have walkable neighborhoods with tree-lined streets and a mix of different housing types with local services, such as primary schools, branch libraries, and small convenience stores and restaurants within walking distance (see figure 3-5).

In the rapidly growing fringes of the metropolitan area such neighborhoods are hard to find. Most new building takes the form of what are called development tracts, often containing hundreds of houses, all of similar size on similar lots. The houses are bigger and better equipped than many of the houses in the older neighborhoods. But, while it is possible to walk to a few nearby houses, most trips have to be made by car. Zoning districts that favor a single size of lot are a strong force in shaping these areas, as are regulations that prohibit any kind of commercial use within these residential tracts. Certainly the large-scale residential tracts are a

Figure 3–5 This view of a neighborhood in West Seattle shows the mix of house sizes and types that are found in older urban and suburban neighborhoods. Regulations have permitted some larger, newer houses to be built in what had been the sideyards of older, smaller homes. This street is within walking distance of a K-8 school, several parks, convenience stores and coffee shops, a community center, and a bus line that runs to downtown Seattle, which is only 20 to 30 minutes away.

reflection of the market, but this development pattern is fostered in many ordinances—a template waiting for builders to implement (figure 3-6).

The founders of the Congress of the New Urbanism began to propose alternatives to this suburban pattern back in the 1980s. At first, New Urbanist developments were approved under planned unit development (PUD) ordinances, with the special designs for narrower streets and more closely spaced houses regulated by the developer as part of the plan submitted for approval. However, many local ordinances contained requirements that did not permit the complete New Urbanist community design, even under the PUD. As a response, the New Urbanists drafted a traditional neighborhood development (TND) ordinance, which could be applied in place of the PUD in areas where new houses are built. Zoning in many locations has now been changed to permit such walkable areas, but it is an alternative procedure. Like the PUD ordinances dating from the 1960s, a TND approval is given to a street and building plan for an individual

Figure 3–6 The design and layout of this tract of expensive houses in Scottsdale, Arizona, is closely determined by development regulations. The area offers a pleasant lifestyle and may be preferred by many people to the older type of neighborhood, but the houses are all of similar size and living there requires being totally dependent on automobiles. Some people who would like a new, large house might also like a range of housing types in the neighborhood, as well as shops and community buildings within walking distance. Simple changes in zoning ordinances could make such an alternative much easier to build.

development as an exception to the street plan and the lot dimensions required by the main provisions of the zoning and subdivision regulations.

The creation of a TND usually requires that standard zoning enabling legislation be modified to allow local communities to provide for the mixing of residential, commercial, and civic buildings. The procedure for establishing TNDs is usually through a zoning district amendment, an overlay zone, or a floating zone. For example, in 1999, the Wisconsin state legislature amended Wisconsin law to mandate that every city and village with a population of at least 12,500 adopt a specifically enabled traditional neighborhood development ordinance by 2002.[8] This requirement affects approximately 60 cities and villages in the state. The law defines traditional neighborhood development as "a compact, mixed use neighborhood where residential, commercial, and civic buildings are within close proximity to each other."[9] The law also specifies that the ordinance is not required to be mapped. The TND requirement is meant to provide an option for developers seeking an alternative approach to conventional development. While the legislature did not require cities and villages to map the ordinance, local communities may, at their option, map TND districts. Cities and villages therefore may treat the ordinance requirement as a zoning district designation, an overlay zone, a floating zone, or as a modified approach to PUDs.[10]

While there have been several hundred new traditional neighborhoods created in the United States, they represent a small fraction of residential development every year. Here are some ways to make new walkable neighborhoods a more common occurrence.

Change density requirements to units per acre and reduce the minimum lot size. Consider an 80-acre piece of undeveloped land that is zoned for 10,000-square-foot lots, or about four houses to the acre. The size of a walkable neighborhood, as defined by Clarence Perry in an often-cited article published in 1929,[11] is 160 acres, so 80 acres can be considered a substantial part of a walkable neighborhood. That 80 acres is about the size of Seaside, a community on the Gulf Coast of Florida that was an early example of the revival of walkable neighborhood design in the 1980s. Seaside was built in accordance with a private development code that both permitted and required an unusual arrangement of narrow streets and closely spaced houses. The code is enforced through recorded covenants. While many suburban development tracts are smaller than 80 acres, many are larger; they can be several thousand acres. Development at a large scale has become the usual practice in the outlying areas of cities and suburbs. A quarter-acre lot is a typical suburban lot size, although some are much larger—and these days, many are much smaller.

In the typical situation, the developer will accept the zoning template already in force and will want to maximize the development potential of the land. This results in a plan that divides the property into as many lots as possible and devotes as little land to streets as the ingenuity of the surveyor or engineer can devise. Even so, the developer is unlikely to realize the full capacity of 320 houses on 80 acres because of the land area occupied by streets, but the land will be completely developed with houses that are all on the same-sized lots.

Now consider an alternative. Let us say that the local government continues to limit the development to four houses an acre in this zone and continues to permit only single-family houses, but reduces the minimum lot size to 2,500 square feet, which would be the lot size for a typical attached row house. This change would be to the underlying zoning district; in other words, the developer would have this flexibility "as of right." A developer could build 320 attached town houses on 80 acres, which would end up leaving almost three-quarters of the site undeveloped because the density remains four units to the acre and the attached town houses use much less land than single-family houses on 10,000-square-foot lots. The resulting plan would certainly be walkable, but it is unlikely to be what the developer wants to build. A more plausible mix could be 80 lots with 100-foot frontages (10,000-square-foot lots), 80 lots with 75-foot frontage, 80 lots with 50-foot frontage, and 80 of the attached town houses with 25-foot frontage. This mix would result in the development of about three quarters of the site (including the streets), which would give useful flexibility to preserve the kinds of natural resource or fragile environmental land areas that should not be built on—another good reason for changing the regulations in this way.

Of course, the mix of four lot types is only one of a list of possible choices a developer could make while still meeting the regulatory purpose of the ordinance to create a single-family house district at a density of four units to the acre. If the local government wishes to add some apartments to the permissible house types while retaining the four units per acre density and the minimum allocation of 2,500 square feet of land per unit, the list of potential configurations grows longer. To mention an extreme example: four 80-unit apartment complexes would use up the permitted density for the entire 80 acres. The higher density parts of the development are the most likely to be walkable, but the flexible lot-size aspect of the regulation by itself, although it makes walkability more attainable, would not necessarily produce a walkable neighborhood. There are some additional requirements, which belong in the subdivision ordinance.

Figure 3-7 illustrates the kind of alternative site plans that would be possible by right if residential density requirements were maintained and the minimum lot size were reduced. On the left is a map of a tract of land where standard large-lot zoning requires the entire site to be developed with lots and houses that are close to the same size. On the right is an alternative plan for the same number of houses, but some lots are much

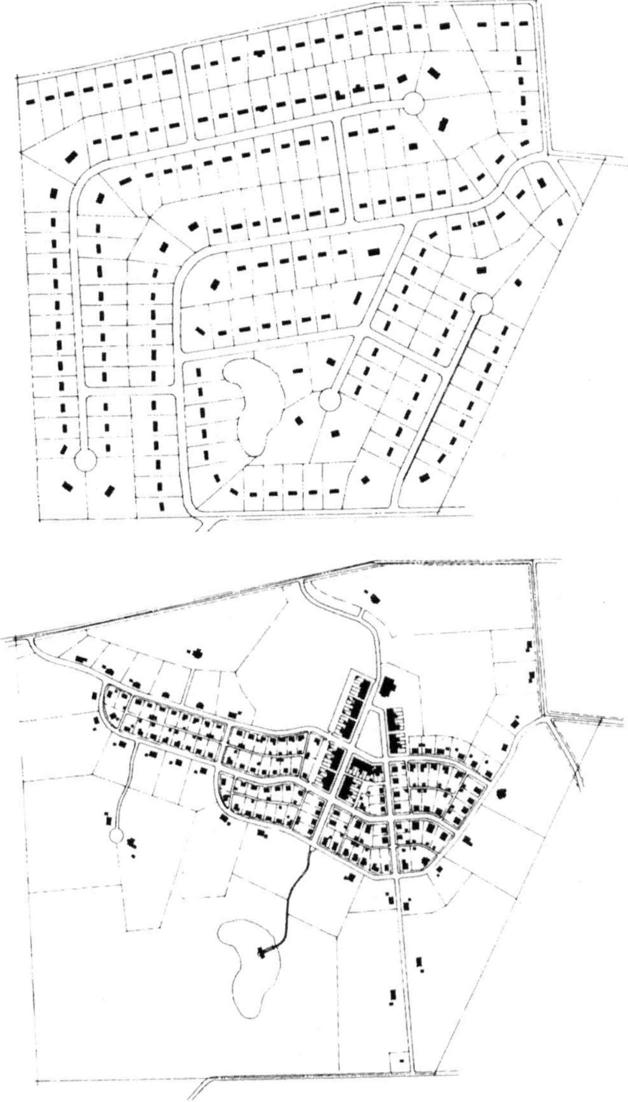

Figure 3–7 The diagram on top shows a typical layout required by most zoning ordinances where every house and lot is approximately the same size. On bottom is an alternative layout, also for single-family houses at the same density, but which offers a much wider range of choices, while preserving substantial parts of the site as open space. There are some estate lots that are much bigger than the typical lot. There are also some attached houses on much smaller lots. The site plan shows the different types of houses with a much more walkable relationship. This kind of alternative layout is possible in many places as a planned unit development but requires a complicated set of discretionary approvals subject to extensive public comment. By simply changing the regulations to reduce the minimum lot size to that of an attached town house, and at the same time keeping the area as a location for single-family houses at the same overall density, a developer can decide on such a diverse layout, subject only to administrative review and approval under the subdivision ordinance. Because smaller lots require less of the site to be developed, this kind of layout also makes it much easier to comply with requirements that portions of a development site be left unbuilt for environmental reasons.

larger, some are similar in size, and others are much smaller town house lots. In addition, substantial portions of the site are shown as open space. This type of design is possible in a PUD or a traditional neighborhood development, but their approval requires a lengthy, special procedure, as discussed in chapter 1. Our suggestion is to permit this flexibility by right in residential zones when the land under development is larger than a defined minimum size. The number of houses remains the same, and, in this example, they are all single-family units. The land plan would still need to be reviewed and approved in accordance with the subdivision ordinance, but that is a relatively simple administrative procedure, unlike applying for a PUD or TND approval, which is a discretionary rezoning decision involving a public hearing process and approval by the local planning commission and town or city council.

Although this "as of right" alternative may not be possible without enabling legislation in states where local zoning regulations are strictly governed by the provisions of state enabling legislation (Dillon's Rule states[12]), this change in minimum residential lot size should be possible as long as the maximum density in the zoning district does not change. The rationale for this kind of change would be similar to that for a PUD or a TND district, which allows for a variety of housing types through different lot sizes without changing the overall density. To the extent that there is existing development within a zoning district, as noted earlier, it is possible to add a provision to the zoning district indicating that lot sizes that predate the change in zoning are still deemed conforming. The zoning district for this purpose is explicit in allowing for a variety of zoning lot sizes; the existing zoning district lot sizes would simply be an example of a lot size permissible under the zoning regulations.

Add walkability requirements to subdivision regulations. We also propose adding the following provisions typically included in TND ordinances, and sometimes in PUD ordinances, to the subdivision ordinance as a means of introducing elements of walkability into most new residential developments, rather than relying on a special exception process.

Eliminate dead-end streets. Dead-end streets tend to reduce walkability by making pedestrians go a long way around if their destination is not on the street itself. A change to the subdivision ordinance can eliminate dead-end streets as an option in site plans. This change could be limited to development tracts above a specified size, and only in developing or recently annexed areas. In such cases, for example, the subdivision ordinance should require that street layout include access to adjoining property that has not yet been subdivided. There could be a requirement that a right-of-way from the end of all cul-de-sacs and dead-end roads to adjoining property must be part of the street layout and must be shown on street acceptance plans and deeds. The only exception would be where it is demonstrated that the adjoining property will never be developed. Even then, however, a pedestrian and bicycle trail up to the property line should be required unless that is impossible because of environmental conditions such as wetlands or a steep grade.[13]

Limit block perimeters. If dead-end streets are strictly limited or eliminated, the result will be that all the streets in a development will need to link to one another or to surrounding streets to form blocks. Limiting the perimeter of a block can improve walkability. A limit often recommended is 1,800 feet, producing blocks of 200 × 700 feet or 250 × 650 feet. This limit can also produce a block that is 450 feet square, which would be a difficult block to use in a residential zone, as it can produce a large area in the center of the block with no street access. However, this decision is best left to the developer, as a private central park within a block or a large lot development within the block could be a desirable element of a site plan. Blocks with longer perimeters can be made more walkable by including dedicated cross-block pedestrian walkways and bikeways, which can reduce the effective perimeter for a pedestrian to 1,800 feet or less. Our proposal is to make approvals for exceeding the maximum block size conditional upon inclusion of cross-block walkways that meet design standards and requirements for their safety and maintenance. Such a subdivision provision might look like this:

> Block perimeters may not exceed 1,800 linear feet as measured along the inner edges of each street right-of-way. Blocks may also be broken by a civic space provided that space is at least 50 feet wide and will provide perpetual pedestrian access between the blocks and to any lots that front the civic space. Block perimeters may exceed this limit, up to a

maximum of 2,000 linear feet, only if one or more of the following conditions apply:

(1) The block contains a parking facility mid-block that serves a mixture of uses.
(2) The block contains valuable natural features that should not be crossed by a street.[14]

Require a uniform build-to-setback line on all block frontages. Having several different types of lots along a block can be highly desirable, but can also produce a chaotic appearance along the street. Uniform setback lines are typical requirements in zoning and subdivision codes. We suggest adding a build-to line requiring that the majority of the street frontage of a building be constructed coincident with this line. In our proposal, build-to and setback lines would normally be combined into a single line. Incorporating these lines into the subdivision plan for each block frontage could produce a relatively uniform streetscape despite variations in lot sizes, or it could be a means to create a variety of open spaces along the street (figure 3-8).

Require streets designed for walking and cycling. Typical subdivision ordinances require wide streets and large turning radiuses, making walking and cycling difficult. The average right-of-way for a typical suburban street has traditionally been 50 feet.[15] The current right-of-way widths in the regulations can be kept, but the way the land is used within the right-of-way should change. Making streets walkable requires essentially the same measures as those discussed in chapter 1 to make the streets environmentally friendly by creating what are known as "complete streets"—a term publicized by Smart Growth America.[16] Within a typical right-of-way, the portion devoted to paved traffic lanes should be narrower, with much more space devoted to sidewalks and trees, rain gardens for drainage, and landscaped utility easements. The right-of-way should be wide enough to permit a utility easement, a sidewalk at least five feet wide, and a tree lawn, also at least five feet wide on both sides of the street. Trees can and should be included at an appropriate spacing. The right-of-way should also include a drainage swale on both sides of the pavement, designed so that storm water from the street will flow into the rain garden and thus into the ground. Then, traditional curbs, gutters, and drainage pipes should

Figure 3–8 A build-to line is a simple, objective way to organize buildings along a street. This example of regulations for a planned development adjoining the downtown of Buena Vista, Colorado, uses both build-to lines (the thin dark lines on the map) and build-to zones (the wider gray lines), a somewhat more flexible requirement to accommodate buildings with varied facades that may include entrance porches and bay windows. Note that some of the build-to zones are also set back from the street, which modulates the arrangement of buildings.

not be necessary in most subdivisions, and the savings in the costs of providing them will support the greater investment in landscaping and green infrastructure. A separate bicycle way is probably not necessary on smaller local streets, but the subdivision approval should include rights-of-way for bicycles to connect to and help implement a regional bicycle plan. Figure 3-9 shows one way to design a complete street in a 50-foot right-of-way.

Permit street layouts that include alley access. Most advocates of traditional neighborhood design prefer removing driveways from street frontages completely, making the garage access from an alley or lane at the rear of the house lot. The streets are more walkable because there are no interruptions to the street by driveways and no blank garage doors in view. If enough houses are built with a rear access, the costs for the developer in providing the alley or lane can be competitive with paving all the driveways of the individual houses. The subdivision ordinance should always permit this option. However, it may not be possible to have separate service lanes in every subdivision. How do we keep the convenient relation of garage-to-house that home buyers require today and preserve the walkability of the streets where the garages were almost hidden behind the houses?

Place front-facing garage doors back from the street and make driveways narrow where they cross sidewalks. In the traditional neighborhoods before World War II—neighborhoods valued today for their diverse housing types, walkable streets, and compact development—garages were usually separate structures set back almost to the rear lot line. This contributed to the walkability of the streets, as most of the frontages were occupied by houses and other buildings. Today, however, people expect to be able to drive into their garages and walk straight into the house, so the garages have inevitably come forward into more prominent locations. Suburban families almost always own more than one car, so garage doors and driveways are wider.

A garage facing the street can be set back behind the front facade of the house and still be connected to the main house structure. If the front of the house is at the combined build-to and setback line for the block, a garage door can be set back an additional 20 feet and still permit entering from the garage directly into a hallway or a kitchen. Alternatively, the garage can be built farther forward but entered from the side or rear,

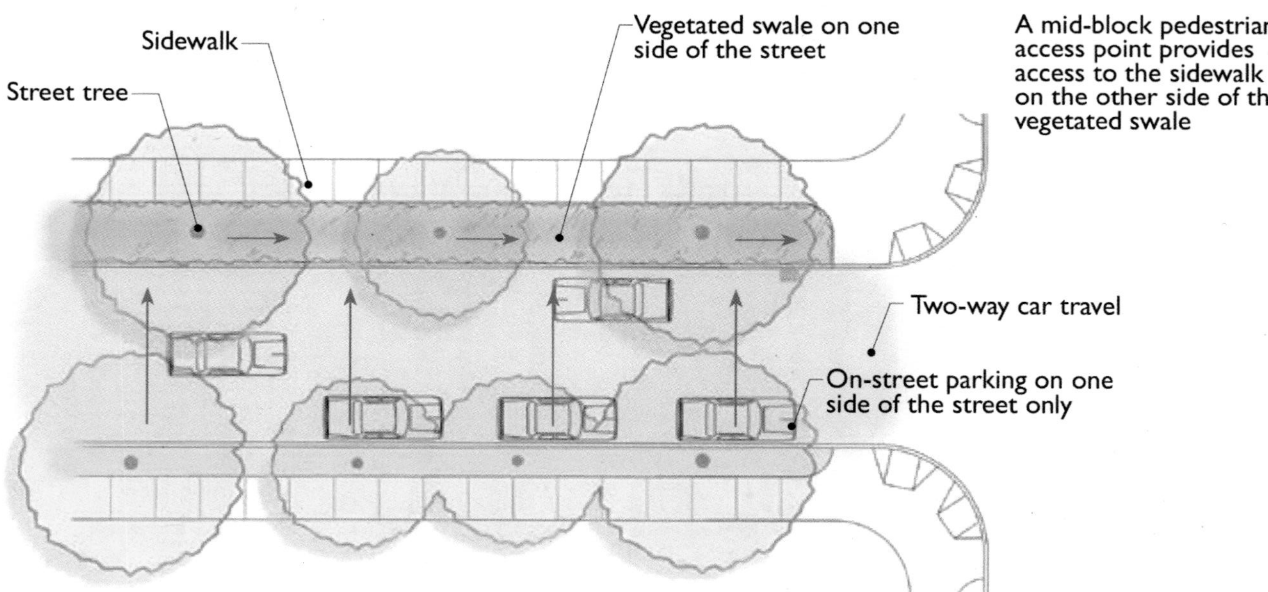

Figure 3–9 This street right-of-way diagram is from the *Stormwater Management Handbook: Implementing Green Infrastructure in Northern Kentucky Communities*, prepared for the U.S. Environmental Protection Administration. The drainage swale, comparable to the one shown in figure 1–4, is on one side of a residential street. The street is pitched to drain to the side with the swale, unlike the typical street, which is designed for water to flow into gutters on both sides. There is a midblock bridge across the swale for pedestrians to cross at the corners. This landscape design fits easily into the 50-foot-wide right-of-way typically required for residential streets. If parking is considered desirable on both sides of the street, the same right-of-way still would leave enough room for two, much narrower traffic lanes. Cars could still pass each other, but would need to move at slow speeds. Such a "traffic calming" device can be desirable in a residential neighborhood.

provided the lot is wide enough for the driveway to swing around the side of the house and permit enough maneuverability for the car to get into the garage. With garage entrances set back, it is possible to limit the width of the driveway from the street past where it crosses the sidewalk to only one lane (a common specified width is 10 feet) with the driveway widening out once past the sidewalk to allow convenient access to the garage and more space for parking. Shared driveway access for not more than two houses is an additional way of limiting the prominence of driveways.

Keeping garage door width to a size sufficient for a single car is an effective design technique for reducing the prominence of garage doors when they face the street. Two single doors next to each other will be much more in scale with a pedestrian environment than one wide door. In any case, the width of a garage door opening should always be limited to a distance suitable for two cars. If there is a third garage, it should have a separate single door. Garage doors for multifamily residential-use parking structures should never face the street. This objective is attainable relatively easily as lots for multifamily buildings will be larger than individual house lots.

Allow lane houses and garage apartments as accessory uses. An additional residential use can be permitted on single-family lots if the size of the additional unit is strictly limited and there is a clear set of design standards, with design exceptions requiring review. Adding an apartment over a two-car garage produces a unit of about 500 square feet. A two-story unit occupying the same footprint as a two-car garage would be about 1,000 square feet, which should be an upper limit. This kind of housing can be desirable for small households, and although the costs per square foot are likely to be comparable to other residential construction, the small size makes such units more affordable. Such housing is especially appropriate on lanes and alleys because more people will then be using these areas, and each new unit can have a completely separate entrance from the main house. Adding density and variety to residential districts to achieve neighborhood walkability and enable more affordably sized housing units are valid public policy objectives that can justify these needed modifications to the regulations. Community opposition to the increase in neighborhood densities that would result from allowing lane houses and garage apartments is less likely because the owners of the house lots where these units will be built will benefit (figure 3-10).

Site Plan

These illustrations show the overall site layout for the Prototype. Below is the "base case" option. To the right are variations of a reversed plan and rotated plan to address access from an alley.

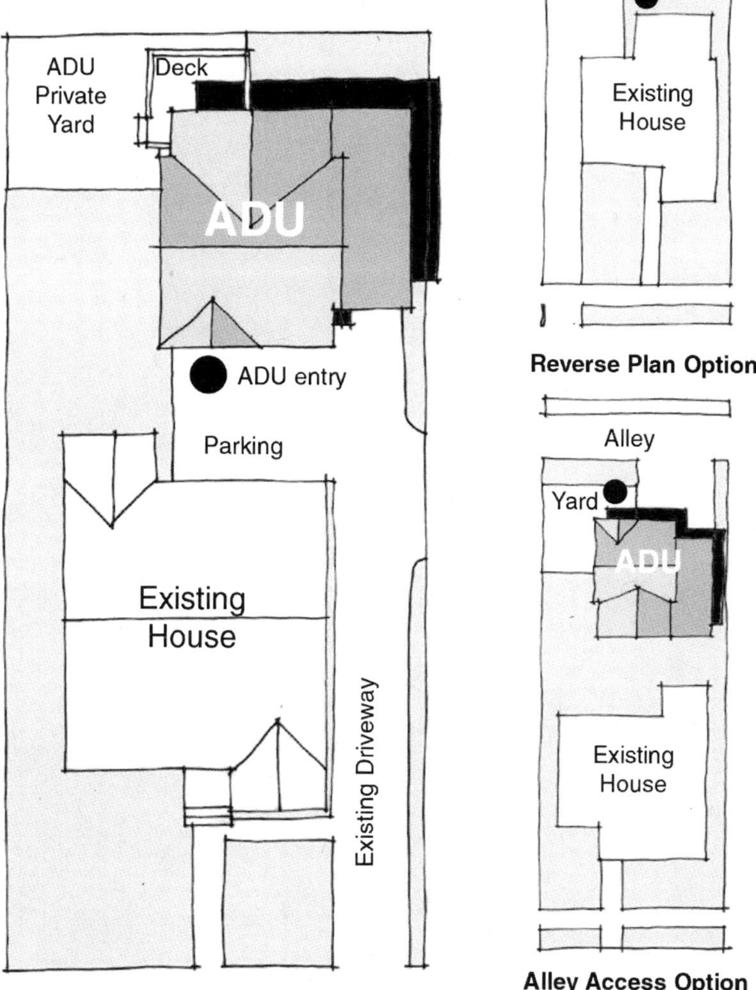

Figure 3-10 Permitting a second residence, an accessory dwelling unit, in a single-family residential zone can potentially double the density without making big changes in neighborhood character. These alternative configurations, from a manual prepared by the city of Santa Cruz, California, show how detached garages can be replaced with a building that combines a garage and a small apartment, with its own parking and a small private yard. The diagrams show how the same design can work for driveways on either side of the main house with access from an alley, if there is one. There is more information about accessory dwelling units in chapter 5, which discusses affordable housing.

Community support for accessory uses that increase available affordable housing is likely to be greater if a community has adopted a neighborhood infill-development strategy as part of a comprehensive planning process. The comprehensive plan must identify new neighborhood locations and existing neighborhoods of appropriate size and scale in which these kinds of accessory uses are most appropriate. Once these appropriate locations have been identified, standards must be established to ensure compatibility with the existing development patterns within those neighborhoods. In addition, such accessory uses may need to be subject to a discretionary review approval process, unless studies have been done on a neighborhood-by-neighborhood basis to ensure that the appropriate standards and design guidelines are adopted.

Require land to be set aside for open space. Subdivision ordinances often require that the developer set aside a portion of the land as open space. Flexible lot size makes it easy for a developer to accomplish this without losing the number of house lots allowed. In addition, it is possible to identify portions of the subdivided land that are not suitable for development and preserve their natural state as much as possible. These places should receive priority for being included in an open space set-aside. The principal legal issue, when open space is required as part of the subdivision process, is whether, when the amount and location of the open space goes beyond natural resource or fragile environmental areas, such a requirement could constitute an unconstitutional exaction because it exceeds what is necessary for the subdivision design. If a community requires the dedication of open space as part of a subdivision approval, it must justify that requirement as part of a comprehensive planning process that identifies the need and extent of open space.[17]

If land is set aside from development, it is important to determine how it should be maintained. It can be deeded to the local government or the parks district if the government is prepared to accept it. It can be managed by a homeowners association or appended to individual lots—with restrictions—in which case its maintenance becomes the responsibility of the lot owner. If land is preserved for environmental reasons, its use for recreation will need to be carefully defined and managed. This is most effectively accomplished through a conservation easement granted to a private, usually not-for-profit entity that is charged with the legal responsibility for implementing the provisions of the conservation easement.

Neighborhood Convenience Stores and Schools Within Walking Distance

Our objective in recommending changes to residential zones to permit flexible lot sizes, and require connected streets and limited block perimeters, is to facilitate the creation of walkable neighborhoods, removing obstacles to their creation. Building new neighborhoods that can match the best neighborhoods in older parts of cities and suburbs will also require other supportive public policies. A walkable neighborhood should have foot or bike access to local shops and primary schools.

A density of four units to the acre, 640 families on 160 acres, does not provide enough people to support even a small local shop. Clarence Perry, in a diagram illustrating his 1929 essay, situates retail space at one corner of a neighborhood shared with the corners of three other neighborhoods. The four neighborhoods together should be able to support a small convenience store, and perhaps more, if the location is on a main street. Developers using TND ordinances have sometimes set aside land for a shop, and some have also subsidized it as a necessary amenity. The most successful shops located in new traditional neighborhoods that are otherwise isolated from other walkable areas offer a mixture of coffee, baked goods, prepared food, groceries, and staples. It is a worthwhile public policy to permit a small parcel of land to be set aside for neighborhood commercial use, subject to being part of the subdivision approval, but that parcel is unlikely to attract a store unless the retail location can serve a sufficiently large trading area. However, walkable residential neighborhoods located close to commercial centers along commercial corridors can become sought after places to live.

Clarence Perry's diagram also showed a neighborhood primary school. Part of his definition of a neighborhood was the residential area that would support a primary school. Perry's assumed residential densities were higher than are typically mapped in developing suburban areas today, and primary schools were much smaller. Today, a walkable primary school needs to be located where it can serve several neighborhoods. Even then, the economics of building the school would improve greatly if the school could share land and facilities with other public uses such as a branch public library, a recreation center, a senior center, or a combination of these uses. A cluster of such neighborhood services in a walkable location would be a highly desirable outcome, but it would be complicated to achieve because schools, libraries, and departments of parks and recreation all have separate administrative decision-making structures. Coordinating capital investment among these separate administrations is well beyond the reach of development regulation. Appropriate locations would need to be identified as part of a public facilities and services master plan in advance of development. Based on fiscal impact analysis prepared as part of the plan, subdivision approvals could require that developers contribute proportionately to the costs of the public facilities and services needed to accommodate their development proposals within these neighborhood areas.[18]

Use of Floating Zone to Guide Site-by-Site Development

New development usually goes forward site by site. The problem for planning departments seeking to promote an innovative development concept like a mixed-use center or a walkable neighborhood is to encourage developers to consider these options without the planning department's losing its ability to help shape what happens for an entire district or neighborhood. Some developers will own enough land to create an entire business district or walkable neighborhood, but many do not. We have recognized this situation in making suggestions for mixed-use and flexible residential development that can proceed on a site-by-site basis. However, compact, walkable, mixed-use centers and walkable neighborhoods can be created more easily and reliably if the local government, as part of its comprehensive planning process, identifies potential future locations in a comprehensive plan. The potential for locating compact, walkable business centers and neighborhoods can be created by using a concept called a *floating zone*, a land-use zone that is established in the zoning text but is not mapped. In effect, the zone "floats" until a developer, taking into consideration the market and the comprehensive plan policies and zoning standards for the zone, makes application to have the zone apply to a particular geographical location. If the developer's application satisfies the standards in the zoning text for the zone, the local legislative body may apply the floating zone to the desired location and designate the zone on the official zoning map. Unlike an overlay zone, whose provisions usually supplement those of the underlying zoning district, the floating zone, when adopted for a particular location, replaces the existing zoning district. Identifying potential locations for future floating zones in a comprehensive plan would permit coordination of street and public open-space designs as well as the location of important public facilities. There also are forms of development such as office parks, hospital complexes, college and school campuses, and other large-scale developments that require coordination among their component parts. For example, identifying an appropriate location for a campus area in the comprehensive plan where a "campus" floating zone could be applied would help to guide such development, using the same procedures and criteria we have outlined for mixed-use centers.[19]

Notes

1. Treatment of chronic disease accounts for 75 percent of all health care spending—projected to reach $5.4 trillion a year by 2024. See Brad Broberg, "Walkable Communities: The Prescription for Better Health," *On Common Ground*, Winter 2016.
2. For discussions about the connection between walking and public health, two basic texts are Lawrence Frank and Peter Engelke, *Health and Community Design: The Impact of the Built Environment on Physical Activity* (Washington, DC: Island Press, 2003), and Howard Frumkin, Lawrence Frank, and Richard J. Jackson, *Urban Sprawl and Public Health: Designing, Planning, and Building for Healthy Communities* (Washington, DC: Island Press, 2004), chap. 5.
3. Richard J. Jackson, with Stacy Sinclair, *Designing Healthy Communities* (San Francisco: Jossey-Bass, 2011), 20.
4. Jeffrey Spivak, "Q&A with AARP—Livable Communities," *Urban Land*, April 26, 2011, *http://urbanland.uli.org/Articles/2011/June/SpivakWalkable;* see also Benjamin Davis, Tony Dutzik, and Phineas Baxandall, *Transportation and the New Generation: Why Young People Are Driving Less and What It Means for Transportation Policy* (Frontier Group/U.S. PIRG Education Fund, April 2012).
5. See *National Household Travel Survey* (Washington, DC: Federal Highway Administration, 2009). A new survey is under way with release promised in early 2018.
6. See Frumkin, Frank, and Jackson, *Urban Sprawl and Public Health*, 74.
7. See Jan Gehl, *Cities for People* (Washington, DC: Island Press, 2010). The well-known passage from Kierkegaard quoted by Gehl is from a private letter, not one of Kierkegaard's books, and can be found on page 412 of *Soren Kierkegaard's Journals and Papers*, Vol. 5: *Autobiographical, Part 1: 1829–1848*, trans. Howard V. Hong and Edna H. Hong, ed. Gregor Malantschuk (Bloomington: Indiana University Press, 1978).
8. 1999 Wisconsin Act 9 (the biennial budget act), generally effective 10/29/99, as amended by Act 148 (the trailer bill), effective May 25, 2000.

9. *A Model Ordinance for a Traditional Neighborhood Development*, adopted by the Wisconsin Legislature, July 28, 2001 as a follow-up to the requirement in section 66.1027 of the Wisconsin Statutes. The text of the model ordinance can be accessed at *www.reconnectingamerica.org/assets/Uploads/bestpractice160.pdf*.

10. This discussion of the Wisconsin law is based on Robert J. Sitkowski, Anna M. Breinich, and Brian W. Ohm, "Enabling Legislation for Traditional Neighborhood Development Regulations," *Land Use Law & Zoning Digest* 53, no. 10 (October 2001): 3–10.

11. Clarence Arthur Perry, "The Neighborhood Unit," in *Regional Survey of New York and Its Environs*, vol. 8, *Neighborhood and Community Planning* (New York: Regional Plan of New York and Its Environs, 1929).

12. See explanation of Dillon's Rule in chapter 1.

13. See, for example, Wayne Feiden, *Commentary on Updating Subdivision Regulations in Massachusetts* (Haydenville, MA: Highland Communities Initiative, a program of The Trustees of Reservations, n.d.)

14. Gina Gregory and Reggie Copeland, *An Ordinance Regulation to Amend the Subdivision Regulations for the City of Mobile, Alabama Codes to Create New Walkable Street Standards That Enables Traditional, Walkable Village and Neighborhood Centers Within the City of Mobile* (City of Mobile, May 15, 2008).

15. From a study by University of California professor Eran Ben-Joseph, *Residential Street Standards & Neighborhood Traffic Control: A Survey of Cities' Practices and Public Officials' Attitudes*, made available on the website of the National Association of City Transportation Officials, *Nacto.org/docs/usdg/residential_street_standards_benjoseph.pdf*. See also Michael Southworth and Eran Ben-Joseph, *Streets and the Shaping of Towns and Cities* (Washington, DC: Island Press, 2003), for a history of conventional street standards, as well as the authors' discussion of the best ways to design streets today.

16. Smart Growth America created a National Complete Streets Coalition in 2004.

17. See discussion of "exactions" in chapter 7.

18. See discussion of *Nollan* and *Dolan* cases in chapter 7.

19. See generally, Brian W. Blaesser, "The Floating Zone," chap. 4 in *Discretionary Land Use Controls: Avoiding Invitations to Abuse of Discretion* (St. Paul, MN: Thomson-Reuters, 2017).

4

Preserving Historic Landmarks

Zoning regulations assume there are no existing buildings on the land. Within a base zoning district, the extent of permitted development is a calculation made primarily from the dimensions of the property, along with restrictions such as permitted floor area, height, and setbacks. If some buildings will remain, their space must be subtracted from whatever additional construction is allowed, but, in many situations, the permitted development under the zoning makes the land worth more as a building site than the value of existing buildings. The economic concept of highest and best use reinforces the lack of interest in existing structures. The property owner has a market incentive to seek to realize the full development potential of property, particularly if acting in concert with associated investors. Another factor against retaining buildings is modernist architectural design, which had its origins in the 1920s and became dominant after World War II—just at the time when the concept of zoning became almost universal, adopted through state enabling acts. The modernist assumption is that only a few buildings constructed in the past are worth preserving, and then only for sentimental reasons. The market incentive to realize full economic value from property, the disdain once held by the architectural profession for older buildings, and the indifference of zoning toward the presence of existing buildings have been a powerful combination of forces militating against the retention of older buildings. Many older buildings that today would be considered highly valuable have been demolished, and the pressures for demolition have not diminished.

Gradually a countervailing force—the historic preservation movement—emerged. It has helped develop a set of legal requirements for preserving buildings and create incentives for property owners to preserve architecture of special value.

Historic preservation began in order to save irreplaceable cultural artifacts—an early example was Stonehenge, the prehistoric monument in Wiltshire, England, first protected by the Ancient Monuments Act of 1882 and then more completely when the land was purchased by a private owner and given to the government in 1918.[1] Early efforts at preservation also included buildings at sites of important historical significance. The only way to assure preservation was ownership of the land and buildings by an entity sympathetic to preservation. An example is the organization created to preserve George Washington's plantation, the Mount Vernon Ladies Association, which purchased the estate from members of the Washington family in 1858.

The Old and Historic District in Charleston, South Carolina, is an early example of the growing recognition that entire areas of each city have a character beyond the individual buildings, and, if preservation is to be meaningful, the whole area should be protected. A zoning ordinance enacted there in 1931 created a Board of Architectural Review with the ability to examine and approve, or disapprove, changes to buildings within the district. However, there was no authority to prevent demolition.[2] Much of the reason historic Charleston continued to survive was a weak real estate market until the 1960s, when attitudes toward older buildings began to change and other preservation tools became available. The Old and Historic District was declared a National Historic Landmark in 1966.

In the United States, two events in the early 1960s helped define the future of historic preservation: the conservation of the old buildings surrounding Lafayette Square, across from the White House in Washington, DC, and the demolition of Pennsylvania Station in New York City.

At Lafayette Square, the federal government proposed to demolish the historic nineteenth-century town houses on two sides of the square, plus what is now known as the Renwick Gallery on an adjacent corner, to make room for two new government office buildings. The plans were drawn up by a respected architectural firm and approved by the Fine Arts Commission. Demolition was ready to begin when the president's wife, Jacqueline Kennedy, intervened. Remarkably, she set in motion a sequence of events that led to the appointment of a new architect, John Carl Warnecke, who prepared a design that preserved all the old buildings fronting on the square as well as the Renwick Gallery. As part of the project, Warnecke designed a connecting structure for a vacant lot facing the square, which, while not a replica of a historic building, was comparable to the surrounding houses in materials, height, and the scale of the window and door openings. Behind the older buildings, Warnecke designed two new, substantial office towers that rose to the full permitted height and were not in a historical style, although Warnecke used red brick for the facades that was more in keeping with the domestic appearance of the buildings on the square than the usual white limestone or concrete government buildings (figure 4-1). These heresies against architectural modernism were part of a more general adjustment in the architectural profession's approach to historic buildings that began around that time.[3] Warnecke's techniques have since become an accepted way to make zoning and historic preservation compatible.

Figure 4–1 Jacqueline Kennedy and architect John Carl Warnecke standing by the model of the planned redevelopment of Lafayette Square during a press conference announcing the revised plans in October 1962. The model shows how the historic buildings along the square would be preserved, with a new federal office building set back behind them. The segment of the frontage on the square where there are three rectangular openings is actually part of a small, new building on a vacant lot, in scale with its neighbors, which serves as the entrance to the offices.

Pennsylvania Station, one of the great examples of civic architecture in the United States, was demolished to build an office building and a sports arena, after a zoning change was unanimously approved by the New York City Planning Commission. The protests after the loss of the station, with its grand marble concourse and glass-roofed train shed, led to the establishment of the New York City Landmarks Preservation Commission in 1965 with the power to designate buildings as historic landmarks. Designation gives the commission power to decide whether changes to a landmark are appropriate. The commission can deny a certificate of appropriateness for the demolition of a landmark building, which is appealable to the courts. Few owners have defied the commission and engaged in a public fight over demolition.

The demolition of Pennsylvania Station and preservation of the buildings around Lafayette Square were two important events that led the federal government to take a more active role in protecting historic sites and structures through the passage of the National Historic Preservation Act (NHPA) in 1966.[4] The NHPA was the first federal preservation law that applied to privately owned landmarks. The NHPA authorizes the secretary of the interior to establish and promulgate regulations for the National Register of Historic Places, which is composed of districts, sites, buildings, structures, and objects that are significant in American history, architecture, archeology, engineering, and culture.[5] The standards for being listed on the National Register are general, with the key requirement being that a structure must be at least 50 years old unless it is part of a historic district.[6] This National Register incorporated an earlier national list dating from 1935.[7] The NHPA also created a mechanism for placing buildings and districts on the National Register, including establishing historic preservation offices in every state to review, and in some cases generate, applications for the National Register.[8]

This authoritative list of buildings and places that ought to be preserved has been an important influence, as the National Register interacts with other legislation. Listed buildings can qualify for tax credits if their renovation meets standards set by the Department of the Interior, a major incentive for preserving and reusing historic buildings. Under the National Environmental Policy Act (NEPA),[9] federal agencies are required to examine the consequences of "major federal actions" on historic buildings.[10]

State historic preservation enabling legislation grants to local governments the authority to protect historic districts or sites by establishing preservation commissions. In addition to the statutory delegation of power to local governments for local preservation, local governments may also have home rule authority to regulate historic areas and sites.[11] The scope of authority of local preservation commissions, as defined by state law, can vary. Most state legislation requires that a survey and study be undertaken to identify and document important buildings and features in an area before designation. Some states require that local district proposals must be reviewed by a state preservation agency before they can take effect.[12] Louisiana is an example where the state created a local district directly—the famous French Quarter (*Vieux Carré*) of New Orleans—established in the Louisiana constitution.[13] Other state-established districts are in Charleston, South Carolina, and Nantucket, Massachusetts. A local historic preservation commission, or board, charged with making decisions on requests for alterations and additions to historic buildings, new buildings, or the demolition of historic buildings, typically renders its decision by what is called a "certificate of appropriateness."

When a historically designated structure is private property, the ability of the owner to alter or demolish the structure depends on the power delegated to the local preservation body under state law. In the case of demolition, the local preservation body is authorized to delay but not prevent demolition for a period of time while efforts are made to preserve the property.[14] In other jurisdictions, the local commission is authorized to deny a certificate of appropriateness to demolish, subject to judicial review.[15]

Historic preservation statutes generally have been held not to violate the Equal Protection Clause[16] even if they apply to some historic properties and not to others in a particular area.[17] To satisfy due process, a determination that a property should be included in a historic district should provide that the property owner be given the opportunity to be heard and be represented by counsel.[18] While the designation of historic properties through local commissions empowered by state law generally satisfies the rational basis requirement for equal protection and due process, the additional question is whether the restrictions imposed on private property as a result of a historic designation status violate the takings clauses of the federal Constitution and state constitutions. Here too, the courts have generally upheld historic preservation regulations on the ground that they do not deprive property owners of the reasonable use of their property.[19] The courts have not yet viewed restrictions based on a historic designation as a form of "exaction" subject to review under the U.S. Supreme Court's cases for determining the constitutionality of an exaction.[20]

At the same time, a distinction can be made between the establishment of a district composed of many individual properties such as the French Quarter of New Orleans, and the historic designation of property that is essentially isolated, a great distance from any other designated historic properties. The economic impact of regulation within a historic district is shared by everyone for the common good (the principle known as the "average reciprocity of advantage").[21] An isolated designation may cause financial hardship to the owner that is not shared by anyone else and may be subject to the challenge that the designation is arbitrary, in violation of the due process and the equal protection clauses. For this reason, the better approach to local historic designations is through establishing historic district regulations based on a local government study to support the delineation of such a district. Support for designating an individual landmark needs to be based on its very special historical or architectural significance, such as Grand Central Station in New York City.

New Development in a Historic District: Keeping in Keeping

A historic district can be designated in accordance with the procedures under the NHPA, by state statute, or by a local government pursuant to the requirements of state law. Municipalities frequently rely on National Register designations in making local designations of historic districts and landmarks. The federal system creates three categories of property within the district: historic buildings, contributing buildings (which, while not among the buildings that caused the district to be created, are nevertheless a significant part of its character), and other properties that are within the boundaries of the district. The categorization of "contributing properties" and "other properties" within the boundary of a historic district should be based on a survey of properties, completed as of a date certain to ensure that property owners have notice of such determinations and that these property-type categories will not be applied on an ad hoc basis by the local preservation commission.

In a historic district, requirements for the appearance of buildings as seen from the street can be much stricter than restrictions in a zoning or subdivision code. For example, property owners may be able to select paint colors only from an approved list. New, energy-saving windows that do not conform to the district standards for window design may not be permitted. Guidelines for new development on a vacant lot, or the site of a nonhistoric, noncontributing building, may require that the structure conform substantially to the character of the district. This requirement may be further defined in terms of making the building similar in height and scale, placement on the site, materials, colors, and the size and shape of window and door openings.

A widely accepted theory among architects is that the best work of any period is always compatible with other work of comparable quality from other periods of history. Leaving aside the question of what can be defined as best work, this proposition can only be substantiated, if at all, by looking at groups of buildings constructed before the Industrial Revolution when the available technology imposed similar limits on building heights, window openings, materials, and other elements that go into the design of a building. Today's building construction techniques enable so many variations of size, shape, and material that the odds are against adjacent buildings having a compatible design unless that compatibility is mandated by some kind of regulation. Architects respond by saying that such regulations stifle creativity and force designs that are little more than fake historic buildings and are a guarantee of mediocrity. An expression, originating in Great Britain and meant to be derisive, refers to such buildings as "keeping in keeping." There are other architects who see nothing wrong with a faithful reproduction of historic buildings, provided the design details are accurate. It is also possible that a design can either reinterpret the requirements of a historic district or break them in a way that creates a building that many people agree would be a wonderful addition to the area.

Using Height Limits and Setback Regulations to Reinforce a Historic District

Many historic districts are old, prestigious residential areas whose original homeowners could afford exceptional architectural design. Such historic districts are most often overlay districts whose boundaries cover one or more base zoning districts and include nonhistoric or noncontributing buildings and vacant parcels. Often the permitted new development is still residential and not much larger than what is already in the district, but zoning regulations, based only on lot size, can permit infill buildings on large lots or the amalgamation of several lots to produce a bigger and taller structure. The historic character of that area may be preserved by adding height and building placement regulations for new construction that can take place on vacant parcels or on the sites of noncontributing buildings. The height limit should be based on the prevailing height of buildings in the historic district. Infill buildings can be regulated to ensure that their spacing and placement are compatible with existing development. For example, if the historic houses in a district are generally set back a similar distance from the street, the building placement provisions can require infill buildings to conform to the same setback. The local historic preservation commission would need to review the architectural character of an infill building to determine if it meets the requirements of the historic district.

In historic overlay districts, the underlying zoning can allow for potential development much larger than the existing buildings. If there is a strong real estate market, the pressure to realize the full value from the property can be difficult to resist. In such circumstances, either the underlying zoning district regulations can be amended to help shape new development in ways that can be compatible with the existing historic character or provisions can be added to the historic overlay district. Historic buildings are likely to be constructed at the front property line. In that situation, placing a build-to line and a height limit at the front property line and requiring a setback of a substantial distance, for example, 50 feet, before the building can be taller, is a way of requiring the design strategy used by John Carl Warnecke at Lafayette Square in Washington (figure 4-2). If you are standing on the sidewalk facing a four-story building and look up, any taller structure attached to the building will appear to be disconnected from it and a substantial distance away. If this strategy is followed consistently within a district, higher densities can be achieved, and the area as seen from the street will still have some of its historic character. If the low building at the street frontage is a historic building, not a new infill building, enough should be preserved of the older building that it can still function, providing interior spaces at a historic scale that are different from the new buildings behind them. This

Figure 4–2 Aerial view of Lafayette Square showing how the two new federal office buildings are fitted in behind the rows of historic buildings fronting the square on Jackson Place, on the right, and Madison Place, on the left. The red-brick tower on the Jackson Place side is the New Executive Office Building. The matching tower of the Markey National Courts Building fits into the block on the opposite side of the park. The historic buildings fronting the square are preserved and adaptively reused, a very different outcome from what is often described as a *facadectomy,* where portions of a historic facade are incorporated as part of the front of a new building.

policy, if followed in issuing a certificate of appropriateness, avoids what are called *facadectomies*, where only the front facade of the original buildings is salvaged during demolition and the new building is constructed to incorporate the facade. The effect can be relatively pleasing and can preserve something of the original architectural scale, but if there are no functioning original spaces behind the facade, it is not really preservation.

Rezoning Buildings in a Historic District for New Uses

Sometimes there is not much of a real estate market for historic buildings because the area is zoned for uses for which there is no longer market demand. New York City in the late 1960s helped start a new trend in landmarks preservation with the rezoning of the area known as SoHo, an acronym for south of Houston Street. An old industrial loft district, with many nineteenth-century cast-iron-front buildings, had fallen into disrepair, partly because it was in the path of a Robert Moses expressway plan and partly because such buildings were no longer appropriate for most modern warehousing or manufacturing.

When the expressway plan was canceled and the facades caused the district to be up for landmark designation as the Cast Iron District, the city rezoned the area from industrial to a special industrial district that also permitted residential occupation of lofts in smaller buildings to increase the economic viability of the buildings. Artists had been moving into these lofts illegally, so it was clear there was a market. At first, residents were restricted to artists, on the somewhat contrived theory that artists were a category of industrial workers who needed to live near their work. The question then arose: Who is an artist? A board was created to make this determination, but eventually the provision was found to be unworkable. Ultimately, the entire SoHo district permitted residences, and, as commercial uses had always been allowed in the underlying industrial zone, the ground floors increasingly have become occupied by shops, art galleries, and restaurants, while some of the original industrial uses remain. Some adjustments to the building code were also needed to make loft buildings with large floors, which consequently had deep spaces a long way from windows, acceptable as residences.[22]

The district has been such a real estate success that most artists can no longer afford to live there. The change in development regulations reinforced the historic district designation very well by creating an economic basis for preserving the buildings. SoHo has become a prototype for revitalizing historic loft districts in many cities, where these versatile old buildings have possible alternative uses as homes or offices. Loft living has now become so popular that developers are building new lofts in places where genuine old factory and warehouse buildings have already been converted to different uses.

To facilitate the conversion of loft buildings to residential use and artist lofts, existing provisions in the relevant residential and commercial zoning districts that impede such conversion must be eliminated, while keeping or adding provisions that allow for a mix of residential, commercial, and light manufacturing uses. For example, in New York City, the zoning allows the conversion of nonresidential floor area to residential use only if floor area that is appropriate for certain commercial or manufacturing uses is preserved, either in the same building or elsewhere within the district. The amount of floor area that must be preserved depends on the size of the floors in the building being converted. This space is preserved by deed restriction. A special permit process is used to allow for the reduction of the loft space required to be preserved for industrial or commercial use if the City Planning Commission determines market conditions no longer warrant or support keeping the space industrial or commercial.[23]

Saving Historic Main Streets

In many smaller cities, the original retail businesses along historic main streets fell on hard times and the future of the buildings became endangered, usually from competition from malls and big-box stores on a highway by-pass at the edge of the community. The National Trust for Historic Preservation—a private organization chartered by Congress—created a Main Street program to help save historic buildings in these retail districts. A pilot program was begun in 1977, a series of Main Street programs began in 1980, and a National Main Street Center was established in 2004, which consolidated the previous programs.[24]

The older buildings, reconceptualized as an asset by becoming part of a historic district, turn out to be the key to future retail success. The Main Street programs use a wide range of preservation methods beyond district designation. Perhaps the most important has been making sure there are funds to pay a manager who is responsible for the long-term viability of the whole district. Other important measures include public investment in street improvements and landscaping, merchandising advice for store owners, shared parking, and capitalizing on the character of the area to create a distinctive retail identity. These actions have proved effective in making Main Street historic districts into successful shopping destinations. Changes in the local zoning are often needed for the district to succeed: the most important change is usually to the existing retail zoning to permit a mix of uses, particularly on the upper floors of buildings. When these buildings were originally constructed, it is likely they had either office space or apartments on the upper floors, but conventional zoning codes often permit only specific retail categories in commercial districts that would have been mapped on local main streets. It is much easier to preserve a retail building if there are other uses returning income to the owners. Allowing parking requirements to be satisfied off-site can be important in maintaining existing structures that were built before automobiles became widely used. The National Trust for Historic Preservation advises groups interested in preserving Main Streets to begin by obtaining a historic district designation if possible.[25] When a Main Street becomes successful, zoning measures similar to those used to reinforce historic districts should be in place, such as a height limit, build-to lines, and other building placement requirements. If there is no historic district, a design-review district could be an alternative, with guidelines intended to reinforce the main street character and operations.

Transferable Development Rights

The technique of transferable development rights (TDR) is based on the legal concept that ownership of real property is ownership of a combination of rights that pertain to that property. For that reason, ownership of real property is frequently described as owning a "bundle of sticks." Each stick in the bundle represents one of the rights of ownership, such as the right to possess, including the right to minerals below the surface, the right to exclude others from one's property, and, of course, the right to make productive use of one's property, usually understood as the development right. Ownership of the entire bundle of rights is known as ownership in fee simple absolute. However, because each property "right" is a separate "stick" in the bundle, each such right can be conveyed or transferred to another person or entity.

TDR is a market-based mechanism intended to discourage development of property within a designated "sending area." The sending area contains attributes that the local community wants to protect from development, such as valuable environmental resources, open space, or historic landmarks. Under a TDR program, a property owner in the sending area can agree to restrict development on the property by entering into a conservation easement or similar deed restriction that is noted on the land records and encumbers the property forever. In exchange for this restriction, the property owner receives one or more transferable development rights. These *transferable development rights*, as the term suggests, can be transferred (sold) to a property owner in a receiving area who wants to build more than would otherwise be allowed by the development regulations applicable in that area. The receiving area is a designated district where denser development is determined by the local government to be appropriate and is encouraged. The receiving area should meet two important criteria: be desirable for development from a market perspective and have the necessary infrastructure available.[26]

TDR programs have existed in this country since 1965, when New York City adopted its Landmark Preservation Law, which allowed development density to be transferred from a lot containing a historic structure to an adjacent parcel.[27] Many local TDR programs have been established under home rule authority without the benefit of statewide enabling legislation. Some programs have been established under statewide legislation that offered little specific guidance on program development. Some of these programs are considered successful. However, well-drafted state enabling legislation increases the likelihood that a local TDR program will succeed.[28]

Under a TDR program there must be a method of valuing the development rights that are transferred. For example, a local TDR ordinance may define development rights in units per acre, in square feet of floor area, or in units of height of structures, among others. The ordinance may establish rights in terms of credits that may in turn be sold. When an existing building does not use up all the permitted floor area, the unused development rights can be transferred to another site. Under New York City's zoning law, such a transfer has always been possible if the building's owner purchased a next-door parcel and merged it to form a single property.[29]

Grand Central Station, New York City's other great civic arrival hall besides Pennsylvania Station, had been under threat of demolition since the 1950s to make way for the much larger building that was possible under the zoning law. The New York City Landmarks Commission designated Grand Central Terminal as a historic landmark. When the city landmarks commission designates a landmark, the landmark owner, under the ordinance, is subject to several restrictions. These include a requirement that the landmark owner obtain a certificate of appropriateness from the commission for any alteration of the landmark or for any construction on the site. The zoning ordinance also provides economic relief to the landmark owner by allowing the transfer of any development rights it cannot use under the zoning ordinance to contiguous parcels on the same city block that are under different ownership.

The landmark owner and a developer filed an application to construct a 55-story high-rise office building in the air space over the terminal based on a design by the well-known modernist architect Marcel Breuer. The commission rejected this proposal as an "aesthetic joke." The landmark owner did not submit another plan for the office building to the commission; instead, it filed an action claiming that the landmark law was a taking.[30] It asked for injunctive relief as well as damages for the "temporary takings" that was alleged to have occurred. The state's highest court did not find a taking.

In an appeal before the U.S. Supreme Court, the landmark owner conceded that a mere diminution in value is not a taking, but argued that a taking had occurred because the landmark regulation applied only to individual selected properties. This argument set up a distinction between a building designated as a landmark and historic district regulation applied to landmarks in an entire district. Justice Brennan, writing for the majority, first appeared to treat this argument as raising an equal protection objection to the landmark ordinance as "reverse" spot zoning, that is, singling out a particular property for discriminatory treatment. But he rejected this argument by holding that the designation of landmarks in the city had been carried out in accordance with a comprehensive plan. The landmark owner also attempted to distinguish landmark regulation from historic district ordinances by arguing that landmark regulation does not impose "identical or similar restrictions." The owner claimed that landmark regulation "is inherently incapable of producing the fair and equitable distribution of benefits and burdens of governmental action" characteristic of zoning and historic district ordinances. This argument appeared to be a claim that landmark regulation is a taking because it does not confer an "average reciprocity of advantage."[31] Justice Brennan rejected this, holding that a taking does not occur just because a regulation has a more severe impact on some landowners than others.

Finally, Justice Brennan noted that the air rights over the terminal were transferable to other sites under the transfer of development rights option. These rights might not have constituted just compensation if a taking had occurred, but they would "mitigate whatever financial burdens the law has imposed."[32] There have actually been purchases of Grand Central Terminal development rights in accordance with this historic landmark ordinance.

Transferring development rights seems like an easy way for everyone to win. Old buildings remain, and property owners realize the full potential value of their property. But air-rights transfer is complicated, and the potential results need to be studied carefully before implementing such a program. One complication is that the market for the development rights may not exist at the time a landmark building is designated. Another set of complications involves the areas designated as receiving sites for development rights. The areas immediately around Grand Central that were the receiving sites were zoned for an amount of development comparable to Grand Central. The extent of development rights that could be purchased in these receiving areas was limited to 20 percent in addition to what would otherwise be possible on each receiving site. But what happens if areas designated as receiving sites are zoned for far less development? Presumably, this lower zoning would be based on objective factors. If one property owner is suddenly able to build a much larger building by purchasing rights, why are the surrounding properties still limited in what they can build? It can be argued that the zoning authorities have now accepted that the area is appropriate for larger buildings. Therefore, by this reasoning all the properties should be zoned for the higher density, without their owners' having to purchase development rights.

An example of unexpected consequences from development rights transfer is another New York City zoning provision, adopted around the same time as the Grand Central District, which has permitted developers to buy up the unused development rights from adjacent properties without purchasing the underlying land or buildings. It was regarded at the time as a minor technical change, and for years it did not seem to have much effect. But "adjacency" has since been interpreted to mean that once a development has bought the air rights from an adjacent property, it could also buy the rights from the property adjacent to that property, permitting the development proposal to work its way down a block acquiring the rights for more and more potential development. The result has been a series of new buildings that are far taller than would otherwise be possible (see figure 4-3). The adjacent buildings, probably not designated landmarks, are likely to be preserved permanently, as a new building on each site could be no larger than the existing building. The environmental value of preserving the structures and building materials of existing development is now recognized, but New York City has found itself with what opponents of the transfer process call an "accidental skyline." The opposition is currently proposing a moratorium on transfers while the practice is restudied.[33]

Figure 4–3 This graphic by New York City's Municipal Art Society shows the location and size of unusually tall, new residential buildings under development as of 2013. The height of these slender towers, which the society calls an "accidental skyline," came as a surprise to even such vigilant watchdogs over New York City development as the Municipal Art Society. The towers are made possible by a combination of new building technologies and the amalgamation of development rights transferred from contiguous properties, which do not need to be in the same ownership as the site of the tower. These amalgamations, permitted by the zoning ordinance, are private transactions, and the results only appear when building begins. One alternative would be to require a public hearing and approval by the NYC Planning Commission of development transfers larger than a predetermined threshold, as the basic intention of the zoning had not been to permit such towers.

Methodology for a Transferable Development Rights Program

To increase the likelihood that a TDR program will be successful, TDR enabling legislation should require the following provisions:

- Include comprehensive definitions of terms.
- Create specific local program objectives to identify sending areas.
- Provide clear standards for delineating receiving areas and regulating development within the areas.
- Require that receiving areas have sufficient demand for new development to absorb TDRs.
- Require that local TDR programs follow steps to guide the initial allocation of TDRs and to measure and establish values.

- Provide standards for the market analysis conducted to ensure a reasonable balance between the supply of and demand for TDRs to incentivize use of TDRs.
- Create standards to guide the administration of local programs to ensure programs are equitable, simple to administer, and have clearly defined procedures for the acquisition, transfer, and use of TDRs.
- Require that the local government responsible for program implementation has, or hires, the expertise necessary to design, implement, and monitor the program.
- Outline provisions that define the circumstances under which exceptions to standard restrictions placed on property following the sale of TDRs may be permitted, if the state enabling legislation authorizes such exceptions.
- Create variance provisions to ensure the flexibility of local TDR programs and provide a way to address undue hardships.

A Simple Administrative Change to Help Protect Historic Buildings

Existing buildings do not appear on zoning maps, and the text, as noted earlier, is written so that the full zoning potential is based on the dimensions of the property. Additionally, zoning regulations often impose requirements for a building site, such as a setback, which make it difficult to preserve existing buildings and to meet the requirements of historic districts.

As discussed in chapter 1, simply placing the outline of buildings on the zoning district maps and calling out buildings protected by landmark or historic district designations on these maps will help clarify administration by placing all the legal requirements on the same page. Most local governments now have the geographic information systems to make this change practical.

Notes

1. Land continues to be purchased around Stonehenge, which has gradually been restored to a grassland setting. For the early history of Stonehenge preservation,

see Joseph L. Sax, "Origins of Cultural Property Protection in England," *California Law Review* 78 (1990): 1543–1567.

2. See Robert R. Weyeneth, *Historic Preservation for a Living City: Historic Charleston Foundation, 1947–1997* (Columbia, SC: University of South Carolina Press, 2000).
3. See Kathleen P. Galop, "The Historic Preservation Legacy of Jacqueline Kennedy Onassis," *Forum Journal* 20, no. 3 (2006); also Jonathan Barnett, "Those Old Buildings on Lafayette Square," *Architectural Record* 143 (April 1968): 147–154.
4. 16 U.S.C. § 470 to 470w-6 (1966).
5. Ibid., § 470a (1(A)).
6. 36 C.F.R. pts. 60 and 63. The regulations provide for a number of procedural steps for listing. These steps make the process less subjective.
7. Prepared under the Historic Sites Act of 1935.
8. In 1980, the NHPA was amended to provide that a property owner (or property owners, where a district is involved) must be given the opportunity to object to or concur with the listing. If there is an objection by a sole owner or by a majority of owners in a district, the property may not be listed. See 16 U.S.C. § 470(a)(6).
9. 42 U.S.C. §§ 4321–4361.
10. Section 101 of NEPA states: "It is the continuing responsibility of the Federal Government to use all practicable means, consistent with other essential considerations of national policy to . . . (2) assure for all Americans safe, healthful, productive, and aesthetical and culturally pleasing surroundings; . . . (4) preserve important historic, cultural and natural aspects of our national heritage, and maintain, wherever possible, an environment which supports diversity and variety of individual choice; . . . (6) enhance the quality of renewable resources and approach the maximum attainable recycling of depletable resources." See also *Aluli v. Brown*, 437 F. Supp. 602, 608 (D. Haw. 1977), *judgment rev'd on other grounds*, 602 F.2d 876 (9th Cir. 1979) ("An EIS must consider the possible effects of major federal actions upon historic and cultural resources").
11. See discussion of home rule in chapter 1.
12. See, for example, N.C. Gen. Stat. §§ 160A-400.1 et seq. See also Ark. Stat. Ann. § 19-5003 A; Ga. Code Ann. § 23-2606a(b)(1); N.C. Gen. Stat. § 160A-399.5(2); Pa. Stat. Ann. tit. 53. § 8002.
13. La. Const. of 1921 art. XIV, § 22A; see also art. VI, § 17. See also *Maher v. City of New Orleans*, 516 F.2d 1051 (1975), *cert. denied*, 426 U.S. 905 (1976) (upholding constitutionality of the architectural control ordinance applicable to the French Quarter as a means to preserve the "tout ensemble" of the historic district). State-established districts were also created in Charleston, SC, and Nantucket, MA.

14. See, for example, Ind. Code Ann. § 36-7-11-14(b) (60 days to a year); Va. Code § 15.1-503.2(c) (delay period based on the value of the building—the greater the value the longer the required delay).
15. See, for example, Ill. Rev. Stat. Ch. 24, sec. 11-48.2-1 et seq.; Mass. Gen. Laws Ch. 40C; D.C. Code Ann. §§ 5-1001 to 5-1015.
16. See discussion of this constitutional principle in chapter 7.
17. See *City of Santa Fe v. Gamble-Skogmo, Inc.*, 389 P.2d 13 (N.M. 1964).
18. See *Donnelly Associates v. District of Columbia Historic Preservation Review Board*, 520 A.2d 270 (D.C. 1987).
19. See, for example, *First Presbyterian Church of York v. City of York*, 360 A.2d 257 (Pa. Commw. Ct. 1975); *Mayor of Annapolis v. Anne Arundel County*, 16 A.2d 807,833 (Md. 1974).
20. *Nollan v. California Coastal Comm'n*, 483 U.S. 825 (1987); *Dolan v. City of Tigard*, 512 U.S. 374 (1994); *Koontz v. St. Johns River Water Management Dist.*, 133 S. Ct. 2586 (2013). See discussion of these cases in chapter 7.
21. The average reciprocity of advantage principle was explained by the U.S. Supreme Court in *Keystone Bituminous Coal Association v. DeBenedictis*, 480 U.S. 470 (1987). In that case, in upholding a law that limited the extent of underground mining of coal to prevent subsidence damage to structures on the surface, and the resulting public nuisance, the court explained: "Each of us is burdened somewhat by such restrictions but in turn, we greatly benefit from the restrictions that are placed on others. These restrictions are properly treated as part of the burden of citizenship" (491).
22. This explanation is drawn from a presentation by Donald H. Elliott given at a conference at the Harvard Graduate School of Design, October 9, 2014. Elliott was chairman of the New York City Planning Commission at the time the regulations for SoHo were enacted.
23. See NYC Planning Commission Zoning Resolution, art. 1, chap. 5: Residential Conversion of Existing Buildings (effective 9/21/11), *www1.nyc.gov/site/planning/zoning/access-text.page*.
24. Additional information about the National Main Street Center can be found at their website *www.preservationnation.org/*.
25. See *A Citizen's Guide to Protecting Historic Places: Local Preservation Ordinances* (Washington, DC: National Trust for Historic Preservation, 2002).
26. See generally Arthur C. Nelson, Rick Pruetz, and Doug Woodruff, "Designing Receiving Areas," chap. 9 in *The TDR Handbook: Designing and Implementing Transfer of Development Rights Programs* (Island Press, American Bar Association, 2012); Peter J. Pizor, "Making TDR Work," *APA Journal* (Spring 1986): 210.
27. Rick Pruetz, *Saved by Development* (Burbank, CA: Arje Press, 1997), 9.

28. As of 2010, twenty-five states had adopted TDR enabling legislation. See Nelson, Pruetz, and Woodruff, *The TDR Handbook*, 105. The New York legislature enacted TDR enabling legislation to more broadly authorize the implementation of TDR programs at the local level by cities, villages, and towns. N.Y. Gen. City Law 20-f; N.Y. Village Law § 7-701; N.Y. Town Law, § 261(a).

29. According to the *New York City Zoning Handbook*, "A zoning lot merger is the joining of two or more adjacent zoning lots into one new zoning lot. Unused development rights may be shifted from one lot to another, as-of-right, only through a zoning lot merger." *City of New York Zoning Resolution*, art. I, chap. 2: Construction of Language and Definitions. The actual paragraph is (2/2/1/)(f)(3).

30. *Penn Cent. Transp. Co. v. City of New York*, 438 U.S. 104 (1978).

31. See the definition of "average reciprocity of advantage" in note 21 of this chapter.

32. *Penn Cent. Transp. Co. v. City of New York*, 438 U.S. 104 (1978), 135.

33. *Accidental Skyline Report* (New York: Municipal Art Society, 2013).

5

Creating More Affordable Housing and Promoting Environmental Justice

Exclusionary Zoning

A major reason for the shortage of affordable housing[1] in this country, particularly in suburban areas, is the negative impact of certain zoning techniques and other development regulations on the production of houses and apartments that people with low or moderate incomes can afford to rent or buy. Local community zoning policies make it too expensive or impossible to develop affordable housing. These policies include large lot requirements in single-family zones, large frontage and building setbacks, the exclusion of multifamily units, the imposition of minimum floor-area requirements and bedroom limitations, and the prohibition of mobile homes. The term *exclusionary zoning* describes this array of zoning practices along with growth management control techniques such as development exactions (impact fees), urban growth boundaries, and rate of growth controls, when they are imposed for growth control rather than growth management.

Exclusionary zoning forces developers to look for land outside communities with these zoning restrictions, often in cities and towns that are farther from employment centers. As the National Association of Homebuilders (NAHB) has observed: "In many high-growth markets, teachers, police officers, fire fighters, and other public servants are commuting 50 to 100 miles to work each day because they can't find affordable housing to rent or buy close to their jobs. . . . Growth boundaries, large-lot zoning, and resistance to infill development are pushing people to satellite cities in search of homes that are affordable to middle income families."[2]

Faced with exclusionary zoning practices, developers seek farmland or other undeveloped land at the edge of or beyond suburban areas to rezone and develop for housing. Agricultural land or undeveloped land can look like a good buy for housing development because the price reflects its lack of infrastructure: the existing water and sewer services, as well as electricity and gas systems, cannot support higher-density housing. The schools, police and fire services, libraries, road networks, and all the other services are not sufficient either. Even in these areas, land-use control mechanisms can increase development costs that ultimately impact the price of housing, but the bigger issue is the cost of making such sites suitable for higher-density housing.

Development Impact Fees

The costs of extending needed infrastructure to these undeveloped areas are typically imposed on the developer through a system of impact mitigation fees administratively, on an ad hoc basis, or through an ordinance that establishes a schedule of fees. These fees can cover the full range of development-related improvements to capital facilities and services, such as roads, water, sewer, fire, emergency medical services, police, parks, and schools. Alternatively, the local community may decide to address the need for new infrastructure through an *adequate public facilities ordinance*. Under this approach, the local government may deny approval of any new developments unless the infrastructure needed to accommodate a development has already been built or will be built in time by the community, or by the developer, to serve the development.

The effects that the development-impact mitigation fees have on the property values in these areas depends on the nature and extent of the local impact fee system and the local market for land. Initially, the imposition of impact fees may decrease the price a developer would otherwise be willing to pay for raw land in an impact fee area, because the impact fee will increase the cost of development.[3] Although some of this cost may be shifted backward from the developer to the owner of the undeveloped land, in a competitive housing construction market it is also likely that the developer will seek to pass the higher development costs to the ultimate homebuyer, meaning new home purchasers will be likely to bear most of the additional development costs through higher housing prices.[4] If impact fees are imposed in distressed, non-growth, or less desirable areas, however, there is greater risk that builders and developers will not be able to recover their increased costs and will have to absorb the fees or simply choose not to develop new housing.[5]

Large-Lot Zoning

Communities in which most or all of the land is zoned for large single-family lots leave no sites where smaller houses and apartments can be built. This restriction has an exclusionary effect that is difficult to overcome because local communities oppose rezoning land to higher single-family residential density or multifamily use. As a result, action at the state level, both by judicial doctrine and statute, has been the remedy in certain states. For example, in New Jersey, as a result of two exclusionary zoning lawsuits, *Mount Laurel I* in 1975[6] and *Mount Laurel II* in 1983,[7] the state imposed an affirmative obligation on every "developing municipality" to provide a realistic opportunity for its fair share of low- and moderate-income housing. In *Mount Laurel I*, the New Jersey Supreme Court held that strict zoning restrictions (for example, large minimum lot sizes and prohibitions against mobile homes and apartment houses) that increased the size and cost of housing were contrary to the general welfare[8] and had the practical effect of excluding poor and middle-income persons from the township, in violation of the state's constitutional guarantees of due process and equal protection. However, because the elimination of the zoning restrictions did not, by itself, lead to the construction of low-income housing, the New Jersey Supreme Court, in *Mount Laurel II*, upheld the trial court's use of a so-called builder's remedy—namely, the right of a development project applicant, who prevails before a trial court on its constitutional claim, to seek direct court approval of its application, in this case a mobile home park. In 1985, the New Jersey legislature responded to the Supreme Court's *Mount Laurel* doctrine by enacting the Fair Housing Act.[9] In *Mount Laurel III* in 1986,[10] the Supreme Court approved the transfer of pending cases to a nine-member Council of Affordable Housing (COAH) that had been authorized by the state's recently enacted Fair Housing Act.[11] The builder's remedy was eventually eliminated under COAH's regulations. But affordable housing was not being built under the COAH. In 2015, the New Jersey Supreme Court expressed its displeasure with this circumstance and decided to again follow *Mount Laurel I* and *Mount Laurel II*, stating, "We conclude that towns must subject themselves to judicial review for constitutional compliance, as was the case before the Fair Housing Act was enacted. Under our tripartite form of government, the courts always present an available forum for redress of alleged constitutional violations or, alternatively, for towns seeking affirmative declarations that their zoning actions put them in compliance with *Mount Laurel* obligations."[12]

The court's holding that towns were once again subject to judicial review for state constitutional compliance means that they are now also subject to all the remedies available through exclusionary zoning litigation, including a builder's remedy.

A handful of other states have statutory or judicial exclusionary zoning doctrines that make it possible to challenge large lot size and other exclusionary zoning techniques.[13] Massachusetts has a unique statute, known as the Comprehensive Permit Law.[14] The law encourages the construction of state or federally subsidized low- or moderate-income housing by authorizing local zoning boards of appeal (ZBAs), after receiving input from other local boards and officials, to grant a single permit to an eligible developer. The ZBA may override local zoning and other requirements and regulations that are inconsistent with affordable housing needs, if planning and environmental needs have been addressed. The ZBA may not override state requirements. A developer whose Comprehensive Permit application is denied, or approved with conditions that make the project "uneconomic," may appeal the decision to the state Housing Appeals Committee (HAC).

Beyond these relatively few state statutory or judicial doctrines to address exclusionary zoning, various exclusionary zoning techniques persist in communities around the country and severely impact the availability of affordable housing. One zoning technique that is advocated by some to address exclusionary zoning is the adoption of "inclusionary zoning" ordinances.

Inclusionary Zoning

The term *inclusionary zoning* is used to refer to both mandatory and voluntary inclusionary zoning programs. Mandatory inclusionary zoning requires housing developers "to dedicate a certain percentage of their constructed projects to low or moderate income housing."[15] This technique may be applied to both rental and owned units and to single and multifamily housing.[16] A mandatory inclusionary zoning program may couple its mandate with incentives such as density bonuses and reduced parking requirements, but it typically requires that the developer either dedicate a percentage of the number of units (for example, 10 or 15 percent) of a market-rate development project to low- or moderate-income households, construct the equivalent number of affordable units off site, or pay a fee in lieu of constructing such units.

Whether a municipality has the authority to adopt a mandatory inclusionary zoning program depends on the applicable zoning enabling statute, whether that authority is preempted by other state statutes, and the holdings of state and federal court regulatory takings decisions. The fundamental question underlying inclusionary zoning is whether it is right to place the burden of producing affordable housing on the individual developer rather than the community at large, particularly where an existing housing shortage is sought to be rectified. The requirement that a market-rate development include an affordable housing percentage is a form of exaction, subject to scrutiny under *Nollan/Dolan* and the unconstitutional conditions doctrine articulated in *Koontz*.[17] In light of ongoing litigation around the country over the complex constitutional questions raised by mandatory inclusionary zoning, the better practice is a voluntary, incentive-based approach by which density bonuses, zoning dimensional waivers, fast-track permitting, and other types of incentives are offered under the ordinance to offset the developer's subsidy of affordable units by reducing the per-unit cost of the development.[18]

Another possible source of funds for inclusion of affordable housing in market-rate developments would be government subsidy programs for low- and moderate-income housing. In 2014, the federal government provided about $50 billion in housing assistance specifically designated for low-income households. The subsidy programs include the Housing Choice Voucher program and project-based rental assistance in buildings that include housing for low-income tenants. The Low Income Housing Tax Credit, made available to developers of housing for low-income families, accounted for the equivalent of $7 billion of expenditure in 2014, according to the Congressional Budget Office.[19]

These funds have not been used in many areas outside central urban neighborhoods because of the lack of available sites. David Rusk, in a book originally published in 1993 entitled *Cities Without Suburbs*, stated that if all the housing subsidy money that had been spent in cities had instead been distributed throughout the metropolitan region, concentrated poverty could have been eliminated by the time the first edition of his book was published. Of course, there is no way to rewrite the history of low-income housing, and making housing subsidies available in new areas will not overcome the past. However, Rusk's chief argument is that central cities cannot solve their serious social problems if people who live in poverty are concentrated in parts of the city and denied access to living in other areas of the city and the surrounding suburbs. Concentrated poverty by itself, according to Rusk, is a major cause of high-crime areas and low education attainment. If poverty could be deconcentrated, families would live better lives and local governments would see decreases in crime, better school outcomes, and more manageable social services.[20]

Local Zoning Changes to Support Creation of More Affordable Housing

The political reality is that the type of comprehensive affordable housing legislation that has been enacted in a few states, and is necessary to overcome exclusionary zoning practices, is unlikely to be enacted in other states in the foreseeable future. There is no evidence that the courts in other states are inclined to adopt the activist judicial approach of the New Jersey Supreme Court. However, there are changes in zoning that can help achieve affordable housing goals on an incremental basis. These changes are less likely to be controversial because they do not conflict with community land-use planning policies that support mixed-use, infill, or accessory uses. Simply put, it is possible to change the zoning in places where the necessary infrastructure and community support systems already exist. Moreover, these changes can increase the property value for owners when new housing is added, potentially taking much of the land cost out of the price.

Affordable Housing in Commercially Zoned Land in Developed Areas

Chapter 3 explained why commercially zoned corridors along arterial streets can be considered land banks, as so much of the land is covered with at-grade parking. Most of these linear commercial districts do not permit residences. Adding attached houses and apartments to the permitted uses provides new possibilities for the owners and creates suburban sites where affordable housing can be part of the new housing offered. If the new residential uses are allowed in addition to the existing commercial floor area, the opportunities become more attractive. Because traffic peaks for residential and commercial uses are different and some of the development costs are shared, permitting both uses on the same site can be an appropriate public policy.

As so much of the land in these commercial districts is used for parking, the cost of the land for new uses, if developed by the current owner, depends on the cost of replacing the parking in a smaller land area. Often these spaces are seldom or never used, an indication that the required parking ratios in the regulations are set too high. In these redevelopment situations, minimum parking requirements should be eliminated. The parking availability still must meet the requirements of lenders and tenants, but it may be possible to reduce the amount of parking for the commercial development, making room for housing. Alternatively, a single-story parking deck—a relatively inexpensive form of structured parking because half of the parking is still at ground level—can cut in half the land area needed for the commercial parking. The cost of decanting the cars into the structured parking can be considered the land cost for the new housing.

To ensure that the most appropriate commercial corridors for such up-zoning are identified and notice is given to affected property owners, corridor planning studies should first be done and approved as part of the comprehensive planning process. However, the rezoning for a particular site should be conditioned on approval of a redevelopment plan, otherwise land values will rise for owners who have no intention of proposing any development, which will raise the potential cost of building housing for the next owner. The economics for many housing types include structured or garage parking as part of the development cost; with the right design, the needed parking can be included in the land area freed up for residential development. If the whole site is redeveloped and apartments are built over retail, the two uses can end up occupying the same building footprint. Some or all of the land cost can be taken out of the development calculations for housing in these situations, which can make the houses and apartments easier to develop and more affordable.

Second (Accessory) Dwelling Unit on Existing House Lots

Another opportunity to add to the housing supply without significantly increasing land costs is to build a second, small house or apartment on an existing single-family property, provided the lot is large enough and the location is within a region with supporting services. A hundred years ago, servant's quarters were sometimes built over detached garages. Such spaces have often been remodeled into garage apartments and rented out by the owner. The garage apartment set the precedent for a more complete second dwelling unit, which is permitted to occupy the same lot as a single-family house. Attic or basement apartments can also be accessory dwelling units in a single-family zone. Generally, these units are known as accessory dwelling units (ADUs)[21] and are usually defined to mean a self-contained apartment in an owner-occupied single-family home: either inside the principal dwelling, attached to it, or in a separate structure on the same property.[22] These additional units can be integrated into the fabric of existing single-family neighborhoods with little change to the character of the neighborhood. Figure 5-1 illustrates ways in which an additional dwelling unit can be added directly to an existing house.

According to a 2008 study by the U.S. Department of Housing and Urban Development,[23] as a result of planning and zoning policy changes urged by advocates of Smart Growth and New Urbanism in the 1990s, municipalities began to adopt programs to permit ADUs as an inexpensive way to increase the affordable housing supply and to address the existence of the illegal units. Typical general standards for such units are:

- No more than two dwelling units are allowed in a structure and no more than two dwelling units on a lot.
- No boarders or lodgers are allowed within either dwelling unit.
- The structure must be connected to the public water and sanitary sewer systems.
- The owner of the property on which the accessory unit is to be created must occupy one of the dwelling units.
- The accessory unit must be designed so that its appearance is comparable to a one-family dwelling.
- At least two off-street parking spaces must be provided for the principal dwelling unit.

Attached ADUs

How can ADUs that are added to existing structures be designed to maintain the building scale, architectural character, and yard patterns found in the surrounding neighborhood?

- Is the primary residence containing the ADU of a compatible scale with nearby residences?
- Is the ADU addition visually subordinate to the original building? Do the massing, scale, and the location of an addition allow the original building to remain visually prominent?
- If the ADU addition is taller than the original building, is it set back from the primary facade?
- Is the ADU entrance visible from the street front? Does it maintain the appearance of a single-family home?
- Are the materials and windows of the ADU compatible with those in the original house?
- Is the ADU roof or attic addition in scale and compatible with the original structure?
- Are dormer or roof additions subordinate to, and set back from, the primary facade so the original roofline can be seen from the street?
- Does the ADU have yard setbacks, street orientation, use of front porches and other design elements found on your block?

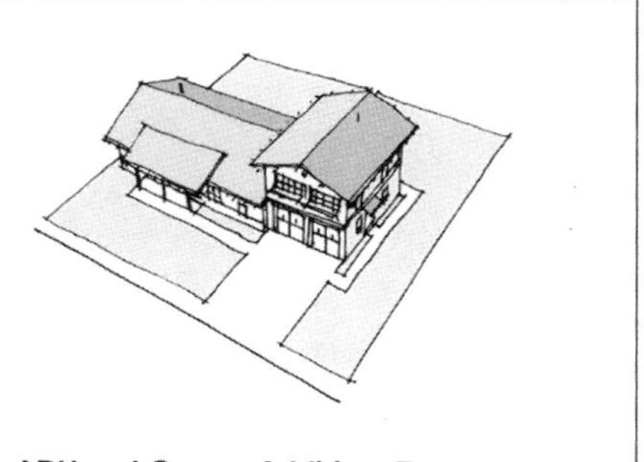

ADU and Garage Addition–Front
- 5' side yard setback
- 20' rear yard setback
- Parking in garage and driveway

ADU and Garage Addition–Side
- 5' side yard setback
- 20' rear yard setback
- Parking in garage and driveway

ADU and Garage Addition–Rear
- 5' side yard setback
- 20' rear yard setback
- Parking in garage and driveway

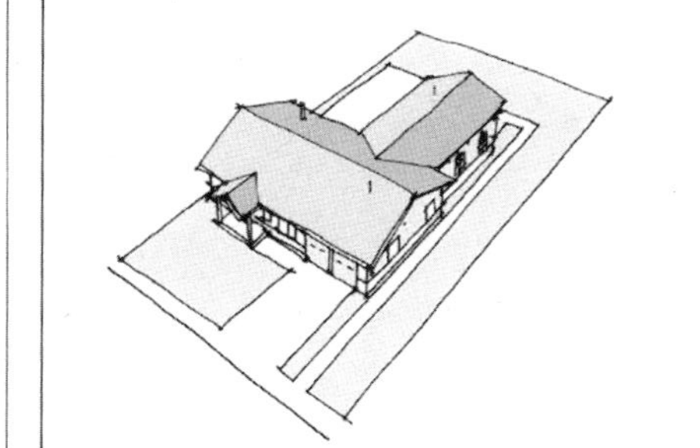

One Story Backyard Addition
- 5' side yard setback
- 20' rear yard setback
- Parking in garage and driveway

Figure 5-1 This illustration, from the manual on accessory dwelling units prepared by the city of Santa Cruz, shows different pre-approved ways to attach an additional dwelling unit directly to an existing house.

- Deed restriction must prevent the accessory unit from being sold separately, limit the accessory unit to an approved size, and provide that the permit for the accessory unit will be effective only as long as the main residence or the accessory unit is occupied as the principal residence by the owner of record.

The authorization of ADUs in communities is now widespread, but many communities impose a discretionary review (special permit) requirement before such units may be approved. Without including a by-right alternative, that is, the right to build an ADU without government review other than for a building permit, such a requirement can be a barrier to this affordable housing solution because of the time and cost required for an owner to obtain approval. The better practice is for a community to allow for both the by-right and the special permit alternatives. For the by-right alternative, the community should determine the basic dimensional characteristics that make up the character of the residential neighborhoods in which ADUs will be permitted and establish standards that allow for a by-right accessory dwelling unit consistent with those characteristics. In Lexington, Massachusetts, for example, the zoning regulations allow ADUs by-right if they conform to the following standards:

- The lot area must be at least 10,000 square feet.
- The accessory unit must be located inside the principal structure.
- The maximum gross floor area of the accessory unit may not exceed 1,000 square feet.
- The accessory unit may have no more than two bedrooms.
- There can be no enlargements or extensions of the principal dwelling except for minimal additions necessary to comply with building, safety, or health codes or for enclosure of an entryway or a stairway to a second or third story.
- The entire structure containing the accessory unit must have been in legal existence for a minimum of five years at the time of application for the by-right accessory unit.[24]

Any proposal that does not conform to these by-right standards requires authorization by special permit from the Board of Appeals.

size & height

unit size

The maximum floor area of a laneway house is determined by multiplying the lot area by 0.16. This results in maximum unit sizes of approximately 56m^2 (644ft^2) on standard 33' x 122' lots, and 84m^2 (900ft^2) on 50' x 122' lots. The maximum size of a laneway house is 900ft^2, regardless of lot size.

These floor area limits include upper and ground floor living space as well as enclosed parking (where it is provided). A 40ft^2 exclusion for storage is available for all laneway houses. The storage space can be provided in the form of closets or as a separate storage room (e.g. for bikes, garden tools).

The floor area of a laneway house must be a minimum of 26m^2 (280ft^2), with a possible relaxation down to 19m^2 (204ft^2).

Stairs, underheight space, areas below sloped ceilings, and open-to-below space are not counted as floor area.

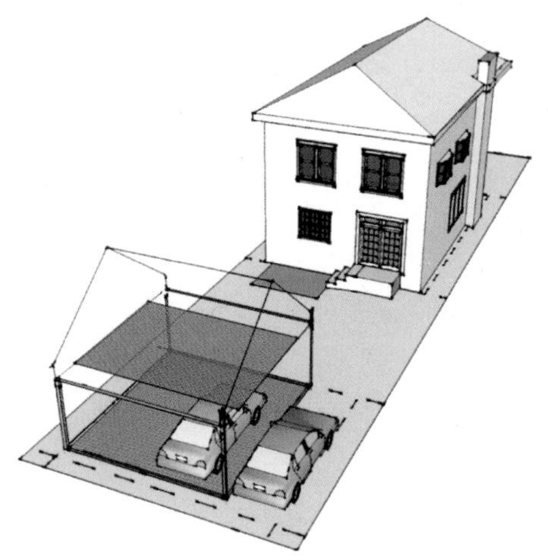

Figure 5-2 Vancouver's *Laneway Housing How-To Guide* shows how to apply for building a "laneway house," which is a more genteel name for an alley. This illustration summarizes what is permissible.

The city of Vancouver, British Columbia, has made "laneway houses"—a lane being a more socially neutral term for an alley—a significant part of its housing policy (figure 5-2). Any homeowner can apply to build a laneway house on any lot in a single-family zone if the lot is more than 9.8 meters (32 feet) wide. A laneway house on lots more than 7.8 meters (25 feet) is permitted by special exception. The laneway house must have its own access from a lane or be located on a lot that extends between two streets. The floor area may not exceed 0.16 times the site area, or 83.6 square meters (900 square feet), whichever is smaller. The largest laneway house is thus limited to the size of a small two-bedroom apartment, and the average house is smaller. There are setback requirements, height limits, and other controls, and each proposed house must be reviewed and approved. According to the city of Vancouver, more than 2,000 of these

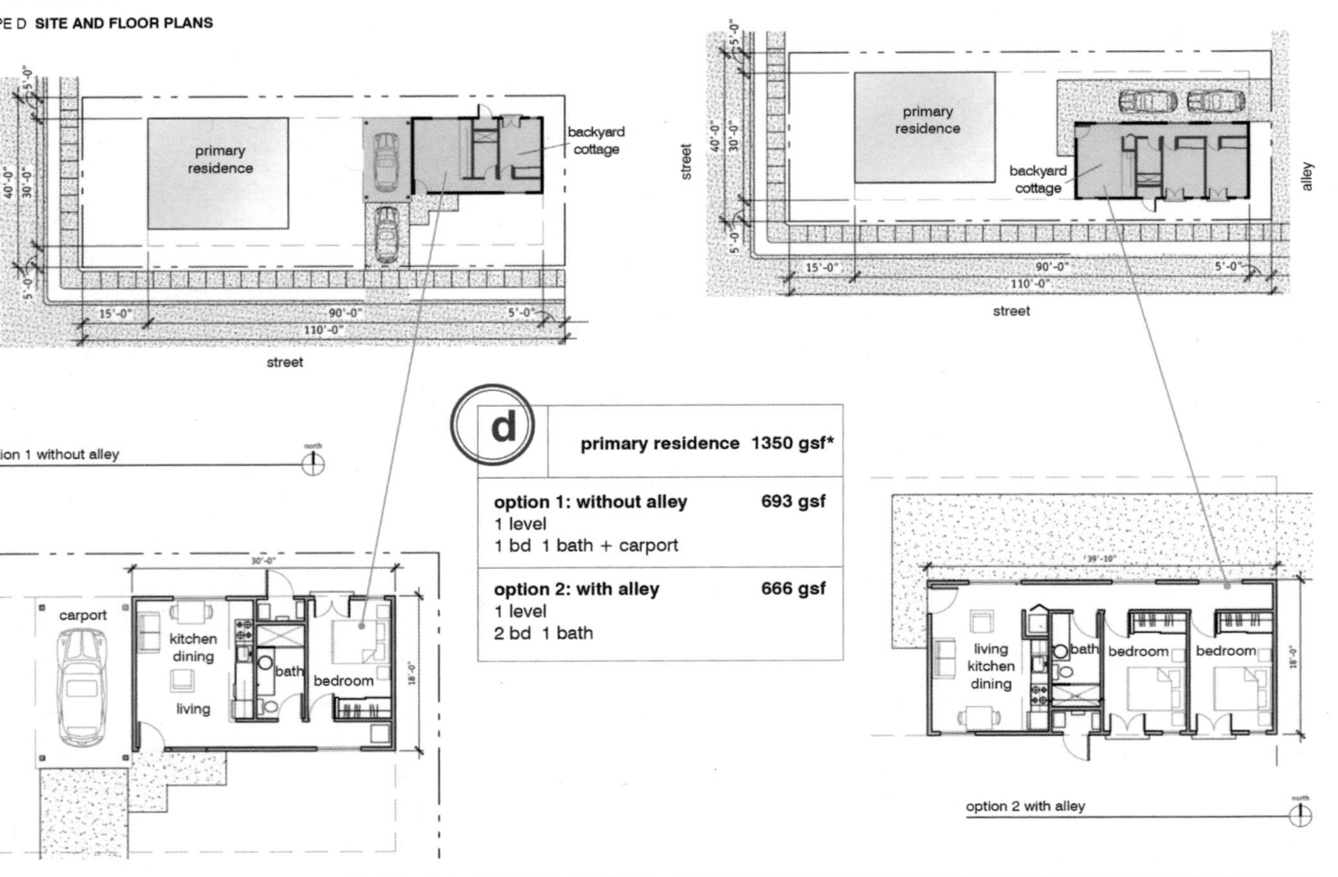

Figure 5-3 Seattle's backyard cottage is that city's version of a permissible accessory dwelling unit. This illustration from the city of Seattle's manual shows that a backyard cottage works especially well on a corner lot.

laneway houses have been built since they were first permitted in 2009. They cost as much to build per square foot as any other house, but their small size makes them less expensive. As the site already belongs to the owner there is no separate land cost, which contributes to affordability. The houses are suitable for single people or small families who might not otherwise be able to live in central, single-family neighborhoods in this very expensive city.[25]

Seattle, Washington, permits accessory dwelling units of up to 800 square feet on single-family lots, except lots in shoreline districts. Unlike Vancouver, Seattle does not require these accessory units, called backyard cottages, to have their own entrance from a public right-of-way (figure 5-3). However, the owner must live in one of the units at least half of the year and own at least half of the combined property. The principle behind requiring an owner-occupier is that if tenants are causing a nuisance, such as making too much noise, the owner will suffer along with the neighbors and will have a strong incentive to deal with the problem immediately.[26]

Permitting a Range of House Lot Sizes Within the Same Zone

As discussed in chapters 1 and 3, there are numerous reasons to allow flexible lot sizes within a development while maintaining a fixed overall density. It is possible to design more walkable communities with this flexibility and to avoid building on portions of a site that are less suitable for development. These objectives can also be realized by using planned unit development (PUD) or traditional neighborhood development (TND) provisions. But making lot-size flexibility possible in all new subdivisions above a certain size can make it easier for more developers to achieve these objectives, as the only approval required would be for the subdivision itself. As noted previously, subdivision ordinances will also need amending if flexible lot sizes are permitted by the zoning.

Another reason for flexible lot sizes is relative affordability. It is possible that the smaller lots will have a lower land cost, although that calculation depends on whether there are land set-asides for public uses or environmental reasons. The cost of this undevelopable land may need to be assigned to all the units within the development. Even if the land cost per lot is not reduced, smaller lots will increase the variety of housing types available and some could be less expensive.

Increasing Density

Increasing the number of dwelling units permitted on a parcel by changing the zoning classification will reduce the cost of land per unit for the owner who succeeds in having the zoning density increased. But once the possibility of a density increase is established, surrounding properties could also increase in value. While there may be good reasons to up-zone an individual property, raising housing densities is not a good long-term strategy for affordability except in the context of comprehensive plan-based changes for a significant section of a community. When considering apartment house densities, it is also important to remember that achieving lower land costs per unit may be offset by the higher construction costs per unit required for apartment buildings, especially if the buildings are big enough to require fully fireproof construction and multiple elevators.

Opening up suburban commercial corridors to apartments and attached houses can increase the variety of housing types available. Accessory housing units can increase the diversity of housing options in single-family districts. Flexibility in lot sizes can increase the diversity of housing options in new developments. The first two options increase residential densities, but they do so within the context of a defined program and not as a simple, open-ended zoning change. More flexible lot sizes can be accomplished without increasing the overall density.

Promoting Environmental Justice

Environmental justice involves both substantive and procedural rights. That all people have the right to a clean and healthy environment where they live, work, learn, and play is a substantive right. At the same time, people who may be affected by environmental decisions should have a procedural right to a meaningful voice in the decision-making process, regardless of their race, income, age, or other factors that might marginalize them. The environmental justice movement argues that the distribution of environmental harms and benefits should be fairly apportioned among all communities.[27] At the federal level, in 1994, President Clinton addressed the issue of environmental justice through Executive Order 12898.[28] At the local level, planning and land-use regulations can be effective means to promote environmental justice because comprehensive plans, and zoning to implement those plans, determine the location, density, and affordability of housing, and the location of industrial development, transportation, and open space—all of which have an impact on the quality of residential life.

Making suburban areas available for a variety of housing types—some of which could be subsidized to make them more affordable—and increasing residential densities in some areas, intersect with environmental justice by recognizing that many people with the least economic resources live in the least desirable places, often areas of concentrated poverty. This reflects the historical fact that poor people have usually had to live in the less desirable areas. Housing for industrial workers was often built around factories, subjecting these families to industrial pollution. Residents were not consulted about planning decisions that would affect them, and their political voice was not strong. Today the negative impacts of some land uses continue to make some urban areas less desirable, even after the factories have been closed or demolished. The environmental justice component of the affordable housing argument is that yes, some of these disadvantaged places are affordable, but no one should have to live in them.

A major focus of environmental justice today is on the neighborhood. What can be done about conditions for people living near industrial, or formerly industrial, areas amid the lingering effects of decades of bad industrial practices? The following are ways that development regulations can address these concerns at the neighborhood level.

Reconsidering the Permitted Uses and Locations of Industrial Zones

Every metropolitan region's planning organization (MPO) should conduct a study of the current and future needs for industrial uses that may present problems for neighboring residents. These uses can range from traditional problem operations such as cement plants, to newer concerns like wind turbines and power lines. Plans to accommodate these uses should be based on sound environmental principles that consider location, wind direction, and other factors that can mitigate negative effects of industrial operations. The plans should fairly apportion the obligation to accommodate these uses among the communities that make up the metropolitan planning area. There are political problems with changing the status quo in these industrial locations, but there will be long-term benefits when the region creates better opportunities for industry in more suitable locations, with more space and better relationships between industry and transportation. The process could free older communities from the disproportionate burden incurred from conditions created long ago.

Rezoning and cleaning up unneeded industrial sites. Communities are often reluctant to rezone industrial properties, even those that are mostly vacant, because they are concerned about eliminating jobs and about foreclosing the opportunity to create future jobs. This is one reason that industrial properties should be subject to a careful regional study of future industrial needs. If it is clear that former industrial jobs are not coming back to an area, that site can be remapped as a commercial zone that permits a mix of office and light industry and thus is still available as a place of employment or, in some locations, can be remapped for residences or a mix of residences and retail. Making the cost of these sites competitive in the regional real estate market may also require that the local government clean up accumulated industrial pollution.

Assembling abandoned properties. Areas of concentrated poverty are likely to include many abandoned former factories and residences. Some entire blocks are vacant; in other situations, there is a mixture of occupied and vacant buildings and lots. These vacant properties have potential value because they have all their necessary utilities, but the combination of on-site contaminants and unclear ownership of many scattered properties means that few private investors will be interested in acquiring land in these areas. Some cities are now creating land trusts. Properties that a city has acquired through tax delinquency can be transferred to the trust. The trust can acquire other properties. Land can be cleared of contaminants, and structures that still have value can be stabilized. The trust can then put these properties together into tracts that are large enough to interest private investors, or perhaps government agencies, that would not want to go through the intricate process of clearing titles and cleaning up contaminants but will find the assembled properties attractive. Once such a trust begins to make sales, the money can be recycled into acquiring and clearing more properties.

Development regulation can be helpful by permitting large-scale development on multiple properties, even if the properties are not contiguous. Successful implementation of such policies can reduce the concentration of poverty in neighborhoods with high abandonment.

All land banks need some initial funding to put together the first group of properties and prepare them for sale to potential developers. One source of funding is federal grants. In 2008, Congress passed the Housing and Economic Recovery Act, which allocated approximately $4 billion for assistance to state and local governments to stabilize communities by reusing abandoned and foreclosed properties.[29] Foreclosed houses in relatively good condition can be reused, but the act also allocated funds to establish land banks, demolish blighted structures, and redevelop demolished or abandoned properties.[30] Another source of funds for land banks could be grants applied for under the 2009 American Recovery and Reinvestment Act. Both laws were part of the economic stimulus enacted to combat the effects of the Great Recession that began in 2007.[31] Another continuing source of federal funds has been the Treasury Department's Hardest Hit Fund, begun in 2010, for states suffering the most from the economic recession.[32] Community development block grants are also a potential source of funding, as are community-based philanthropic foundations. Among the cities and counties that have land banks are Cleveland and Cuyahoga County, Ohio; Detroit, Michigan; Fort Collins, Colorado; Fulton County/City of Atlanta, Georgia; Jackson, Mississippi; Little Rock, Arkansas; Philadelphia, Pennsylvania; and Minneapolis–Saint Paul, Minnesota.

Detroit's Land Bank Authority, which began operation in 2014, has sold about 3,500 vacant lots to neighboring properties under its Side Lot program. Eighty-one closings were completed under a program to sell restorable abandoned houses.[33] Based on a report by a task force in 2014, Detroit's Blight Elimination Program demolishes structures no longer considered usable. The task force identified about 85,000 blighted properties, and estimates that the job of removing structures and cleaning up the lots could take five years at a cost of $850,000,000.[34]

Minnesota's Twin Cities Community Land Bank's Living Cities Initiative is targeting sites within half a mile of transit stations along the city's three light-rail corridors to build or restore 400 to 600 affordable units close to transit.[35] The Fulton County/City of Atlanta Land Bank has conveyed some 350 properties to developers on which to construct affordable housing.[36] Cleveland's land bank has helped create a development

The City of Cleveland Land Bank at Work

Residential Side Yard Expansions

The Land Bank has worked with numerous community development corporations and residents in programing Model Block & Neighborhood Stabilization Program strategies to transform distressed areas throughout the city with strategic demolitions, yard expansions & the installation of attractive public green spaces. Aside from the obvious visual and physical impacts, the projects strengthened the community by engaging residents in the design, development and maintenance phases of the projects, restoring a deep sense of pride throughout these communities.

New Housing: Trailside

Trail Side is a dynamic new urban development in historic Slavic Village. Slavic Village Development and Third Federal Savings & Loan along with its project partners at the City of Cleveland and Zaremba recently celebrated the groundbreaking of Trail Side Slavic Village, a 12 acre site abutting the new Morgana Run Trail that will add 58 new homes to the neighborhood.

Commercial Expansion: OTC

Founded in 1969, Ohio Technical College has grown from a small diesel mechanics program to a nationally recognized college that offers courses in trending industries such as High Performance Racing and Alternative Fuel Technologies. The City of Cleveland has supported its need to expand over the years through land sales for facility expansion, parking, and neighborhood green space.

Business Development

Three Land Bank owned parcels assembled originally through the Re-Imagining Cleveland initiative enabled Mansfield and Brenda Frazier to create a 3/4 acre vineyard containing 300 vines of Traminette and Frontenac grapes. Another focus of their project is to provide education & training in the areas of horticultural practices and entrepreneurship to participants in a local prison reentry program.

Social Enterprise

One of the nation's 1st urban garden zoning districts (26 acres), the Urban Agricultural Innovation Zone, has paved the way for large projects such as Rid-All Green Partnership & the Kinsman Farm. Ohio State University Extension supported this effort by assembling a collection of grants from the USDA, Ohio Dept. of Agriculture & the City of Cleveland totaling $940K while continuing to provide technical assistance to community gardeners throughout City, as it has for the past 30 years.

Lots starting at $200! Bring your plans to us...catalyze your dreams!

CITY OF CLEVELAND
Mayor Frank G. Jackson

601 Lakeside Avenue, Room 320, Cleveland, Ohio 44114 (216) 664-4126

www.city.cleveland.oh.us>city departments>community development>landbank

CITY OF CLEVELAND

Department of Community Development

Figure 5–4 A flyer advertising Cleveland's Land Bank. One of its programs sells vacant lots acquired by the city. Homeowners can expand their properties by acquiring a vacant lot next door. The land bank has also put together groups of vacant parcels to create sites for new housing and has helped create a vineyard on land in the Hough district, which has suffered decades of abandonment and disinvestment. The land bank is a force for improving disadvantaged urban neighborhoods, although the individual changes are small ones. As the population of the whole city is shrinking, opening up residential land to new uses can make sense.

of 58 new houses in the city's Slavic Village neighborhood, supplied land for a vineyard in the Hough neighborhood, and put together a 28-acre urban agricultural innovation zone. The land bank will also sell individual vacant lots, including lots next door to occupied buildings made available under the sideyard expansion program. The bank invites applications: "Lots starting at $200! Bring your plans to us . . . catalyze your dreams!"[37] (figure 5-4).

These land banks are aiming for incremental change by making the most of relatively low funding. They have yet to address the problems of widespread abandonment to an extent that would transform distressed neighborhoods into places that attract large-scale investment.

Summing Up

Development regulation can help open up locations for affordable housing in developing areas and add infill development in commercial corridors and neighborhoods. Rethinking industrial development regulations can help eliminate concentrations of pollution in cities. Abandonment can be addressed by revising regulations to make redevelopment easier, but the abandonment problem also requires substantial infusions of capital to effect change at the scale needed in many cities. And, of course, addressing the full range of social inequities in our society requires a much broader series of actions than can be managed through development regulations.

Notes

1. *Affordable* is usually defined as within the means of a family whose income is at or below the median income for a defined locale. For example, the Town of Cary in Wake County, North Carolina, in its 2020 Affordable Housing Plan, assesses the local housing needs in terms of the area median income (AMI) of renters and home buyers: low income (30 to 50 percent of AMI), moderate income (51 to 80 percent of AMI), and middle income (81 to 120 percent of AMI). See Town of Cary, North Carolina, *2020 Affordable Housing Plan*, *www.townofcary.org/Assets/Planning+Department/Planning+Department+PDFs/affordablehousing/2020affordablehousingplan.pdf.* The NAHB-Wells Fargo Housing Opportunity Index measures the percentage of homes sold that a family earning the median income can buy based on standard mortgage underwriting criteria. See *www.nahb.org/generic.aspx?sectionID=135&genericContentID=533* (August 1, 2007). Another common standard is that a family pay no more than 30 percent of its annual income. 42 U.S.C. § 12745(a) (2006). This standard is used in Connecticut,

C.G.S. sec. 8-30g(6), *Affordable Housing Land Use Appeals* (chap. 126a), to define the affordable units to be set aside. This statute, like many others, also defines income eligibility as 80 percent of AMI.

2. National Association of Home Builders, *Growth Restrictions Push Cost of Housing Higher*, October 17, 2000, *www.nahb.com/news/ growth%20htm*. Echoing this concern about the impact of land-use controls on the production of affordable housing, the Fannie Mae Foundation captioned its November 2000 conference "Fair Growth: Connecting Sprawl, Growth Management and Social Equity." Noting that smart growth has been primarily concerned with protecting open space, curbing sprawl, and improving regional transportation, the Foundation advocated "Fair Growth" as a set of "land use practices that attempt to curb urban sprawl without endangering housing affordability and access to jobs for minorities and low income residents." Stacey H. Davis, *Only Smart Growth is Fair Growth,* Fannie Mae Foundation Housing Facts & Findings, Winter 2000, *www.knowledgeplex.org/kp/new_content/commentary-editorial/relfiles/hff_0204_perspectives.html.*
3. Ronald H. Rosenberg, "The Changing Culture of American Land Use Regulation: Paying for Growth with Impact Fees," *Southern Methodist University Law Review* 59 (2016): 177, 214.
4. Studies in various jurisdictions such as Illinois, California, Texas, and Colorado have examined the effect of impact fees on development and other costs and have concluded that impact fees increase the cost of housing, primarily because they result in higher development costs. See, for example, Bret M. Baden, Don L. Coursey, and Jeannine M. Kannegiesser, *Effects of Impact Fees on the Suburban Chicago Housing Market*, Policy Study No. 93 (Arlington, IL: Heartland Institute, November 19, 1999); Maria Dresch and Steven M. Sheffrin, *Who Pays for Development Fees and Exactions?* (Sacramento and San Francisco, CA: Public Policy Institute of California, 1997); Mark Dotzour, *Fiscal Impact Studies: Does Growth Pay for Itself?,* National Association of Home Builders, *www.nahb.net/growth_issues/fiscal_impact/growth_pays.html*; Larry D. Singell and Jane H. Lillydahl, "An Empirical Examination of the Effects of Impact Fees on the Housing Markets," *Land Economics* 66 (1990): 82, 89. Based on these studies, one should expect land development costs to rise in those jurisdictions in which impact fees are imposed, even where they are imposed fairly and consistently.
5. Dresch and Sheffrin, *Who Pays for Development Fees and Exactions?,* 75.
6. *Southern Burlington County N.A.A.C.P. v. Mount Laurel Tp.*, 67 N.J. 151, 336 A.2d 713 (1975).
7. *Southern Burlington County N.A.A.C.P. v. Mount Laurel Tp.*, 92 N.J. 158, 456 A.2d 390 (1983).
8. The New Jersey Supreme Court applied a regional concept of the general welfare as opposed to general welfare based on local interests. See John M. Payne, "Reconstructing the Constitutional Theory of Mount Laurel II," *Washington University Journal of Law and Policy* 3 (2000): 555, 558.

9. N.J. Stat. Ann. §§ 52:27D-301 et seq.

10. *Hills Development Co. v. Bernards Tp. in Somerset County*, 103 N.J. 1, 510 A.2d 621 (1986).

11. N.J. Stat. Ann. §§ 52.27D-301 et seq.

12. *In re Adoption of N.J.A.C. 5:96 and 5:97 ex rel. New Jersey Council on Affordable Housing*, 221 N.J. 1, 19–20, 110 A.3d 31, 42 (2015).

13. In Pennsylvania, *Appeal of Kit-Mar Builders, Inc.*, 439 Pa. 466, 268 A.2d 765, 766-767 (Pa. 1970) (holding "absent some extraordinary justification, a zoning ordinance with minimum lot sizes such as those in this case [two- and three-acre zoning] is completely unreasonable"); in New York, *Berenson v. Town of New Castle*, 38 N.Y.2d 102, 378 N.Y.S.2d 672, 341 N.E.2d 236 (1975) (adopting two-tier test for exclusionary zoning: (1) whether the local legislative body has provided a properly balanced and well-ordered plan for the community and (2) whether the municipality has met regional housing needs in view of the need for county and metropolitan residents to live near their employment or for various other social and economic reasons. Persons challenging alleged exclusionary zoning must show that a municipality, in enacting an ordinance, acted with exclusionary intent or failed to give proper consideration to regional housing needs); in Michigan, *France Stone Co., Inc. v. Charter Tp. of Monroe*, 802 F. Supp. 90 (E.D. Mich. 1992) (noting that under Michigan law "it is both unconstitutional and unlawful to exclude a legitimate land use from the borders of a municipality, and a showing of exclusionary zoning destroys the presumption of the zoning's validity").

14. Mass. Gen. Laws, chap. 40B, §§ 20–23.

15. Theodore Taub, "Exactions, Linkages, and Regulatory Takings: The Developer's Perspective," in *Exactions, Impact Fees and Dedications: Shaping Land Use Development and Funding Infrastructure in the Dolan Era*, edited by Robert Frielich and David W. Bushek (Chicago, IL: American Bar Association, 1995), 125–163.

16. Municipal Research and Services Center, *Affordable Housing Techniques: A Primer for Local Government Officials,* Report No. 22, March 1992, *www.mrsc.org/Publications/textaht.aspx*, 12.

17. See discussion of exactions and the unconstitutional conditions doctrine in chapter 7.

18. When needed infrastructure costs are imposed by a community, the developer includes these project-related infrastructure costs in its pro forma in calculating a return on cost or other rate of return calculation, which, if acceptable in light of the housing market and the requirements of lenders and investors, will lead to a decision whether to go forward with the development.

19. Congressional Budget Office, *Federal Housing Assistance for Low-Income Households*, September 9, 2015, *www.cbo.gov/publication/50782.*

20. The most recent edition of David Rusk's *Cities Without Suburbs,* based on 2010 census information, was published by the Woodrow Wilson Center Press in 2013.

21. Accessory dwelling units are also sometimes referred to as accessory apartments, guest apartments, in-law apartments, family apartments, or secondary units.
22. See 2007 Smart Growth/Smart Energy Toolkit, *http://www.mass.gov/envir/smart_growth_toolkit/*.
23. U.S. Department of Housing and Urban Development, Office of Policy Development and Research, *Accessory Dwelling Units: Case Study* (Reston, VA: Prepared by Sage Computing, June 2008).
24. Town of Lexington, Massachusetts, Zoning Bylaw, art. V, § 135-19, Accessory Apartments.
25. For an introduction to the building rules, see "Building Your Own Laneway House," *http://vancouver.ca/home-property-development/building-your-laneway-house.aspx*.
26. For the rules for backyard cottages, see Seattle Department of Construction and Inspections, "Establishing a Backyard Cottage," *www.seattle.gov/DPD/Publications/CAM/cam116b.pdf*.
27. *Environmental Justice for All: A 50-State Survey of Legislation, Policies, and Cases*, 4th ed. (San Francisco, CA: University of California Hastings College of the Law and the American Bar Association, February 15, 2010), viii.
28. Executive Order 12898, "Federal Actions to Address Environmental Justice in Minority Populations and Low-Income Populations," states that "each Federal agency shall make achieving environmental justice part of its mission by identifying and addressing, as appropriate, disproportionately high and adverse human health or environmental effects of its programs, policies, and activities on minority populations and low-income populations in the United States and its territories and possessions, the District of Columbia, the Commonwealth of Puerto Rico, and the Commonwealth of the Mariana Islands." 59 Fed. Reg. 7629 (Feb. 16, 1994).
29. Housing and Economic Recovery Act of 2008 (Pub.L. 110-2889, 122 Stat. 2654).
30. Ibid., Title III, §§ 2301–2305.
31. *Revitalizing Foreclosed Properties with Land Banks* (U.S. Department of Housing and Urban Development, 2009).
32. *www.treasury.gov/initiatives/financial-stability/TARP-Programs/housing/hhf/Pages/default.aspx*.
33. Detroit Land Bank Authority, "Building Detroit," 2015, *www.buildingdetroit.org/reports/completed-side-lot-sales/*.
34. *http://report.timetoendblight.org/*.
35. *www.tcclandbank.org/publications.html*.
36. *www.fccalandbank.org/*.
37. *www.city.cleveland.oh.us/CityofCleveland/Home/Government/CityAgencies/CommunityDevelopment/LandBank*.

6

Establishing Design Principles and Standards for Public Spaces and Buildings

Public spaces, sometimes referred to as the *Public Realm*,[1] consist of all those places where the public has access. This seemingly simple definition applies to a range of different circumstances. Many public spaces belong to government, and thus to the public, including streets, parks, schools, libraries, recreation centers, and the open spaces associated with them. There is also a large category of privately owned spaces, such as the malls in shopping centers and lobbies in office buildings or hotels, where visitors and potential customers are welcome but their presence and behavior is subject to control by the owners. There is an intermediate category of privately owned public plazas and other types of spaces that have been built in response to government incentives, giving to the public some form of access and use.[2] Governments also own many parcels of land, such as storage yards for equipment or land along the edges of highways, that could become public spaces but are currently managed as places with restricted access.

Public Spaces and Urban Form

Urban form is generally understood to mean the spaces, places, and boundaries that make up the physical shape and structure of a city.[3] The urban form of the city is shaped by its natural features—the hills, streams, and valleys that make up a city's land form—and by its transportation components, street system, highways, railroads, and the location of the airport. The urban form is also shaped by the city's land-use policies and regulations, which determine the locations of the different categories of development, the parks and open space areas, and the street and block patterns. Regulations also affect the form, massing, and arrangement of buildings.[4] All these elements help define the nature and extent of public spaces, but buildings—their location, form, massing, and orientation—have the most influence over the shape and quality of adjacent public spaces.

Managing the Relationship Between Private Buildings and Public Spaces

Many decisions about public spaces are made directly by governments through capital improvement programs. However, development regulations can be used to influence the relationship between private properties and public spaces. Controlling the relationship between buildings and public spaces in urban areas is one of the oldest forms of regulation, going back to the height and setback regulations that were adopted in Paris in the eighteenth century (figure 6-1). These Parisian regulations were a model for early zoning ordinances like the New York City 1916 Zoning Resolution (figure 6-2).

Beginning in the 1950s, the substitution of metrics, such as floor area ratios[5] and open space ratios,[6] for height and setback regulations greatly diminished the connection between regulating private property and shaping public space. The new regulations focused on the buildings themselves and gave priority to separating them, rather than relating them to one another. The unanticipated consequences of these new ways of regulating included tall buildings in formerly low-rise neighborhoods, buildings that did not relate to streets and sidewalks, and blank walls or service elements fronting on sidewalks or other public spaces. Concerns about these problems have shown that there need to be new ways to regulate height, frontages, and the relationship of buildings to streets and sidewalks.

Is the Transect a Necessary Organizing Principle to Regulate Building Form and Public Spaces?

Any discussion of regulating the relationship between buildings and public space, including the design of public streets, must include transect-based regulations, also categorized as form-based codes, which are proposed as a regulatory approach to create a more coherent public environment. We use the phrase *transect-based regulations* rather than *form-based codes* because the *transect*, as a term applied to regulation of development, is a specific concept, whereas *form-based* is a descriptive term that applies to many aspects of regulation. Any zoning ordinance that contains height and setback provisions is regulating building form, and there are many examples of zoning regulations that do not make use of transect terminology that could be described as form based, including some of those we propose in this book. But since the transect concept is associated with regulations that shape streets and building form, we explain why it does not play a part in our recommendations.

A transect—short for transverse section—is a way of describing different natural ecologies at various elevations using a cut-away view that slices through the land and the natural environment. It is best known from the diagrams prepared by Ian McHarg for his book, *Design with Nature*, in which McHarg uses transect drawings to dramatize the ways that landforms and habitats differ. McHarg stresses the importance of recognizing each characteristic type of landform when adding constructed elements to the natural environment.[7]

The transect as a regulatory concept divides the constructed environment into six zones: T1 is a natural zone at the edge of the urbanized area; T2 is a rural zone; T3 is suburban; T4 is a general urban zone; T5 is an urban center zone; and T6 is the urban core zone. Ordinances that rely on the transect formulation apply this natural-systems concept to the organization of cities and suburbs, reasoning that, just as ecosystems can be placed on a transect or continuum, such as the ones used by McHarg (shore-dune-upland or wetland-woodland-prairie), built environments can be described on a scale from natural or rural to the most urban.

Figure 6–1 (next page) Architectural historian Norma Evenson describes the history of building regulations in Paris in her book, *Paris, a Century of Change, 1878–1978* (Yale University Press, 1979). In Paris, beginning in 1607, a royal edict prevented upper floors from overhanging the street: facades were required to be flat. From 1783, the height of buildings in Paris was regulated by a limit related to the width of the street. The wider the street, the taller the permitted height. Additional height was permitted as an attic under what is known as a Mansard roof, as shown in these diagrams. The maximum height was raised in 1854 and again in 1884, as elevators were coming into use, and finally in 1902, when the attic was permitted to assume a curved shape to produce the largest possible amount of floor area. The much-admired coherent street facades of Paris are a product of these regulations. Since 1894, Washington, DC, has also had height limits related to the width of streets.

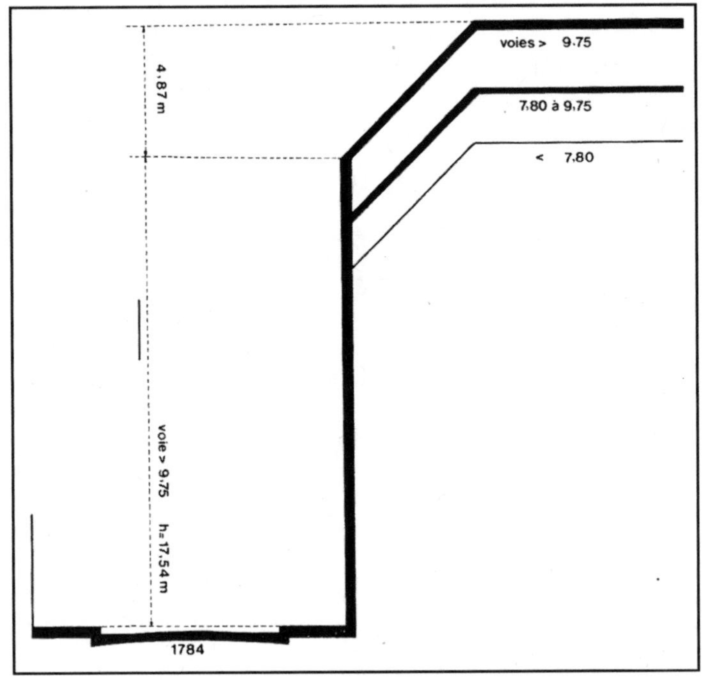
voies > 9,75
7,80 à 9,75
< 7,80
4,87 m
voie > 9,75 h= 17,54 m
1784

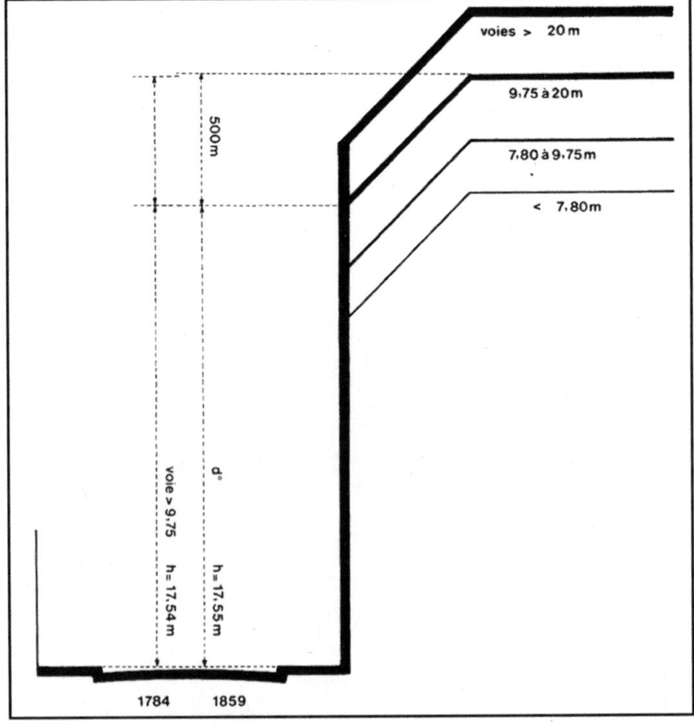
voies > 20 m
9,75 à 20 m
7,80 à 9,75 m
< 7,80 m
500m
d°
voie > 9,75 h= 17,54 m
h= 17,55 m
1784
1859

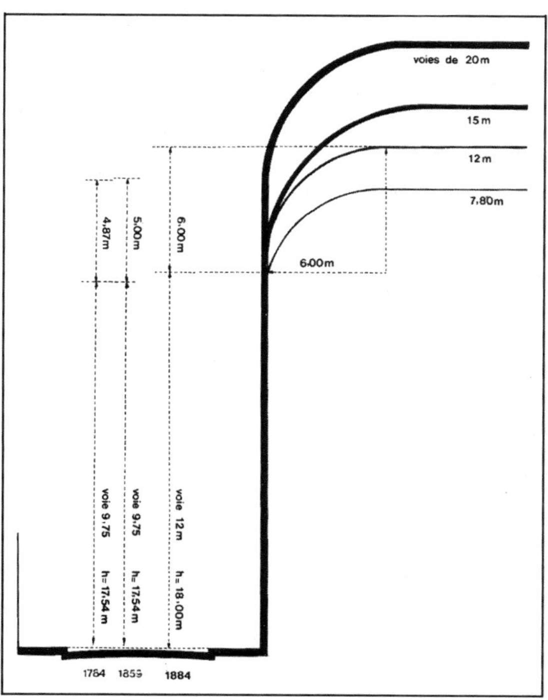
voies de 20m
15m
12m
7,80m
6,00m
4,87m
5,00m
6,00m
voie 9,75 h= 17,54 m
voie 9,75 h= 17,54 m
voie 12m h= 18,00m
1784 1859 1884

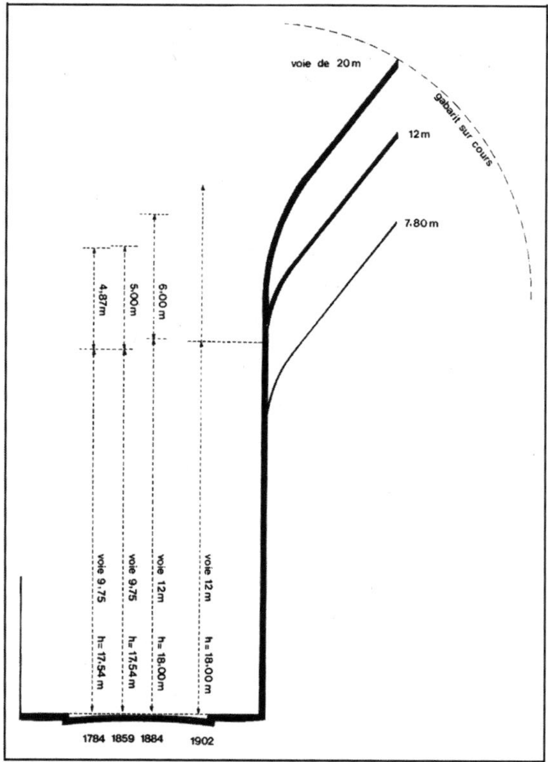
voie de 20m
gabarit sur cours
12m
7,80m
4,87m
5,00m
6,00m
voie 9,75 h= 17,54 m
voie 9,75 h= 17,54 m
voie 12m h= 18,00m
voie 12m h= 18,00m
1784 1859 1884 1902

The transect was proposed by planners, architects, and urban designers who were frustrated with the traditional system of development regulations, particularly with the way these regulations affect urban form as a by-product of other requirements. Transect regulations are put forward as an alternative to the current system of zoning and subdivision regulation.[8] Transect-based regulations grew out of the use of traditional neighborhood development (TND) zones, which were also a response to frustration felt by designers of New Urbanist communities with the regulations in most zoning and subdivision ordinances. As we have discussed, creating a TND is similar to creating a planned unit development (PUD): it is an exception within defined limits that permits a specifically designed project to be developed even when it does not meet the more general requirements in the regulations. Transect-based regulations make designs permitted under a TND ordinance possible by right in all development, an approach that requires the total revision of every zoning and subdivision ordinance.

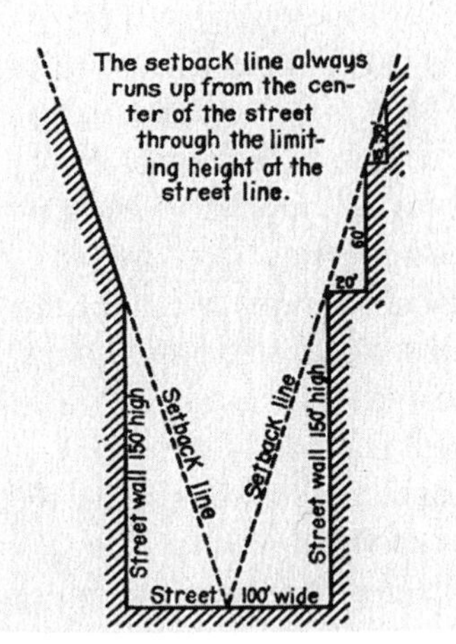

Figure 6–2 The zoning ordinance passed in New York City in 1916 adopted the Parisian method of limiting the height of the building fronting directly on the street, with the maximum height based on the width of the street, although considerably higher than the upper limit in Paris. An angle from the center line of the street defined what is known as the sky exposure plane. Floors above the street-front limit had to be set back within this plane. New York, unlike Paris, placed no absolute limit on height. Once the setbacks had trimmed the size of a tower to 25 percent of the lot area, the building could be as tall as the developer wanted. The Chrysler and Empire State Buildings were constructed under this ordinance.

We agree with many of the objectives of transect-based regulations. But the measures we advocate in this book include many environmental considerations not covered in most transect-based proposals. Our approach to regulating building form and public spaces, and promoting walkability through existing and modified development regulations, does not depend on the use of the transect concept as a regulatory tool. Our alternative proposals make the necessary changes by amending the existing regulations, not by devising an entirely new regulatory system.

Many of the transect-based regulations that have been adopted do not apply to a whole community, but to selected districts with substantial amounts of vacant land and the potential for new construction. Occasionally a transect code has been adopted as an option, which a developer can choose to follow instead of the conventional zoning.[9]

In the locations where a transect-based regulatory system has been adopted, within the limits defined by each zoning category, new development and old are expected to work together as part of a complete design for the six zones in the transect-based code. This physical design is defined by a series of detailed regulatory requirements that address the organization of streets and blocks, the disposition of parking, and provide diagrams of approved ways to relate building frontages to streets—requirements usually found in a subdivision ordinance. These requirements become the formal *regulating plan* when they are mapped and adopted for a specific location. The phrase "regulating plan" is also used in transect-based regulations for the equivalent of a zoning map.[10]

Transect-based regulations respect the form of an existing development context or, where necessary, impose a new, formal, spatially organized system (the transect), making sure that the form is created within its appropriate geographic context. Without the transect as a spatial organizing system, it is argued, a form-based system would only ensure that building form is appropriate for its proximate surroundings. As one commentator put it: "A form-based code can effectively regulate the sustainable development of a building or block . . . [but] if that same building or block is not properly ordered within a cohesive rural to urban context, then the building's form could be just as out of place as a tuxedo at a square dance."[11] This statement perhaps reflects nostalgia for a bygone organization pattern in cities when social classes and incomes were even more segregated than they are today: a place for everyone, and everyone in his or her place.

It requires extensive fieldwork to map the transect zones to apply them to an entire jurisdiction, determining the predominant character of each area and deciding which of the transect zones will be most appropriate. Remapping existing development as a transect zone is difficult because most areas no longer have a uniform spectrum of development that ranges from dense center to rural outskirts. Different densities are mixed together: a development of attached town houses or garden apartments can be right across the street from single-family homes on large lots or an office park.

Codifying these existing conditions can produce a mosaic of relatively small zones that resemble the districts of a zoning map in a conventional ordinance rather than the well-ordered rural-to-urban sequence seen in diagrams describing the transect. Even so, inclusion in a T-zone as described in the *SmartCode*—the cleverly named compilation of transect-based zones promoted as an alternative to conventional zoning and subdivision—requires imposing regulations that dictate precise design elements to achieve the correct building forms required in each T-zone. Many existing buildings will not meet these requirements and will be nonconforming, which makes it difficult to obtain a building permit to make even relatively minor changes. Most jurisdictions try to avoid having large areas where most buildings are nonconforming under an ordinance.

The Miami 21 Code, originally adopted in 2009, is an example of a complete revision of a citywide zoning ordinance that uses the transect concept in the new regulations.[12] However, this code is far more complex than the simple six-zone continuum that is intended to be the essence of transect regulations. Miami 21 adds so many subcategories that there are as many zoning districts as in a conventional ordinance. There are seven different subcategories within the T6 zones, three district zones, and a civic zone. In addition, the T1, T2, T3, T4, and T5 districts each have three subdistricts: restricted, limited, and open. The district zones also have three subdistricts, as does the civic zone. Although the central purpose of transect-based regulation is to shape the design of streets and the sizes and configurations of the buildings, there are many land-use restrictions similar to those in conventional zoning within Miami 21's zones and special districts.[13] In addition, there are eight special appendix sections with specific regulations for complicated parts of the city, such as Appendix C, the Midtown Overlay District, and Appendix E, the Brickell City Center. At the same time, the regulations for large parts of the city remain essentially unchanged. Only the names of the zones affecting these areas have been revised to conform to the transect nomenclature.[14]

Miami 21 is an impressively detailed set of regulations that demonstrate it is possible to change an entire zoning code to something that can be described as transect-based regulations. However, the most significant innovations in this ordinance concentrate new development in corridors along major streets,[15] something close to what we suggest in chapter 3, which we believe can be done within the context of the existing regulatory system.

It is not necessary to rewrite all the zoning and subdivision regulations and redraw the zoning map to conform to transect zones to achieve the basic objectives of transect-based regulations. We also do not believe that relying on the transect concept for regulatory justification is an appropriate theoretical basis for managing the complexities of twenty-first-century urban development and environmental protection.

Andres Duany and Emily Talen propose a historical justification for applying a transect system, originally a way of describing the natural environment, to understanding urban development.[16] They assert that the *valley section*, as defined by Patrick Geddes, a pioneer of regional planning, in his 1915 book *Cities in Evolution*, is an important intellectual ancestor of the transect.[17] However, Geddes's valley section describes the way occupations are related to landform in a traditional society—the shepherd on the hillside, the farmer on the plain, the sailor on the sea—and how these different social geographies are related to the city as it was at the turn of the twentieth century.

A more relevant theory about urban geography and the morphology of cities is the concentric zone description of urban development advanced by Ernest W. Burgess, Robert E. Park, and Roderick D. McKenzie in 1925.[18] These pioneering sociologists used six zones to describe the development of Chicago, zones organized from the center to the periphery: the central business district, the factory zone, the zone of transition, the working-class zone, the residential zone, and the commuter zone at the rural edge. This sociological analysis was based on observations in the early twentieth century, but by 1925 was already becoming out of date. The economist Homer Hoyt, who worked at the Federal Housing Administration (FHA) in the 1930s, prepared a study entitled *Structure and Growth of Residential Neighborhoods in American Cities* that was published by the FHA in 1939.[19] Hoyt's research showed that residential neighborhoods were no longer arranged in gradations around a central business core and its adjacent ring of factories. Instead, urban activities were organized into sectors extending from the center to the periphery. Industrial development radiated out from the city center along one or more corridors following the railway lines. The poorer residents tended to live in sectors nearest to the industrial corridors, and the middle class along streetcar routes and commuter lines as far from industry as possible, with the rich inhabiting their own exclusive enclave within a middle-class sector.

The concentric zone and the sector theories of urban morphology were reviewed by Chauncy D. Harris and Edward L. Ullman in their 1945 article "The Nature of Cities."[20] They proposed their own urban diagram, which showed cities developing around multiple nuclei. For example, there could be an outlying business district in between what they called medium-class residential and high-class residential areas. These diagrams represent cities immediately after World War II with configurations—familiar to graduates of professional planning programs from their planning history courses—that have been superseded by newer development of cities and city regions. Urban geographers and sociologists no longer think of cities as reducible to simple diagrams; it is now understood that cities need to be described as complex entities that are best mapped as overlapping layers in a geographic information system.

Urban form, whether developed in the early twentieth century or today, is the outcome of a complex variety of factors, including the economic and technological environment of the times, which may become manifest in ways that are difficult to predict. For example, those who study urbanization have noted that technological innovation has changed our perception of location and space and that advances in telecommunication and transportation networks have given both individuals and businesses locational flexibility.[21] These commentators also point out that in the past 50 years, the American landscape has rapidly urbanized horizontally into a salt-and-pepper configuration of "agglomerations"—with densely built-up zones of industries and commercial enterprises located on the peripheries of central cities or formerly suburban areas as well as in traditional centers.[22] We believe that it is not realistic to make rapidly evolving areas conform to a preconceived concept about how entire cities and regions should be organized. Rather, the challenge we address in this book is how to make the necessary changes to the existing regulatory framework to modernize it and remove blind spots about the environment and city design. In this chapter, we are concerned with how to use and modify existing regulations to improve the relationship of buildings to streets and other public spaces.

Design Standards for the Relationship Between Private Properties and Public Spaces

What is the public interest in the design of private properties when the buildings are visible from, and relate to, the community's streets and public spaces? In this book, we make a distinction between the general size and configuration of a building or site and the architectural design of a building because there are different bases for the public interest in each. There are also significant regulatory issues around the design of streets, as streets are an important part of every community's public space inventory.

There are three categories of size and configuration issues that should be addressed for buildings: its placement in relationship to the front property line and to adjacent buildings (that is, height limits, build-to lines, and setback lines); the land uses at the street level; and the locations of entrances, including those for garages and service access.

The placement of a building, in relationship to the front property line and to adjacent buildings, defines the formal and spatial characteristics of the area and the building's relationship to public space. Building placement also relates to other buildings and uses along the street. For example, a building set far back from the street leaves open the possibility of a parking lot in front, which is far different from a row of shops or residences along the sidewalk. Placement determines if there is building continuity along a street or separation and discontinuity. The uses at the street level will affect the level of pedestrian activity. Front doors and service entrances should be located where the pedestrian activity is the highest. Where should back doors and service docks be situated? How do these entrances relate to the public space?

To regulate these issues, a local government should consider carefully whether it has the prerequisites for establishing a meaningful, effective, and legally defensible program for addressing the size, shape, and placement of buildings that are adjacent to or form public spaces.[23] Standards for these issues, based on clearly articulated objective criteria, can be implemented through conventional zoning and subdivision ordinances. Such standards should be included in development zones, planned development and subdivision ordinances, and special overlay districts for places of civic importance.

The way a building relates to the street or public space can affect how such places function and serve their multiple purposes. We recommend measures such as setback and build-to lines, ground-floor transparency, and limitations on service entrances and curb cuts on important public streets and spaces. There is legitimate public concern about the height of buildings that can be seen from public spaces; a tall building may cast a shadow on adjacent structures, block light and air, or reduce the ability to use solar or wind energy. These concerns support height limits of some kind.

Height Limits

Since 1894, Washington, DC, has had height limits in relation to the width of streets, when a local law limited apartment buildings to 90 feet and office buildings to 100 feet. This local law was confirmed by acts of Congress in 1898 and 1910, and, while it has been modified since, strict limits are still in force.[24] The District of Columbia's height limit is perhaps the most significant city-design regulation in the United States, as it has helped define the entire low-rise, monumental character of the city.

Height limits in a zoning ordinance are a well-established way to manage the design character of residential neighborhoods. The limits usually are set for the number of stories and as an absolute height in feet. A height limit as a specific measurement raises the question, height above what? This can be answered by specifying height above grade, which must be defined. Defining grade on a sloping site can be done by taking an average, or by specifying the highest point on a site—or the lowest.

Height Limits and Floor Area Ratio

In the early days of zoning, height limits were the principal way of limiting the size of buildings. When floor area ratios are used, there may be no height limits at all. When building shapes and sizes are regulated primarily by floor area ratios and by requirements that buildings be set back a defined distance from a property line, decisions about a building's height are left to each property owner, often arousing strong community opposition. We have already described the importance of enacting a height limit in historic districts in chapter 4, but a limit based on the prevailing height of existing older buildings in the neighborhood can help keep new development in scale with what the neighboring property owners expect when looking at buildings from streets or other public places. There are usually alternative design possibilities that allow a property owner to use the permitted floor area within the height limit.

When the floor area ratio is too high to be accommodated under a height limit based on prevailing development, a limit can be set on the portions of the building closest to the street, with a higher building allowed behind a setback line. New York City's Special Madison Avenue Preservation District sets the height of what it calls the "street wall" at 110 feet along Madison Avenue and 60 feet along a side street, requiring a setback above the street wall of 10 feet on the avenue and 15 feet on the side street.[25] The street-wall height limits are based on the width of the streets from building frontage to building frontage. If the new building is adjacent to an existing building that is lower, that building determines the maximum height of the street wall.

Another method imposes a height limit that is directly related to floor area. The City of Coral Gables, Florida, relates height limits to floor area by reducing the permitted floor area as the proposed building becomes taller. For example, in an MF (multifamily) 2 district, the buildings with a height greater than 70 feet and with a permitted density of up to 60 units per acre without bonuses—and up to 75 units per acre with bonuses—are limited to a floor area ratio of 2.0 above 80 feet but below 90 feet. The floor area limit declines by 10-foot increments in height to a floor area ratio of 1.55 when the building height is between 140 feet and an absolute height limit of 150 feet.

Setbacks

Setback requirements are another way to shape building form. Minimum setback requirements from side and rear lot lines exist in every zoning ordinance and usually in building codes as well. Setbacks from the front lot line are also very common and can sometimes be a problem if they were established for an existing area where most of the other buildings are built to the street. It is not usually desirable to have a small pocket of noncontinuous open space in front of a small building.

Relating Buildings to Streets and Other Public Spaces

Creating walkable streets, as discussed in chapter 3, is not just a question of dimensions and street organization. Studies by Jan Gehl, William H. Whyte, and others have documented the importance of having things to do and see along a pedestrian route to motivate people to use it.[26] The placement of buildings along a sidewalk or walkway can greatly influence how attractive the route is for pedestrians. Early forms of development regulation, based on heights and setbacks measured from the front property line, encouraged buildings that were built right up to the sidewalk, which had always been the standard way of placing buildings in city centers, with doors and windows close to the public space. When regulations based on floor area ratios replaced height and setback regulations, these traditional relationships were often lost, because it was no longer necessary to place the building along a street, and it could be set back any distance. One simple remedy, which can be added to these new codes without any other changes, is the build-to line.

Add a build-to line where walkability is a policy. A build-to line is the opposite of the familiar setback line. Instead of requiring that a building be set back behind a specific line on a map, the requirement is that the building facade be constructed along a line also specified on a map. To give designer and developer some flexibility, the requirement can be for a percentage of the building to be built at the designated line. To be effective, this percentage must be at least 50 percent; 70 percent is a typical requirement.[27] The build-to line can also be the front property line, but lines at other locations can be specified depending on the desired urban design for the area. The build-to line can also be the same as a front setback line, if there is a front setback requirement in the zoning district and most buildings conform to it.

Set uniform build-to lines along frontages around public parks and plazas. A public space is enhanced if it is defined by building frontages or landscaping and is not bordered by parking lots or an ill-assorted group of structures at varying distances from the edge of the space. Lack of building frontages facing a public space makes oversight into the space difficult, which can cause the space to be less used and more dangerous. Frontage on a public space, such as a park or riverfront, is a privileged position that can confer value on a property. Owners have an incentive to participate in district-based measures that will improve values for all the property owners. This is another situation where an overlay district that includes a build-to line at a defined distance from the public space can promote a more coherent, pleasant, and safer urban experience. The build-to line only becomes effective when a property is altered substantially, but over time the experience of the public space is protected and enhanced.

Front setbacks may be appropriate but should not include parking between public sidewalks and building frontages. It is not always the best policy to set building frontages at the front property line. Sometimes the policy for an area should be for all buildings to be set back a certain distance from the property line to allow for landscaping, or, perhaps, for steps up to front doors. In that situation, creating a uniform frontage for the block would require mapping the build-to line in the same location as the minimum front setback line. Although setting back a building far enough to have parking spaces in front may be considered desirable by retail tenants, it is not a good design policy for the pedestrian. In places where the local government gives priority to supporting and enhancing pedestrian movement and access, it is important that the parking for retail be allowed only behind or adjacent to the retail use, with no cars between pedestrians and front doors. Clear, highly visible signs can direct customers in cars to these parking locations.

On a retail street where the street right-of-way is too narrow for much parking and street parking is a priority, a special district can be enacted where the public sidewalk is rerouted to an easement along a build-to-setback line within the fronting properties. The area between the new sidewalk and the street can be designed for parking (figure 6-3). This is just one example of answering a legitimate concern of retailers or other building owners by imposing a design district that applies to a whole area. It is not a good policy to permit parking lots of different sizes and depths to be developed in an ad hoc fashion between buildings and a public sidewalk where walking is a desirable public objective.

Require ground-floor windows on street fronts. While small retail buildings need transparent store fronts that connect them to the streetscape and invite customers, typical big-box stores and modern hotels are not

Figure 6–3 This photograph of 29th Street in Boulder, Colorado, shows how the sidewalk can be moved back to continue along the building frontage, allowing parking places to be created directly on the street. The angled parking permits more car spaces than would be possible with parallel parking at curbside, and relocating the sidewalk preserves walkability and continuity from store to store, as opposed to the more usual, and much less desirable, method of placing a row of parked cars between the sidewalk and the front of the stores.

designed to relate to streets. The prototypes for these buildings were designed for shopping centers or to be located within parking lots along highways. When a hotel or retail chain builds outside the shopping center or highway environment, its prototype building often has blank walls on the street, creating underused and potentially dangerous spaces along sidewalks, even if the building meets build-to-setback requirements. One way to make such a building support a walkable environment is to require that a percentage of the building on the street front have windows, preferably windows that connect to the ground-floor interior, but at least display windows that provide lighting and visual interest. To be effective, windows should constitute more than 50 percent of the street frontage.[28] Compliance can be worked out through a site plan review process that includes design guidelines, discussed later in this chapter. For example, supermarkets often have a takeout food department and some customers eat on site. When reviewing a development proposal, the reviewer can suggest that this use can be placed along the windows as it is outside the checkout area. Big-box drugstores can have display windows. Hotel restaurants, bars, and assembly areas for ballrooms and conference facilities are enhanced by windows, as are lobbies in apartment buildings.

Regulate loading docks, trash pickups, and parking exits and entrances. Most jurisdictions do their best to avoid interrupting busy sidewalks with driveways and service elements, especially on important retail streets, but sometimes the local regulations do not include provisions that adequately address how and where such elements are permitted. It is possible to map areas with strong pedestrian traffic as restricted curb-cut zones, where curb cuts are only obtainable with a special permit, which cannot be granted if there is an alternative location on a side or back street. The special permit can also be granted with requirements that all loading operations must take place within the building; there can also be limitations on the number and width of curb cuts.

It is possible to limit the visibility of loading docks and trash storage in lower density areas by requiring such activities to take place away from public streets or to be hidden by screening, with the location and screening requirements defined in the ordinance.

Shaping Public Spaces to Enhance Buildings

Modern office, residential, and hotel towers, particularly in suburban locations, often are set back from property lines and have a substantial amount of outdoor space around them. All too often this space is purely ornamental, a good location from which to admire the building but not a useful place. Members of the public are not encouraged to do more than walk through these places, and sometimes access is forbidden. These areas are lost opportunities. It is possible to add activities at the base of these tower buildings, such as restaurants that can offer outdoor tables in good weather, or pleasant spaces with chairs or benches where office workers can take a break. In the context of a busy urban center, these places can, and should, be part of a coordinated public open space plan that enhances walkability. Open space in the wrong location can diminish the positive aspects of a public open space plan designed to give coherence and legibility to an urban district.

Zoning in high-density areas sometimes includes incentives to provide outdoor public space on private properties. The local government can require that development follow specific design guidelines in exchange for these incentives.

New York City has perhaps the most comprehensive set of guidelines for public open space. The city has long offered a bonus of zoning floor area to developments that provide public plazas in high-density residential and commercial zones and, over the years, has developed extensive sets of criteria for how that public space should be designed. William H. Whyte was a consultant to the city in setting the criteria, based on his observations of how people behave in public places.

New York City operational standards for public spaces. New York City's requirements for public open spaces that qualify for a zoning bonus include provisions to make plazas accessible and safe for the public. The spaces must be kept open to the public during daylight hours and be accessible for the disabled. The regulations encourage the use of, but also limit the size of, food-service and other kiosks on plaza space and require 50 percent of the building frontage adjoining the plaza to be retail and service establishments, which, of course, must be uses permitted by the zoning. The intent is to make it easy to get into the plaza and safe to remain there by encouraging active uses that keep the spaces full of people.

New York City design standards for public spaces. New York City's public space requirements also include detailed design provisions governing the orientation of the open space, for example, favoring a plaza open to the south. In special circumstances, plazas can be approved that face east and west, but not north. Other design requirements make access easy, with walking levels only a few feet different, at most, from the sidewalk level. Other requirements address lighting, planting, seating, and signs—eighteen sets of standards in total. Together, they make a useful checklist for designing outdoor public spaces.[29]

Shaping Public Spaces in Low-Density Residential Neighborhoods

Public spaces in residential neighborhoods include streets and parks, as well as the land occupied by public buildings such as schools, libraries, and community centers. The layout of new residential neighborhoods is governed by the subdivision ordinance, by a PUD, or by other special neighborhood planning districts. The usual document submitted for any of these approvals is a street and lot plan. Evaluating the effect of development on the preexisting landscape should be part of such approvals, as discussed in chapter 2.

Public Open Space Plan

Another element that should accompany every submission is a public open space plan that shows all the streets, parks, and areas reserved for environmental reasons. Such a plan makes it easier to envision the experience of living in the community and highlights places where changes need to be made. The following are some actions that should be included in a public open space plan.

Set aside a percentage of the land area for public use. Many ordinances include public use set-aside requirements for all subdivisions and PUDs, with the land that is set aside being used for parks or school sites, which may also be shared with surrounding areas. This is a way of making sure that public space and public uses are integrated into residential communities, not relegated to separate sites reachable only by car.

Set aside a percentage of land area for mixed commercial and residential use. This set-aside should be close to the site perimeter where it can also serve other areas. The ordinance can permit a small percentage of the residential area to have a commercial district overlay zone. The location of this commercial area should be determined as part of the review process and take into consideration relationships to other nearby areas.

Design Standards for Residential Streets

Standards for street design are typically found in the subdivision ordinance rather than in the zoning ordinance because new streets are built when a large tract of land is subdivided into smaller parcels. The developer usually builds the streets, but the streets must meet the standards in the ordinance in order for them to be accepted by the local government and maintained by the public. Government-built streets must conform to administrative standards, which ought to be comparable to those required of private developers.

Street Grade

The grade, or steepness, of the street is a central guideline for street design. Too often, published street design standards assume that the land is flat. In newly developing areas, the street grade should be as close as is feasible to the existing land contours to minimize the need to regrade the land. Site areas too steep for streets without regrading should not be developed for this purpose, if possible. There should be minimum and maximum grade requirements based on safety considerations, as well as drainage requirements for the cross section of the paved areas. As discussed earlier, provisions permitting a variety of different lot sizes within a uniform overall density is a good way to achieve the flexibility needed to leave some site areas close to their natural state.

Traffic Lanes and Traffic Calming Devices

Standards for the width of the traffic lanes in streets depend on the anticipated traffic speed. At one time, local streets were designed to give primacy to drivers by designing for relatively high speeds, which meant wide traffic lanes and a large turning radius at corners. Today, safety considerations for children and pedestrians in residential neighborhoods have led to a preference for lower speeds, and thus for the narrowest practical travel lanes and a relatively small radius of curvature. Older residential streets are frequently fitted with "traffic calming" devices like roundabouts at intersections to reduce speeds on streets that were originally designed to facilitate rapid through-traffic movement. On-street parking is also a traffic calming device, but adding parking lanes on both sides of a street can greatly increase the paved area. This may not be necessary in neighborhoods where every building has a garage and a driveway and the parking on the street is only for visitors. Guidelines need to address on-street parking as well as traffic lane width.

Require complete street designs. The usual 50- or 60-foot-wide right-of-way dimensions for streets in the subdivision ordinance may not be necessary for traffic any longer, but provide ample space for "complete streets"—streets designed and operated to enable safe access for all users, including pedestrians, bicyclists, motorists, and riders of transit where that transportation mode exists. It is necessary to reallocate priorities, with less of the right-of-way given to auto lanes and parking so that sidewalks, tree-planting areas, and bicycle lanes have enough space, and there can be dedicated areas for landscaping and for utilities. The standards for curbs, gutters, and drainage pipes can be replaced by standards for "green infrastructure": that is, using natural ways to absorb drainage from paved areas into the landscape. A twenty-one-foot roadway and a seven-foot-wide parking lane is ample for most residential streets, and in some places a single fourteen-foot traffic lane is sufficient. This provides room for cars to pass one another—very slowly—and the other seven feet can be used for an additional parking lane or more landscaping (figure 6-4). Green infrastructure can take up more right-of-way space than curbs and gutters, but what the developer loses in potential lot size may be balanced by savings in street-construction costs for curbs, gutters, and drainage pipes.

Set design standards for alleys, lanes, and driveways. Moving garage and service entrances off the street and having them face an alley or lane can make the experience of the street more pleasant and more walkable. Alleys only need to be one traffic lane wide, but the lane width must accommodate a sanitation truck and other service vehicles. Alleys work best if they are part of a system, so that the sanitation department can design routes that cover a neighborhood with a minimum of backtracking. Alleys should be laid out to line up with the alleys in adjacent blocks. The developer needs to pay for an additional small street, the alley, but the developer also saves the cost of driveways, which need be only about five feet long if the garage faces the alley—just enough that the driver can see what is coming when the car pulls out of the garage. Both alleys and driveways should be constructed of pervious paving that lets water percolate through and be absorbed by the ground.

The width of front-facing driveways along streets can be limited to one lane for a designated distance into the property, thus providing less interruption to street landscaping, sidewalks, and bicycle paths. This requirement relates to regulations that front-facing garage doors must be set back from the street.

Set standards for street connectivity and maximum block size. As described in chapter 3, it is important for the overall livability of the community to make streets, bicycle paths, and pedestrian pathways connect

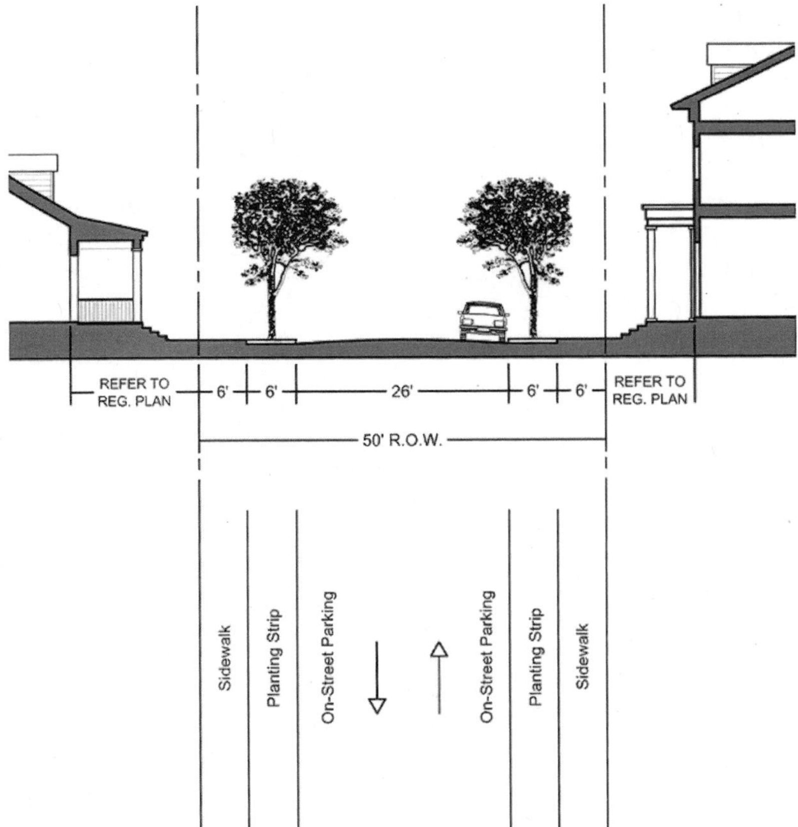

Figure 6–4 This cross section of a fifty-foot right-of-way required for a residential street in Buena Vista, Colorado, follows conventional dimensions but devotes just under half the space to wide tree lawns—which could also be drainage swales—and ample, six-foot sidewalks. With parking on both sides of the paved street, the actual travel lane is reduced to 12 feet. This kind of street is known as a neighborhood give-way street, meaning that one car needs to pull over in front of a driveway or into an unused parking space to let the other car go by. Such streets used to be common in urban neighborhoods, but were abandoned in new developments in favor of wider pavement that allowed higher traffic speeds. They are now coming back in new developments like this one, as a way to discourage through traffic. Residents have their own, off-street parking, so curbside spaces are rarely fully used. However, by taking six inches off both the sidewalks and the tree lawns, the trafficway could become 14 feet, enough space for two cars to squeeze by each other, if the drivers are careful. The frontages on this street are governed by build-to lines and build-to zones, as shown in figure 3-8, hence the instruction, printed on the cross section, to consult the regulations.

to one another to form a convenient network. A strong case can be made against having many dead-end streets in a residential neighborhood. Unless the ends of the streets are connected by pathways, they require pedestrians and cyclists to take a long way around to reach destinations on other streets. Dead-end streets also intensify traffic on neighborhood "collector" streets because they limit the routes in and out of the neighborhood. Some people like dead-end streets because there is no through traffic, but a connected street system designed for low traffic speeds can have much the same effect, without the need for higher-speed collector streets.

Street connectivity can be addressed by a performance specification that sets a minimum number of intersections for a certain number of acres. A more reliable method is to restrict dead-end streets to places where the terrain does not permit an alternative and limit the maximum perimeter of the blocks formed when streets connect. Maximum block perimeters are a good way to make a neighborhood friendly to pedestrians without more rigid specifications. A pedestrian pathway that meets standards for paving, lighting, and landscaping can be approved as an alternative to a street in some situations, so that the route through a block creates a perimeter for pedestrians and cyclists that is less than the maximum block perimeter in the ordinance. The block perimeter for cars is larger. This flexibility can help in situations where the terrain makes connectivity difficult.

Set standards for street landscaping. In addition to providing for the space required to plant trees on both sides of streets, standards can include a requirement that developers provide a minimum number of trees per length of street frontage. There should also be standards for tree size and for the way the tree is planted. There can be minimum planting standards for individual lots in new subdivisions. A list of approved tree species can also be provided.

Using Design Guidelines

Designing private buildings involves a complicated interplay of program, cost, structure, and image. As each building site and program will have special considerations, it is not always possible to write an exact specification for implementing a public policy that affects the designs of private buildings. In these situations, less specific guidelines associated with a review process are needed. The review process can include special expertise from staff or an appointed review board, but the review should always be advisory to the body making the actual regulatory decision, and that body should make findings that indicated how the guidelines were applied in its decision. Equally important, the review process should not be regarded as a procedural means to overcome the substantive deficiencies of vague, poorly written design guidelines. Although there may be circumstances when it may not be possible to write guidelines with the specificity that might be desired, the words used should have settled meanings based on usage and custom and be sufficiently "technical" so as to be understood by design professionals.[30] The guidelines should also describe a range of decisions that are acceptable within a clearly defined building context.

Architectural Guidelines for Private Properties That Relate to Public Spaces

How far can guidelines go to maintain or enhance a specific architectural character? When a historic district is established to identify and maintain the architectural character of an area, there is a clear public interest in maintaining and enhancing that architectural character. The establishment of the district also provides the legal basis for requiring an architectural expression for new buildings that is compatible with the historic character. This interest can be supported by a combination of architectural design standards and guidelines. If the architectural standards are clearly written, design staff can review the compliance of new buildings within the historic district. If the historic district also includes design guidelines, and there is an appointed design review board, the staff review can be coupled with a design review board process. The design review board can conduct advisory review of certain defined issues or provide an administrative appeal process for staff review decisions.

Nantucket Island, in Massachusetts, has a clearly defined historic character, which supports detailed design guidelines, described in a document, *Building with Nantucket in Mind*, that covers the entire island, not just the locally designated historic districts. The guidelines are very detailed. For example, "The use of overhead garage doors is strongly discouraged where highly visible along the street. In historic districts, overhead doors are not appropriate except in places of low visibility."[31] The entire island of Nantucket is a National Register historic district, which provides the justification for detailed character regulations even in parts of the island that have developed recently or are still undeveloped.

Sometimes architectural character is a standard that can be extended beyond a core historic district. Civic activists in Santa Barbara began promoting the use of the Spanish Colonial style after World War I. The landmark city hall was completed in this style in 1922. After a hugely destructive earthquake in 1925, public sentiment favored rebuilding in Spanish Colonial. There was an architectural advisory committee and a temporary architectural review board during rebuilding. Consistent use of stucco wall finishes, tile roofs, wrought iron grillwork, and other hallmarks of this style can be found in the actual historic core of the city and in other areas as well. Conforming to a historic style was a mainstream architectural decision in the 1920s when most buildings were designed according to historic precedents. Santa Barbara's El Pueblo Viejo Historic District was enacted in 1960 and requires the use of historic styles within its boundaries. In 1999, Santa Barbara adopted a comprehensive set of urban design guidelines prepared by the city's planning division after an extensive planning and public involvement process. These guidelines apply to the entire portion of the city built within its original street grid, which is substantially larger than the designated historic district included within it.[32] The guidelines apply "traditional design principles contained in existing City policy documents to development projects within the grid" to preserve the significant characteristics of existing buildings and make new buildings relate to the older ones as closely as possible. The regulations are based on objective considerations, comparable to the policies we recommend in this book, but the illustrations make it clear that the Spanish Colonial style is what is expected (figure 6-5).

Government's authority to apply design standards and guidelines to shape architectural expression is clearest in the context of a designated historic district, or through a discretionary review process such as a PUD. Outside of these two contexts, subject to legal limitations,[33] there are still substantial ways of achieving design coherence. For example, it is generally not possible to prescribe a specific style as happened in Santa Barbara, but design requirements can be established if they are based on a comprehensive urban design plan that establishes the basis for criteria

This large building appears smaller due to the variations in height and roofline and the use of recesses and projections. Reference Guidelines: 2.2.1 and 2.2.2.

- ❖ Use variations in height and roofline to reduce the perceived height of the building;
- ❖ Use planter walls to reduce the apparent height of the building;
- ❖ Organize the façades of a large project or building into several visually distinct parts to create the appearance of several smaller buildings;
- ❖ Use roof overhangs to decrease the vertical appearance of the walls;
- ❖ Use color to visually reduce the size, bulk, and scale of the building; and
- ❖ Use recesses and projections to visually divide building surfaces into smaller scale elements (see guideline 2.2.2).

2.2.2 The use of recesses and projections is encouraged to divide the surfaces of buildings into smaller scale elements, as follows:

- ❖ Large or long, continuous wall surfaces should be avoided. As a general principle, building surfaces should be relieved with a change of wall plane that provides strong shadow and visual interest;
- ❖ Use recesses to define courtyards, entryways, circulation routes, or other outdoor spaces that are accessible from the exterior of the building;
- ❖ Expression of wall thickness is desirable. Reveals, returns, and deep recesses at door and window openings are encouraged;
- ❖ Recessed balconies, arcades, and loggias create a sense of depth in the building walls, contrasting surfaces exposed to the sun with those in shadow;
- ❖ Use projections to emphasize important architectural elements, such as stairs, towers, balconies, and verandas; and
- ❖ Use materials with textural interest to break up large wall surfaces.

Figure 6–5 This is a page from the City of Santa Barbara's *Urban Design Guidelines for the City Grid*, the grid being the part of the downtown Santa Barbara area that was built on the original city street system. The grid is larger than the El Pueblo Viejo Landmark District, which is contained within the grid and has its own set of very detailed guidelines requiring that buildings be designed in what is defined as the Spanish Colonial style. The urban design guidelines are also a very detailed set of instructions. They are written objectively, but clearly a Spanish Colonial style would be the most direct way to meet the requirements, as the drawing demonstrates.

that are general enough to apply to all buildings and are supported by language that explains the reasons for adopting measures to implement the plan. For example, the Urban Design Element of the City of Omaha, Nebraska Comprehensive Plan contains design objectives and policies that apply to the entire city. These objectives and policies provide the basis for the urban design implementation measures in the form of guidelines that were prepared and adopted as part of the city's zoning ordinance.[34] The guidelines in the Omaha Zoning Ordinance address the design of building exteriors, including the proportion and visibility of entrances, the proportions and organization of windows, how buildings should relate to sloping sites, and the screening of rooftop heating and ventilation elements. These plan implementation measures, as established in the zoning ordinance, apply when these building elements are visible from a public street, public space, or parking lot. This section of the ordinance is introduced with the following language:

> *Findings.* The city council finds that the creation of high quality building design within the city is a major goal of the urban design element of the city's comprehensive plan, and further finds that the adoption of guidelines regarding the elevations of such buildings will help to achieve this goal.
>
> *Purpose.* The purpose of these guidelines is to improve the quality of building design within the city and improve the city's image as defined by its built environment. While these guidelines attempt to set forth what is generally acceptable building design, the city intends by these guidelines to encourage innovation and creativity in the design of such buildings.[35]

A special zoning district that applies to a whole area can contain specific provisions that require building design features that serve a significant public function. For example, if a study established the basis for public-benefit design considerations within a geographical area, a special district could require that the entire building frontage along a particular street include a ground-level arcade. Requiring that every building have a ground-floor arcade would be central to such a district design concept, as an arcade that is interrupted from building to building would not be an effective public space. Because an arcade is a public amenity that imposes costs on the developer, the local government will have to offer some form of financial incentive, such as a density or intensity of use (floor area ratio) bonus, to induce the developer to provide the public amenity. This should occur unless the developer's project is subject to some type of discretionary approval that provides a valid basis for exacting the amenity from the developer. Under either approach, the minimum height and width of the arcade can be specified, as can the number of support columns as a percentage of the arcade frontage.

If a community has not legally established the basis for imposing a coherent design concept that applies to all construction, it can still address some design issues that relate more specifically to health and safety issues. For example, standards can stipulate that reflective building facades not focus sunlight on undesirable places, such as in the eyes of oncoming drivers. Another possibility would be regulations that require wind-tunnel tests of buildings with unusual shapes to determine their effect on the microclimate around the building.

Some form-based codes have been adopted that use rules about architectural design to define a community's character. The codes are less detailed than Nantucket's, but far more explicit than can be found in most ordinances. If the regulations are intended to cover an entire community, defining an overall design character as a basis for regulation would require the careful design-based comprehensive planning process that occurred in Omaha.[36] It is much easier to require a specific design character for an individual property if the regulations are for a special district—especially if it is a government-sponsored redevelopment where land is owned or acquired by the public sector, or for a private greenfield site, if the owner wants to create a specific character for the development.

Design concepts based on community character are more easily imposed as part of the private developer's overall discretionary approval. For example, the town of Celebration, Florida, has required all buildings to follow "pattern books" based on historic architectural styles. But these design regulations were imposed on new construction at the Walt Disney Company's discretion. When a privately financed development is approved as a subdivision, a planned development, or a special neighborhood development, the developer can make design controls part of the documents to be approved or can keep them separate. The developer may want builders to prepare designs in a specific style or to create uniformity by having windows of similar dimensions, or by using roofs pitched at a predetermined angle. Making these design elements part of the approved plan can ensure that completed development continues to maintain its design character. Such requirements are typical of so-called New Urbanist communities. However, they are private initiatives; they do not begin as a regulatory requirement. The developer can use covenants recorded with the individual properties to enforce design provisions and leave long-term compliance to a homeowners' association.

Publicly Owned Land as a Public Space Resource

The important decisions about designing public buildings, parks, and publicly owned open space generally take place within the context of public capital programs, not through regulation. However, it is good practice for each locality to have a design review board that can make suggestions about how to improve public projects. A major issue for each such project is whether it makes the most of its potential to improve the experience of surrounding areas. A review board could also look at a locality's inventory of publicly owned space and suggest other uses that might improve the design in different parts of the local jurisdiction.

In summary, we believe that most, if not all, of the objectives that might lead a community to consider replacing all its current development regulations can be attained more simply and effectively through modifications within the existing framework of zoning and subdivision ordinances.

Notes

1. The term *Public Realm* appears to have originated in sociology literature to refer to "the unique social and psychological environment provided by urban settlements." See Lyn H. Loftland, *The Public Realm: Exploring the City's Quintessential Social Territory* (Hawthorne, NY: Aldine De Gruyter, 1998). The Public Realm is an important organizing principle for New Urbanism and is defined as "those parts of the urban fabric that are held in common such as plazas, squares, parks, thoroughfares and civic buildings." Duany Plater-Zyberk and Co., *The Lexicon of the New Urbanism* v3.2 (2002), A5.
2. See Jerold S. Kayden, New York Department of City Planning, and Municipal Art Society of New York, *Privately Owned Public Space: The New York City Experience* (Hoboken, NJ: Wiley, 2000), which identifies and discusses the 500 New York City plazas, parks, and atriums located on private property that are legally accessible to the public.

3. Sam Bass Warner and Andrew Whittemore, *American Urban Form* (Cambridge, MA: MIT Press, 2012).
4. For a more detailed discussion of the ways that planning policies and regulations affect urban form, see the *Urban Form Technical Working Group Draft Report for Portland Plan*, March 25, 2008.
5. Floor area ratios are perhaps better described as multipliers. If the area of a building lot is 10,000 square feet, and the floor area ratio is 10, the permissible floor area is 10 times the lot area, or 100,000 square feet. Zoning floor area, however, is not the same as actual floor area. As the ratio is intended to limit the occupancy of a building, it applies only to occupied floor area, which, depending on the ordinance, may exclude stairs and elevator shafts, mechanical equipment spaces, and, sometimes, above-ground parking. Below-grade spaces are not generally considered floor area for zoning purposes.
6. The open space ratio is the amount of open space required on a residential zoning lot, expressed as a percentage of the total floor area permitted on the zoning lot. For example, if a building with 20,000 square feet of floor area has an open space ratio of 20, then 4,000 square feet of open space would be required on the zoning lot (0.20 × 20,000 sq. ft.) The definition of the open space ratio is adapted from the New York City Department of City Planning Glossary of Zoning Terms, available at *http://www1.nyc.gov/site/planning/zoning/glossary.page*. The definition notes that the open space ratio does not apply in New York City's contextual districts, which have regulations intended to relate new buildings to the existing urban form.
7. Ian McHarg, *Design with Nature* (Garden City, NY: Published for the American Museum of Natural History by the Natural History Press, 1969). In particular, see the second chapter, "Sea and Survival." The edition of this book currently in print is the 25th anniversary edition (New York: Wiley, 1995).
8. While the work of many people has gone into the creation of transect-based regulations, the originator and continued inspirer of the use of the transect concept is Andres Duany, of the Miami firm of Duany Plater-Zyberk and Company. Duany is also one of the founders of the Congress of the New Urbanism. For a prototype for transect-based regulations, see Center for Applied Transect Studies, "SmartCode," 2009, *http://transect.org/codes.html*. Sandy Sorlien, a principal author of the *SmartCode and Manual*, explains the regulatory purpose of the transect-based code as follows: "It would be great if we didn't need regulation to allow walkable, mixed-use, diverse development patterns—but we do. A code must be more than the toothless 'design guidelines,' because the default is so strong in the direction of separated use zoning and autocentric corridors. The code must be regulatory, until such time as the culture regains the wisdom to build compactly again." Andres Duany, William Wright, and Sandy Sorlein, *SmartCode and Manual*, version 9 (Ithaca, NY: New Urban News Publications, 2008).
9. See, for example, the case studies in Parolek, Parolek, and Crawford, *Form-Based Codes.*

10. See generally, Daniel G. Parolek, Karen Parolek, and Paul C. Crawford, *Form-Based Codes: A Guide for Planners, Urban Designers, Municipalities, and Developers* (Hoboken, NJ: Wiley, 2008).

11. Chad D. Emerson, "Making Main Street Legal Again: The SmartCode Solution to Sprawl," *Missouri Law Review* 71, no. 3: 636, 641–642. See, for example, the case studies in Parolek, Parolek, and Crawford, *Form-Based Codes.*

12. The Miami 21 code as amended through May 2015, is available at *http://www.miami21.org/final_code_May2015.asp.*

    The consulting team that prepared the development regulation revisions for Miami 21 was led by Elizabeth Plater-Zyberk of Duany Plater-Zyberk and Company. She was then also dean of the School of Architecture at the University of Miami.

13. For a summary of these zones and subzones, see Miami 21 Code, art. 4, tables 1–4.

14. The Atlas of the Miami 21 Code is available online. *www.miami21.org/pdfs/finaldocuments/miamiatlas-asadopted.pdf.* Using the zoom tool, it is possible to enlarge each area of the city and see both the previous zone name and the new transect name.

15. The T6 zoning as corridors along major streets is also clearly visible in the Atlas of the Miami 21 Code.

16. See Andres Duany and Emily Talen, "Transect Planning," *Journal of the American Planning Association* 68, no. 3: 245–266.

17. Patrick Geddes, *Cities in Evolution, New and Revised Edition* (London: Williams and Norgate, 1949; orig. 1915).

18. R. E. Park, E. W. Burgess, and R. D. McKenzie, *The City* (Chicago: University of Chicago Press, 1925).

19. Homer Hoyt, *The Structure and Growth of Residential Neighborhoods in American Cities* (Washington, DC: Federal Housing Administration, 1939).

20. Chauncy D. Harris and Edward L. Ullman, "The Nature of Cities," *Annals of the American Academy of Political and Social Science* 242, *Building the Future City* (November 1945), 7–17.

21. Alan Berger, *Drosscape: Wasting Land in Urban America* (New York: Princeton Architectural Press, 2006), 61; see also Lars Lerup, "Stim and Dross: Rethinking the Metropolis" in *Assemblage*, no. 25: 82–101.

22. Ibid., 56–57. A region with these agglomerations is often described as a polycentric urban region.

23. See discussion in chapter 7.

24. See Jonathan Barnett, *Redesigning Cities* (Chicago: Planners Press: 2003), 252–253.

25. New York City Zoning Resolution, art. IX, chap. 9, sec. 99–051 (a) and subsections.

26. An excellent discussion of what makes a city street walkable can be found in Gehl, *Cities for People,* 119–133. For a summary of William H. Whyte's findings on walkability, see Barnett, *Redesigning Cities*, 17–25, 236–240.

27. New York City's Special Madison Avenue Preservation District requires building along the street for the entire building frontage, with minor variations to account for possible different configurations of adjacent properties.

28. See, for example, City of Charlotte, "MX-1 Neighborhood Commercial, Mixed-Use Overlay District," 2014, *www.charlottemi.org/wp-content/uploads/2014/08/07a-Mixed-Use-Zoning-Ordinance-Amendment-Language.pdf*: "(1) A minimum of 60 percent of the street-facing building facade between two feet and eight feet in height must be comprised of clear windows that allow views of indoor space or product display areas. (2) The bottom of any window or product display window used to satisfy the transparency standard of paragraph (1) above may not be more than 4 feet above the adjacent sidewalk. (3) Product display windows used to satisfy these requirements must have a minimum height of 4 feet and be internally lighted."

29. New York City Department of City Planning, *New York City Zoning Resolution*, art. III, chap. 7, sec. 70.

30. See Brian W. Blaesser, "Design Review," in *Discretionary Land Use Controls: Avoiding Invitations to Abuse of Discretion* (St. Paul, MN: Thomson-Reuters, 2017). See also discussion of legal principles in chapter 7.

31. J. Christopher Lang and Kate Stout, *Building with Nantucket in Mind* (Nantucket, MA: Nantucket Historic District Commission, 1995) was prepared by the local government to explain all the standards adopted to regulate design and development. *www.nantucket-ma.gov/DocumentCenter/Home/View/12329.*

32. City of Santa Barbara, *Urban Design Guidelines: Street Grid,* adopted by City Council Resolution 99-138 on December 14, 1999.

33. See discussion of legal principles involving architectural design in chapter 7.

34. Omaha Zoning Ordinance, sec. 55-935.

35. Ibid., sec. 55-935 (a) and (b).

36. Some advocates of form-based regulations recognize that detailed architectural design standards are not necessary to address the spatial relationship between buildings, streets, and public spaces. As one advocate states, "The architectural code for a New Urbanist project can be either loose or tight, depending on the context. . . . If a particular community wants more 'everyday urbanism,' then regulations can be relaxed. . . . The debate over the New Urbanism would benefit from less obsession with architectural styles and more attention to the New Urbanism's contributions at the scale of block, neighborhood, district, city and region." Cliff Ellis, "The New Urbanism: Critiques and Rebuttals," *Journal of Urban Design* 7 (2002): 3.

7

Implementing Regulations While Safeguarding Private Property Interests

The development regulation proposals discussed in the preceding chapters relate to three goals that should guide any system of land-use and development regulations: *quality development*, *fairness*, and *efficiency*.[1] The pursuit of these outcomes in the context of development regulation must be informed by an understanding of the fundamental legal principles essential to safeguarding private property interests in both the regulatory and development approval processes. This chapter explains these three goals in relation to these fundamental legal principles to provide a broader framework for understanding issues in the context of the proposals we put forth in the previous chapters.

Regulatory Goals

Quality Development

Not surprisingly, we believe that quality development means development that achieves the policy objectives we have outlined: development that is sustainable, adapts to climate change, encourages walking and mixed use, preserves historic landmarks, creates more affordable housing, promotes environmental justice, and helps to enhance public spaces.

But the term *quality* has a significant element of subjectivity to it. Nevertheless, as applied to real estate development, we can define a set of land-use and development policies to which development should be responsive. Moreover, there is a larger context in which the goal of quality development should be understood if implementation of land-use and development policies is to be successful. In 1972, the Rockefeller

Brothers Fund assembled the Task Force on Land Use and Urban Growth, which concluded in its report[2] that, although no ideal pattern of development existed, it was important to pursue the goal of quality development. Although there have been many references to quality development, no report has made such a thoughtful effort to define what quality development should mean:

> Quality is marked by respect for human and natural values. It is harder to create quality than to preserve it, for creation requires more choices and its goals are inherently complicated. In conservation, quality values are readily translated into physical ideals and, in many cases, the ideals already exist—a community in harmony with its surroundings, a valley preserved in wilderness.[3]

The report further observes that when new development is built, "creation, much more than preservation, must make peace with pluralism":

> The quest for quality development, which respects human values, must recognize that there is no agreement about what constitutes quality. Rather, the broadest possible range of individual choices and lifestyles must be accommodated. But even this guideline does not go far. With rapidly changing values and technology, which individual choices are long lasting and which are fleeting? . . . The contrast between conservation and creation is even clearer in relation to natural values. Many ideals of natural preservation can be stated as absolutes: clean air, pure water, unspoiled wilderness. Any program to achieve these goals obviously requires trade-offs. How much of the ideal can the nation afford? Who should pay? Which natural ideals or places are most important? Despite these difficulties, the ideal itself is clear.[4]

For the constructed environment, quality must be based on resolving conflicting objectives in the most favorable possible way:

> Development, no matter how respectful of nature, does not have the benefit of these absolutes. Its assertion of natural values comes, not in moving closer to an absolute, but in determining how far from it we must unavoidably fall. Or determining how far from it we should fall so that other conflicting objectives may be achieved. Creation must,

> for example focus less on unspoiled landscapes than on the construction without "avoidable" grading or "needless" removal of natural vegetation. It must focus, in sum, less on prohibition than on sensitive accommodation and balance. And it needs, for success, people and institutions willing and able to seek those accommodations and strike those balances.[5]

Achieving this accommodation and balance depends, in large part, on the implementation of policies through development regulations that are drafted with certain fundamental legal principles in mind. Before discussing those principles we briefly outline the other two goals: fairness and efficiency.

Fairness

The concept of fairness is also a broad concept that is not easily defined. However, the U.S. Constitution and the states' constitutions address fairness in large part through the requirement that the government ensure that its citizens are provided "due process of law." In general, due process requires that decisions are rationally made, in a process that is open to the public, on the basis of facts, and within a reasonable period of time. Five criteria are central to the concept of fairness: (1) comprehensiveness; (2) consistency; (3) certainty; (4) proportionality; and (5) finality.

Comprehensiveness. To be fair, the decision-making process should provide the decision makers with as much information, data, and opinion as possible from all interested parties. This ensures that a decision is made comprehensively by considering all the relevant facts and issues.

Consistency. The decision-making process should minimize the possibility that decisions will be made on grounds unrelated to the merits of a development proposal. If there are policies and legal principles in place, the same relevant facts can produce, in two separate instances, a consistent result. It is essential to the concept of due process of law under the U.S. Constitution, which requires that our laws operate the same on all persons, that no one is subjected to biased or arbitrary exercise of governmental power.

Certainty. The criterion of certainty is satisfied when standards are clear, which enables the public to understand policy goals and standards for achieving those policy goals. The decision-making process should encourage the development and effective use of standards and guidelines applicable to decision making. Decisions left to complete discretion, without adequate standards, lead to abuses of power.

Proportionality. The goal of fairness is reached when government is required to show a meaningful relationship between a regulatory requirement imposed on a private development and the projected impact of that development on the public. The burden can be determined just or excessive by measuring the proportionality between the extent of the regulatory burden imposed on the development and the development's impacts.

Finality. Developers will shy away from a jurisdiction whose decision-making processes lack finality even when standards and guidelines are clear for land-use and development approvals. A developer must know at some point that a decision is final, whether favorable or unfavorable, to determine the appropriate next step—whether it is a commitment to invest in a project or a decision to appeal the denial. There is nothing more undermining to the achievement of quality development than a decision-making system that has confusing lines of decision-making authority and fails to provide a final decision within a reasonable time.

Efficiency

Simply put, the goal of efficiency in land-use and development approvals is to produce decisions in less time and at less cost. Efficient decision making can encourage the development community to consider changes in design that support local government policy objectives.[6]

Reasonableness in Development Regulation

The legal analog for fairness is reasonableness.[7] Reasonableness in the context of government actions involving citizens and private property means that there is a *rational basis* for the policy that is implemented or the restriction that is imposed. As noted earlier, reasonableness in the legal sense is best understood in terms of the due process clause under the federal and states' constitutions.

For local government to zone or impose land-use and development regulations on private property there must be a delegation of the state's *police power* to local government. Police power refers to the legislative or policymaking power that resides in each state to establish laws and ordinances to preserve public order and tranquility and to promote the public health, safety, and general welfare. This power is one of the inherent attributes of state sovereignty.[8] As such, its existence does not depend on constitutional or statutory authority. At the same time, a state may, by statute or through its constitution, limit the scope of any of the inherent attributes of its sovereignty such as the police power or the power of eminent domain.[9] The exercise of the police power is limited by the constitutional requirement of due process.

Once the power to zone and to implement other land-use and development regulations has been delegated to local governments and their legislative bodies (a city council, a board of selectmen, or a board of county commissioners), there is another form of delegation from the local government's legislative body to local administrative entities—a planning commission, a zoning board of appeal, or a design review board.[10] These are the decision-making bodies that implement adopted policies. If this local delegation is done without clear policy guidance from the local legislative body, restrictions can be imposed on property owners and on real estate development proposals by local administrative bodies that either exceed their authority or lack proper guidance for making those decisions.

This local delegation process implicates the due process concern for certainty, namely, that the standards for implementing policy are clear. The rule that is intended to prevent regulatory uncertainty is the so-called *nondelegation doctrine* that states that local policy making is the purview of the local legislative body and that legislative power may not be delegated to administrative boards, commissions, or committees. This rule is important because the local legislative body is not required to recite the facts it considered in reaching its legislative decisions. Courts, in turn, give deference to local legislative decisions, granting them a presumption of validity. In contrast, an administrative body is required to make findings of fact when it carries out the policies or purposes previously declared by the local legislative body through an adopted ordinance. If the local legislative body does not provide adequate standards in the ordinance to guide the administrative body when it exercises discretion in implementing the adopted legislative policy, the local administrative body is likely to engage in its own legislative policy making, which violates the nondelegation doctrine.

The rule against delegation of legislative power closely relates to the *void for vagueness doctrine*, which concerns the lack of clarity or certainty in the language of regulation. The doctrine is derived from the due process clause of the Fourteenth Amendment to the U.S. Constitution, specifically the procedural due process requirement of notice. Its purpose is to place a limit on arbitrary and discretionary enforcement of the law.[11] Local courts, when presented with a void for vagueness challenge to a land-use regulation, most frequently echo the U.S. Supreme Court's language, namely, that "an ordinance is unconstitutionally vague when men of common intelligence must necessarily guess at its meaning."[12]

The void for vagueness doctrine is particularly important in the formulation of design standards and guidelines and design review processes. When the design terms that are used in such regulations do not give meaningful guidance to those who are expected to implement and comply with regulations—public officials, applicants, or design professionals, who frequently serve on design review bodies—courts can find that such terms are unduly vague and therefore void.

The due process test for reasonableness in the exercise of the police power is whether the local zoning or other land-use regulation promotes the health, safety, or general welfare of the community.[13] This is the substantive component of the due process clause, namely, whether the regulation furthers some legitimate governmental purpose. This substantive component bars "certain arbitrary, wrongful government actions regardless of the fairness of the procedures used to implement them."[14] As noted, the courts give a presumption of constitutionality to police power regulations. This presumption cannot be overcome if the evidence presented regarding the legitimate purpose of the regulation merely raises questions the answers to which people could reasonably differ. This judicial rule is known as the "fairly debatable rule" or the "reasonably debatable rule." The flip side of this rule is that when the evidence presented does not raise questions about which people could reasonably differ and instead indicates that the government's action was arbitrary, the court may invalidate the regulation on the ground that it is arbitrary and capricious, meaning that the regulation has no substantial relation to the public health, safety, and general welfare.

There are situations in which the purpose of a regulation is reasonable, but the method employed to implement that purpose—a requirement to grant or dedicate a property interest or comply with some other form of exaction as it affects or is applied to a specific property owner or developer's proposal—makes no sense. In those regulatory exaction situations, a standard more rigorous than the rational relationship standard applies. Such a situation occurred in the *Nollan* case[15] decided by the U.S. Supreme Court, where the California Coastal Commission sought to require a lateral beach easement as a condition for granting a permit that would have allowed the expansion of a beach bungalow. The commission asserted that the easement was necessary to maintain "visual access" to the beach. The Court observed: "It is quite impossible to understand how a requirement that people already on the public beaches be able to walk across the Nollans' property reduces any obstacles to viewing the beach created by the new house."[16] The Court explained that there must be an "essential nexus" between the regulation and the government's purpose. In such a situation involving a regulation that is directed at a property interest, the Court held that the standard is not the finding of a "rational basis" between the regulation and the governmental purpose but rather a finding that the regulation "substantially advances legitimate state interest and does not deny an owner economically viable use of his land."[17]

The Court also explained its ruling in *Nollan* as an application of a categorical takings rule. The right to exclude others from one's property is a protected property interest under the Fifth Amendment. An easement giving the public the permanent and continuous right to traverse the Nollans' property would have entailed a permanent physical occupation, which is always a taking, requiring compensation.[18] This takings principle becomes relevant in the context of environmental regulations when they involve required setbacks from natural resource areas. If such setbacks are required on an ad hoc basis, without any analysis to support the extent of setback required, they may be subject to challenge under this categorical takings rule.

As noted earlier, this heightened judicial scrutiny under the *Nollan* "essential nexus" test in matters that pertain to property interests is relevant in situations where regulations in the form of "exactions" are applied to development proposals. This test is discussed shortly regarding the importance of "proportionality" to achieve fairness in development regulation.

Planning and Rational Basis for Regulation

One of the principal ways that local governments can establish a rational basis for their land-use and development regulations is to undertake the necessary planning and related studies that establish the factual bases for policies that, in turn, are implemented through regulation. This planning step is particularly important when local government seeks to impose regulations for historic landmarks, for design or aesthetic considerations, and for environmental and infrastructure mitigation of the impacts of development. It is important to undertake this planning step to satisfy the fairness criteria of *comprehensiveness* and *consistency*. Plans that provide the substantive rationale for regulations ensure that the decision makers will be informed by factual circumstances, data, and public input, thereby increasing the likelihood that decisions will be fair. This planning step will also reduce the possibility that regulatory decisions will be made on grounds unrelated to the facts and related policies that were developed for those regulations. Without the planning and empirical basis for showing the rational relationship between policy and implementation, regulations are vulnerable to challenges under the due process clause and the takings clause of the Fifth Amendment.

Equal Treatment

As noted earlier, one of the important criteria of fairness is consistency, namely, that our laws operate on all persons alike and that persons similarly situated are treated equally under regulations unless there is some rational basis for different treatment. This principle is embodied in the Fourteenth Amendment to the U.S. Constitution, which provides that no state "shall deny to any person within its jurisdiction the equal protection of the laws." The Fourteenth Amendment applies to local governments within states. Under the equal protection clause, a local government must show that a classification of the land-use regulation is justified by a legitimate governmental purpose and that the regulation is administered fairly.

Proportionality in Development Regulation

The extent to which the application of a development regulation is fundamentally fair often comes down to whether the regulatory requirement, typically an exaction, is proportional to the impact of a proposed development. Development regulations, particularly those that address environmental resources, climate change, public services and facilities, and affordable housing, may rely on exactions, in the form of dedication of property or the payment of fees, to offset the impacts of development. These exaction-type development regulations often involve discretionary decision making on an ad hoc basis, which triggers a different type of takings standard when the decisions concern property interests.

Seven years after its decision in *Nollan*, the U.S. Supreme Court decided the *Dolan* case[19] and announced a new federal takings standard with respect to property exactions. In that case, Ms. Dolan, the landowner, owned and operated a plumbing and electrical supply store on property through which a creek flowed and which partially lay within the creek's 100-year floodplain. She applied to the city for a permit to increase her store's size and to pave an adjacent parking lot. The city planning commission approved the permit application subject to conditions that she dedicate the portion of her property within the 100-year floodplain to improve the storm drainage system along the creek and dedicate an additional 15-foot strip of land adjacent to the floodplain as a pedestrian/bicycle pathway. The dedication required by that condition encompassed approximately 7,000 square feet, or roughly 10 percent of the property. The Court held that the required floodplain dedication was unconstitutional because it did not merely prohibit the landowner from building in the floodplain but demanded that she grant a permanent easement for the public to use a dedicated strip of land as a public greenway along the river, thus constituting a taking of property without just compensation. The Court also found that the bicycle and pedestrian pathway exaction was unconstitutional because the city had not met its burden of demonstrating that the additional number of vehicle and bicycle trips generated by the landowner's development reasonably related to the city's requirement for dedication of the pedestrian and bicycle pathway easement. The Court held that the city must make some effort to quantify its findings in support of the dedication of the bicycle path—beyond a conclusory statement that it could affect some of the traffic demand generated.

In deciding *Dolan*, the Court answered the question that had not been answered in *Nollan*: What is the required degree of connection between the exaction and the projected impact of a proposed development?

In *Dolan*, the Court explained that there must be a "rough proportionality" between the exaction imposed and the impact of the proposed development. This test, combined with the *Nollan* test, has resulted in what is known as the "*Nollan/Dolan* Dual Nexus Test." The test requires that a development condition or mitigation requirement must (1) have an essential nexus to some legitimate governmental purpose; and (2) that there must be a "rough proportionality" between the exaction or mitigation requirement and the impact or need created by the proposed development. In addition, with respect to the second element of the test, the Court held that local government, not the developer, has the burden of substantiating the purpose and the amount of the exaction.

Application of the Unconstitutional Conditions Doctrine to Property Rights

The Court in *Dolan* also applied a doctrine called the *unconstitutional conditions doctrine*, which says that "government may not require a person to give up a constitutional right . . . in exchange for a discretionary benefit conferred by the government where the property sought has little or no relationship to the benefit."[20] Under this doctrine, a court may invoke the heightened scrutiny of the "essential nexus" test (substantially advance the legitimate state interest) because the exaction arguably triggers a constitutional right, namely, the right under the Fifth and Fourteenth Amendments to receive just compensation when property is taken for public use.

The Court underscored the importance of the unconstitutional conditions doctrine to regulations that impose exactions on property owners and development proposals in its 2013 decision in the *Koontz* case,[21] a case involving regulation by a River Water Management District established pursuant to the Florida Water Resources Act. Mr. Koontz had sought an approval to build a shopping center adjacent to a highway on 3.7 acres of a 14.2-acre tract, subject to the jurisdiction of the district, which conditioned the granting of a permit on his agreeing to implement one of two alternatives: (1) he could reduce his development to one acre and turn the remaining acres into a deed-restricted conservation area; or (2) he could build on the 3.7 acres, as proposed but deed a conservation easement over the remainder of the property. He also had to agree to hire contractors to make improvements on district-owned property by replacing culverts on its property approximately four-and-a-half miles southeast of his property or by plugging certain drainage canals on other district property some seven miles away. Either of these projects would have enhanced approximately 50 acres of district-owned wetlands.

Mr. Koontz refused to comply with these conditions and sued all the way to the Florida Supreme Court, which rejected his claim that the conditions amounted to an unconstitutional taking. The U.S. Supreme Court heard Mr. Koontz's appeal and reversed the Florida court, making two key holdings. First, the *Nollan/Dolan* Dual Nexus Test applies both when a permit is granted with conditions and when the permit is denied because an applicant refuses to agree to conditions: "Regardless of whether the government ultimately succeeds in pressuring someone into forfeiting a constitutional right, the unconstitutional conditions doctrine forbids burdening the Constitution's enumerated rights by coercively withholding benefits from those who exercise them."[22] Second, the *Nollan/Dolan* Dual Nexus Test applies to monetary exactions. The Court rejected the Florida Supreme Court's reasoning that Koontz's claim under *Nollan* and *Dolan* failed because the River Water Management District asked him to spend money rather than give up an easement on his land. The Court explained that government could easily evade the requirements of *Nollan* and *Dolan* by giving the applicant the choice of granting an easement or making a payment equal to the easement's value—a payment in lieu fee. The monetary obligation burdened Koontz's ownership of a specific parcel of land. His case was similar to the Court's cases holding that the government must pay just compensation when it takes a lien—a right to receive money that is secured by a particular piece of property.[23]

Legal Framework for Implementation

The legal principles outlined earlier provide the implementation framework for the development regulation proposals we present in this book. Adherence to these legal principles is essential if the system of land-use and development regulations we propose is to produce development outcomes that reflect the goals of quality development, fairness, and efficiency.

Notes

1. These goals are not new in the discussion of land-use and development regulations. After development activity declined with the recession that started in 1974 and only began to recover in 1976, it became apparent to observers that the development process was fragile, as evidenced by the number of bankruptcies, withdrawals from business, and extensive price increases for the few housing units that had been completed. It also became apparent that in many areas, growth management and control programs often had a significant impact on the cost of development and ultimately on the cost of housing and other facilities. In particular, the lack of coordination among the increasing number of agencies and jurisdictions with permitting authority over development had led to inordinate delays and consequent increases in development costs. In an effort to improve the coordination needed to achieve public policy objectives in growth management, the Urban Land Institute, with the support of the National Science Foundation, undertook a study of ways to improve coordination in the implementation of environmental and land-use plans and regulations. The resulting report, *The Permit Explosion: Coordination of the Proliferation* (Urban Land Institute, 1976), identifies quality, fairness, and efficiency as important criteria for evaluating coordination mechanisms. In this book we view them as "goals" that should guide regulatory initiatives.
2. William K. Reilly, ed., *The Use of Land: A Citizens' Policy Guide to Urban Growth* (New York: Thomas Y. Crowell Company, 1973).
3. Ibid., 177.
4. Ibid., 178.
5. Ibid., 178–179.
6. See generally, *Development Process Efficiency: Cutting Through the Red Tape* (prepared by Abt Associates for the National Association of Homebuilders, November 2015).
7. *Black's Law Dictionary* defines *reasonable* as "fair, proper, just, moderate, suitable under the circumstances . . . rational." *Black's Law Dictionary*, 6th ed. (St. Paul, MN: West Publishing, 1990).
8. *Marshall v. Kansas*, 355 S.W.2d 877 (Mo. 1962). Other attributes of sovereignty, for example, are the power of eminent domain and the power of taxation.
9. For example, in the wake of the U.S. Supreme Court's decision in *Kelo v. City of New London*, 545 U.S. 469 (2005), the legislatures of some states decided to limit the purposes for which the power of eminent domain could be exercised by prohibiting the use of eminent domain to take private property in order to then transfer it to another private property owner.
10. In some states, such as Ohio, the delegation to the administrative bodies of unincorporated governments (that is, townships) comes directly from the state legislature.

11. *Burien Bark Supply v. King County*, 106 Wash. 2d 868, 725 P.2d 994, 998 (1986).
12. *Union Nat. Bank & Trust Co. of Joliet v. Village of New Lenox*, 505 N.E.2d 1, 3 (3 D Dist. 1987), quoting *Broderick v. Oklahoma*, 413 U.S. 601 (1973).
13. See *Village of Euclid v. Ambler*, 272 U. S. 365 (1926).
14. *Zinermon v. Burch*, 494 U.S. 113, 125 (1980), quoting *Daniels v. Williams*, 474 U.S. 327 (1986).
15. *Nollan v. California Coastal Commission*, 107 S.Ct. 3141 (1987).
16. Ibid., 3149.
17. Ibid., 3146.
18. Ibid., 3146, 3148, and 3150–3151.
19. *Dolan v. City of Tigard*, 114 S.Ct. 2309 (1994).
20. Ibid., 2317. One commentator has defined the doctrine as follows: "The doctrine of unconstitutional conditions holds that government may not grant a benefit on the condition that the beneficiary surrender a constitutional right, even if the government may withhold that benefit altogether." Kathleen M. Sullivan, "Unconstitutional Conditions," *Harvard Law Review* 102 (1989): 1413, 1415.
21. *Koontz v. St. Johns Water Management District*, 133 S. Ct. 2586 (2013).
22. Ibid., 2595.
23. Ibid., 2599.

Illustration Credits

Chapter 1

1-1 United States Geological Survey, Center for Earth Resources Observation and Science, Wikimedia Commons.

1-2 Brandonrush/CC BY-SA 3.0 Unported license.

1-3 Newt82/CC BY-SA 3.0 Unported license.

1-4 From *Stormwater Management Typical Details,* Bureau of Environmental Services, City of Portland, Oregon.

Chapter 2

2-1 From *Homeowners Guide to Retrofitting,* Federal Emergency Management Agency.

2-2 Msbeachbum/CC BY-SA 3.0 Unported license.

2-3 Mkieper/CC BY-SA 3.0 Unported license.

Chapter 3

3-1 Courtesy of Freedman Tung + Sasaki.

3-2 Courtesy of Freedman Tung + Sasaki.

3-3 Courtesy of Freedman Tung + Sasaki.

3-4 Courtesy of Freedman Tung + Sasaki.

3-5 Joe Mabel/CC BY-SA 3.0 Unported license.

3-6 Wikimedia Commons, public domain.

3-7 Drawing by Richard Bono, *Rural by Design*, Randall Arendt. Used by permission.

3-8 Courtesy of Dover, Kohl & Partners.

3-9 From the *Stormwater Management Handbook: Implementing Green Infrastructure in Northern Kentucky Communities,* U.S. Environmental Protection Administration.

3-10 From the *Accessory Dwelling Unit Manual*, City of Santa Cruz, California.

Chapter 4

4-1 Abbie Rowe, White House Photographs, John F. Kennedy Presidential Library and Museum, Boston.

4-2 Carol M. Highsmith Archive, Library of Congress.

4-3 Courtesy of the Municipal Art Society of New York City.

Chapter 5

5-1 From *Accessory Dwelling Unit Manual*, City of Santa Cruz, California.

5-2 From *Laneway Housing How-To Guide*, City of Vancouver, British Columbia.

5-3 From *A Guide to Building a Backyard Cottage*, City of Seattle.

5-4 From *The City of Cleveland Land Bank at Work*, City of Cleveland.

Chapter 6

6-1 From *Paris Projet* No. 13–14, Atelier Parisien d'urbanisme (apur), 1975.

6-2 New York City 1916 Zoning Ordinance.

6-3 Hustvedt/CC BY-SA 3.0 Unported license.

6-4 Courtesy of Dover, Kohl & Partners.

6-5 From *Urban Design Guidelines, City Grid*, City of Santa Barbara, California.

Index

About the Authors

JONATHAN BARNETT is one of the pioneers of the modern practice of city design, a discipline firmly grounded in current political, social, and economic realities. As a professor of city and regional planning and the director of the Graduate Urban Design Program at the University of Pennsylvania, former director of the Graduate Program in Urban Design at the City College of New York, and as a visiting professor, critic, or lecturer at many other universities, Jonathan Barnett has helped educate more than a generation of city designers.

Mr. Barnett worked in the reform administration of Mayor John Lindsay when New York City first established an institutional commitment to city design. *Urban Design as Public Policy*, his account of innovations created in New York, was influential in establishing urban design as a necessary element of local government and in making city design a well-recognized profession.

He has written many books, chapters, and articles about city design. In his recent book, *City Design: Modernist, Traditional, Green, and Systems Perspectives*, now in its second edition, Mr. Barnett explores the history and current practice of the four most important ways of designing cities. He suggests a fifth way that draws on all four approaches. He is also the author—with Larry Beasley, former planning director of Vancouver—of *Ecodesign for Cities and Suburbs*, published in 2015.

Jonathan Barnett has also developed his own extensive consulting practice as a city designer, with long-term consulting relationships with the cities of Charleston, Cleveland, Kansas City, Nashville, Norfolk, Miami, Omaha, and Pittsburgh, as well as the cities of Xiamen and Tianjin in China. He has also been the urban design advisor for two planned communities in Cambodia and several large-scale projects in Korea.

He is currently interested in projects that control growth at the suburban fringe and redevelop bypassed areas in the older parts of metropolitan regions. He has worked on growth management plans for suburban communities in Missouri, Wisconsin, and New York State, and on the redesign of several former railway yards and military bases.

With his students at the University of Pennsylvania, Jonathan Barnett has prepared growth management studies for central Florida, researched the potential effects of sea-level rise in the Delaware River Basin and the New Jersey Shore, and demonstrated methods of incorporating Geographic Information Systems into development regulations in Lancaster County, Pennsylvania.

Jonathan Barnett is a magna cum laude graduate of Yale College and has a master's degree in architecture from the University of Cambridge, as well as a master of architecture from the Yale School of Architecture. He is a fellow of both the American Institute of Architects and the American Institute of Certified Planners. He is a recipient of the Dale Prize for Excellence in Urban Design and Regional Planning, the Athena Medal from the Congress for the New Urbanism, and the William H. Whyte Award from the Partners for Livable Communities for being a pioneer in urban design education and practice.

BRIAN W. BLAESSER is a partner in the law firm Robinson & Cole LLP. He heads the Land Use and Real Estate Development Group in the firm's Boston office. Mr. Blaesser represents real estate owners, investors, and developers in analyzing and securing requisite land use and development approvals from local governments, in negotiating and drafting development agreements, and in handling development projects that involve a wide range of environmental, transactional, and regulatory permitting matters.

Mr. Blaesser formerly served as special assistant attorney general for eminent domain actions brought by the Illinois Departments of Transportation and Conservation and has extensive experience in state and federal trial and appellate courts in real estate and land use litigation, including the takings issue, vested rights, condemnation, U.S. EPA enforcement actions, and violations of Section 1983 of the Civil Rights Act. In his current practice, he handles condemnation matters for landowners and developers. He is coauthor of the book *Federal Land Use Law & Litigation* (Thomson-Reuters, 2017).

Mr. Blaesser has been a lecturer at the Harvard Graduate School of Design in Planning and Environmental Law and Public-Private Development, with an appointment at the Kennedy School of Government. He is the author of the book *Discretionary Land Use Controls: Avoiding Invitations to Abuse of Discretion* (Thomson-Reuters, 2017), and coauthor and coeditor of the books *Redevelopment: Planning, Law, and Project Implementation* (ABA Publishing, 2008) and *Land Use and the Constitution: Principles for Planning Practice* (Planners Press, 1989). Over the years, Mr. Blaesser has also served as a legal consultant on development regulations to a variety of local governments and agencies across the country, including Omaha, Nebraska; the District of Columbia; the City and County of Honolulu; Louisville, Kentucky; Salt Lake City, Utah; Cincinnati, Ohio; and Norfolk, Virginia, as well as the Federal Highway Administration (FHWA) and the Transportation Research Board (TRB).

As another dimension of his real estate development practice, Mr. Blaesser structures public/private partnerships with state and local governments on behalf of developer clients. He is experienced in utilizing public financing mechanisms, such as special assessment districts and tax increment financing, to achieve economic development objectives.

Mr. Blaesser has been on the Massachusetts Super Lawyers list in the areas of real estate, land use, and environmental law since 2004 (© Key Professional Media, Inc.). He has also been listed in *The Best Lawyers in America* in the area of real estate law since 2010 (© Woodward/White, Inc., Aiken, SC) and is ranked in 2017 Chambers USA: America's Leading Lawyers for Business in the Commonwealth of Massachusetts in the area of real estate: zoning/land use. He is a LEED Accredited Professional with specialty in Building Design & Construction (LEED AP BD + C), and has been awarded the Counselor of Real Estate (CRE®) designation.

About the Lincoln Institute of Land Policy

The Lincoln Institute of Land Policy seeks to improve quality of life through the effective use, taxation, and stewardship of land. A nonprofit private operating foundation whose origins date to 1946, the Lincoln Institute researches and recommends creative approaches to land as a solution to economic, social, and environmental challenges. Through education, training, publications, and events, we integrate theory and practice to inform public policy decisions worldwide. With locations in Cambridge, Washington, Phoenix, and Beijing, we organize our work in seven major areas: Planning and Urban Form, Valuation and Taxation, International and Institute-Wide Initiatives, Latin America and the Caribbean, People's Republic of China, the Babbitt Center for Land and Water Policy, and the Center for Community Investment.

Cambridge, Massachusetts